D1540554

CONTENTS

North America Automakers Hammered by 2008 Financial Crisis

Already reeling from the impact of the previous year's trouble in the U.S. subprime mortgage market, American consumers were slammed in 2008 by a sharp decline in home values, rising loan defaults and resulting bank failures, the like of which had not been seen in nearly 80 years. The easy-credit financing of everything from homes to vehicles that had been keeping the economy percolating evaporated virtually overnight.

Not helping matters was rampant speculation in crude oil futures that helped push U.S. gasoline prices through the roof for the third consecutive year, this time clearing $5 per gallon in many areas of the country. Normally cheaper than gasoline, diesel fuel — the life blood of the trucking industry — ran as much as $1 more per gallon in most areas. That only added to the economic stress by driving up retail prices for many commodities.

People fearing for the loss of homes and jobs, and unable to get financing, did not buy new cars and trucks. As a result U.S. new light-vehicle deliveries fell 18% to 13.2 million units, a 16-year low, from 16.1 million in 2007. Thus, in just three years the market dropped by 4.2 million units, or 24.1%, and remained well shy of the record 17.8 million sold in 2000.

Unkind as the year was to the industry in general, it was worse for Detroit's three home-grown auto makers. Chrysler LLC was hit the hardest, experiencing a 30.3% plunge to 1,447,736 in 2008 from the prior year's 2,076,062 deliveries. General Motors Corp. posted a 22.7% sales decline for the year, to 2,955,860 from 3,824,550 in 2007, while Ford Motor Co. fared the best of the group with sales falling 20.3% to 1,941,041 from 2,436,530.

Although import brands performed better overall than the domestics, American Honda Motor Co.Inc., with sales down 7.9%, stood alone among top Asian brands in avoiding a double-digit year-over-year decline. Toyota Motor Sales U.S.A. Inc. suffered a 15% setback, while sales at Nissan North America Inc. were down 11.0% and American Isuzu Motors Inc. officially left the U.S. market.

At the same time, more than 1,000 dealers of all makes, unable to obtain financing for either retail buyers or their own inventories, closed up shop, with an even larger number forecast to go bust in 2009.

Reacting to the light-truck sales downturn, GM announced the near-term closing of at least two pickup and SUV plants and said more shutdowns were on the horizon. Chrysler pulled the plug on its Chrysler Aspen and Dodge Durango large SUVs after the '09 model run, along with the Newark, DE, plant that built them.

Yet, amid all the doom and gloom, auto makers were still bringing exciting new vehicles to market, including the revival of a couple of storied performance nameplates. Chrysler led off with the Challenger, while Chevrolet reintroduced the Camaro, both featuring retro styling harking back to their first-generation muscle car era predecessors.

Increasing use of hybrid powertrains, smaller forced-induction engines, diesels and other mileage-enhancing protocols would become increasingly important to auto makers as they faced the government's stricter fuel-economy standards beyond 2009.

In Canada, as unemployment trended upward, light-vehicle production plunged 19.4%, compared with 2007. The decline allowed Mexico's full-year output to surpass that of Canada, 2.18 million vehicles to 2.08 million. As with other regions around the globe, new-vehicle sales sank along with the faltering economy. Gasoline prices paralleled the upward trajectory seen in the U.S., and led to a 5.9% decrease in light truck sales, while car sales increased by 3.7%, leading to a relatively flat 1% overall decrease versus 2007.

As the economy faltered, struggling automakers followed the lead of their U.S. parent companies and reached out to the Canadian governments. In a bid to keep their Canadian operations viable through the economic downturn, Chrysler and GM requested about C$6 billion ($4.8 billion) in combined financial aid from Canada's federal government and the province of Ontario. The governments jointly decided to provide C$4 billion ($3.3 billion) in emergency loans to the ailing auto makers, while Ottawa also promised accounts-receivable insurance to struggling suppliers.

Even with the troubling economic climate, 2008 saw some hope on the product horizon. Ford announced the Flex, with its distinctive boxy profile, would be joined in 2009 by a uniquely styled Lincoln-brand platform-mate dubbed the MKT at its Oakville, ON plant.

South of the border, Mexico's automotive industry enjoyed a robust start to 2008, but as the year progressed, the global economic crisis took its toll, particularly on new-vehicle demand. Sales of light trucks fell 5.9% from 2007 levels to 439,500 units, according to *Ward's* data. Car sales plunged 7.2% to 580,992.

Despite the drop in sales, the country's production remained largely unaffected by the faltering economy. In fact, full-year 2008 output rose 4.0% to 2,178,397 units. Perhaps Mexico's biggest automotive windfall occurred in late May, when Ford announced it would expand its Cuautitlan assembly plant to accommodate production of its Fiesta B-car in early 2010, which was only part of what the automaker claimed would be the single largest investment ever by an automaker in Mexico. Also included was a plan to build diesels in Chihuahua and additional investment in a new transmission manufacturing facility in Guanajuato.

Nissan continued its reign as the best-selling passenger-car brand in Mexico in 2008, controlling 23.2% of the market. GM took the No. 2 spot with a 20.2% share, while VW claimed 21.2%, down from 21.7%.

In the light-truck segment, the Detroit Three took the top three spots, with Ford holding 21.7% of the market, followed by GM at 18.1% and Chrysler with 17.8%. Nissan nearly edged out Chrysler in 2008, grabbing 17.5% of the Mexican light-truck market. ❏

U.S. Production and Factory Sales of Cars, Trucks and Buses

U.S. VEHICLE PRODUCTION AND FACTORY SALES

Year	Production			Factory Sales		
	Cars	Commercial Vehicles	Total	Cars	Commercial Vehicles	Total
2008	3,776,641	4,896,450	8,673,091	NA	5,104,918	NA
2007	3,924,268	6,828,042	10,752,310	NA	6,946,270	NA
2006	4,366,996	6,893,281	11,260,277	NA	7,058,953	NA
2005	4,321,272	7,625,381	11,946,653	NA	7,798,117	NA
2004	4,229,625	7,730,729	11,960,354	NA	7,846,294	NA
2003	4,510,469	7,576,559	12,087,028	NA	7,605,592	NA
2002	5,018,777	7,260,805	12,279,582	NA	7,285,540	NA
2001	4,879,119	6,545,570	11,424,689	4,884,313	6,223,586	11,107,899
2000	5,542,217	7,231,497	12,773,714	5,504,385	7,022,478	12,526,863
1999	5,637,949	7,387,029	13,024,978	5,427,746	6,699,113	12,126,859
1998	5,554,373	6,448,290	12,002,663	5,676,964	6,435,185	12,112,149
1997	5,933,921	6,196,654	12,130,575	6,069,886	6,152,817	12,222,703
1996	6,082,835	5,747,322	11,830,157	6,140,454	5,775,730	11,916,184
1995	6,339,967	5,655,281	11,995,248	6,309,836	5,713,469	12,023,305
1994	6,601,220	5,638,068	12,239,288	6,548,562	5,640,275	12,188,837
1993	5,982,120	4,873,342	10,855,462	5,961,754	4,895,224	10,856,978
1992	5,666,891	4,024,552	9,691,443	5,685,299	4,062,002	9,747,301
1991	5,439,864	3,349,976	8,789,840	5,407,120	3,387,503	8,794,623
1990	6,077,903	3,689,536	9,767,439	6,049,749	3,725,205	9,774,954
1989	6,821,291	4,035,501	10,856,792	6,807,416	4,061,950	10,869,366
1988	7,137,433	4,084,575	11,222,008	7,104,617	4,120,574	11,225,191
1987	7,099,854	3,812,074	10,911,928	7,085,147	3,821,410	10,906,557
1986	7,829,271	3,490,853	11,320,124	7,516,189	3,500,933	11,017,122
1985	8,186,043	3,452,094	11,638,137	8,002,259	3,464,327	11,466,586
1984	7,773,332	3,151,449	10,924,781	7,621,176	3,175,835	10,797,011
1983	6,781,184	2,443,637	9,224,821	6,739,223	2,433,876	9,173,099
1982	5,073,496	1,912,099	6,985,595	5,049,184	1,906,455	6,955,639
1981	6,253,138	1,689,778	7,942,916	6,255,340	1,700,908	7,956,248
1980	6,375,506	1,634,335	8,009,841	6,400,026	1,667,283	8,067,309
1979	8,433,662	3,046,331	11,479,993	8,419,226	3,036,706	11,455,932
1978	9,176,635	3,722,567	12,899,202	9,165,190	3,706,239	12,871,429
1977	9,213,654	3,489,128	12,702,782	9,200,849	3,441,521	12,642,370
1975	6,716,951	2,269,562	8,986,513	6,712,852	2,272,160	8,985,012
1970	6,550,128	1,733,821	8,283,949	6,546,817	1,692,440	8,239,257
1965	9,335,227	1,785,109	11,120,336	9,305,561	1,751,805	11,057,366
1960	6,703,108	1,202,011	7,905,119	6,674,796	1,194,475	7,869,271
1955	7,950,377	1,253,672	9,204,049	7,920,186	1,249,106	9,169,292
1950	6,628,598	1,377,261	8,005,859	6,665,863	1,337,193	8,003,056
1945	83,786	701,090	784,876	69,532	655,683	725,215
1940	3,728,491	784,404	4,512,895	3,717,385	754,901	4,472,286
1935	3,252,244	694,690	3,946,934	3,273,874	697,367	3,971,241
1930	2,784,745	571,241	3,355,986	2,787,456	575,364	3,362,820
1925	NA	NA	NA	3,735,171	530,659	4,265,830
1920	NA	NA	NA	1,905,560	321,789	2,227,349
1915	NA	NA	NA	895,930	74,000	969,930
1910	NA	NA	NA	181,000	6,000	187,000
1905	NA	NA	NA	24,250	750	25,000
1900	NA	NA	NA	4,192	NA	4,192

N.A. - Not available. Production data does not include Buses.
SOURCE: Ward's Automotive Group

North America Car Production by Model

NORTH AMERICA CAR PRODUCTION BY MODEL

	Canada		Mexico		United States		North America	
	2008	2007	2008	2007	2008	2007	2008	2007
Ford Mustang	—	—	—	—	92,345	144,459	92,345	144,459
Mazda6	—	—	—	—	75,145	54,321	75,145	54,321
AUTOALLIANCE TOTAL	**—**	**—**	**—**	**—**	**167,490**	**198,780**	**167,490**	**198,780**
BMW Z4	—	—	—	—	9,771	25,559	9,771	25,559
BMW TOTAL	**—**	**—**	**—**	**—**	**9,771**	**25,559**	**9,771**	**25,559**
300 Series	62,201	123,004	—	—	—	—	62,201	123,004
PT Cruiser Convertible	—	—	—	11,429	—	—	—	11,429
Sebring Convertible	—	—	—	—	25,592	32,646	25,592	32,646
Sebring Sedan	—	—	—	—	53,664	79,593	53,664	79,593
Chrysler Total	**62,201**	**123,004**	**—**	**11,429**	**79,256**	**112,239**	**141,457**	**246,672**
Avenger	—	—	—	—	82,247	125,292	82,247	125,292
Caliber	—	—	—	—	127,499	163,447	127,499	163,447
Challenger	27,665	—	—	—	—	—	27,665	—
Charger	116,105	123,848	—	—	—	—	116,105	123,848
Magnum	4,733	26,351	—	—	—	—	4,733	26,351
Viper	—	—	—	—	1,545	332	1,545	332
Dodge Total	**148,503**	**150,199**	**—**	**—**	**211,291**	**289,071**	**359,794**	**439,270**
CHRYSLER TOTAL	**210,704**	**273,203**	**—**	**11,429**	**290,547**	**401,310**	**501,251**	**685,942**
Crown Victoria	61,421	70,476	—	—	—	—	61,421	70,476
Five Hundred	—	—	—	—	—	13,349	—	13,349
Focus	—	—	—	—	236,612	191,115	236,612	191,115
Fusion	—	—	206,390	175,462	—	—	206,390	175,462
Ikon	—	—	—	5,975	—	—	—	5,975
Taurus	—	—	—	—	46,546	54,218	46,546	54,218
Ford Total	**61,421**	**70,476**	**206,390**	**181,437**	**283,158**	**258,682**	**550,969**	**510,595**
MKS	—	—	—	—	23,388	—	23,388	—
MKZ	—	—	32,996	36,437	—	—	32,996	36,437
Town Car	18,574	152	—	—	—	21,478	18,574	21,630
Lincoln Total	**18,574**	**152**	**32,996**	**36,437**	**23,388**	**21,478**	**74,958**	**58,067**
Grand Marquis	29,393	53,754	—	—	—	—	29,393	53,754
Milan	—	—	33,368	37,996	—	—	33,368	37,996
Montego	—	—	—	—	—	4,041	—	4,041
Sable	—	—	—	—	12,068	17,879	12,068	17,879
Mercury Total	**29,393**	**53,754**	**33,368**	**37,996**	**12,068**	**21,920**	**74,829**	**113,670**
FORD TOTAL	**109,388**	**124,382**	**272,754**	**255,870**	**318,614**	**302,080**	**700,756**	**682,332**
LaCrosse	50,665	47,889	—	—	—	—	50,665	47,889
Lucerne	—	—	—	—	53,301	81,217	53,301	81,217
Buick Total	**50,665**	**47,889**	**—**	**—**	**53,301**	**81,217**	**103,966**	**129,106**
CTS	—	—	—	—	86,333	55,934	86,333	55,934
DTS	—	—	—	—	32,558	52,226	32,558	52,226
STS	—	—	—	—	14,796	18,836	14,796	18,836
XLR	—	—	—	—	1,451	1,343	1,451	1,343
Cadillac Total	**—**	**—**	**—**	**—**	**135,138**	**128,339**	**135,138**	**128,339**
Aveo	—	—	24,177	—	—	—	24,177	—
Cobalt	—	—	—	—	250,002	226,314	250,002	226,314
Corvette	—	—	—	—	30,897	36,597	30,897	36,597
Impala	308,783	315,114	—	—	—	—	308,783	315,114
Joy/Swing	—	—	36,819	39,707	—	—	36,819	39,707
Malibu	—	—	—	—	251,296	130,598	251,296	130,598
Monte Carlo	—	10,889	—	—	—	—	—	10,889
Monza	—	—	26,848	28,048	—	—	26,848	28,048

North America Car Production by Model

NORTH AMERICA CAR PRODUCTION BY MODEL — continued

	Canada		Mexico		United States		North America	
	2008	2007	2008	2007	2008	2007	2008	2007
Chevrolet Total	308,783	326,003	87,844	67,755	532,195	393,509	928,822	787,267
G3	—	—	6,305	—	—	—	6,305	—
G5	—	—	—	—	58,013	54,138	58,013	54,138
G6	—	—	—	—	157,154	150,397	157,154	150,397
Grand Prix	—	96,124	—	—	—	—	—	96,124
Solstice	—	—	—	—	6,843	24,049	6,843	24,049
Pontiac Total	—	96,124	6,305	—	222,010	228,584	228,315	324,708
Aura	—	—	—	—	64,510	60,853	64,510	60,853
Ion	—	—	—	—	—	27,502	—	27,502
Sky	—	—	—	—	8,902	14,735	8,902	14,735
Saturn Total	—	—	—	—	73,412	103,090	73,412	103,090
Opel GT	—	—	—	—	3,128	4,109	3,128	4,109
GM TOTAL	359,448	470,016	94,149	67,755	1,019,184	938,848	1,472,781	1,476,619
Acura CSX	2,738	3,483	—	—	—	—	2,738	3,483
Acura TL	—	—	—	—	57,207	66,654	57,207	66,654
Honda Accord	—	—	—	15,784	381,533	366,870	381,533	382,654
Honda Civic	299,246	246,374	—	—	114,305	156,032	413,551	402,406
HONDA TOTAL	301,984	249,857	—	15,784	553,045	589,556	855,029	855,197
Hyundai Sonata	—	—	—	—	152,588	133,534	152,588	133,534
HYUNDAI TOTAL	—	—	—	—	152,588	133,534	152,588	133,534
Mitsubishi Eclipse	—	—	—	—	15,944	30,365	15,944	30,365
Mitsubishi Galant	—	—	—	—	38,536	32,445	38,536	32,445
MITSUBISHI TOTAL	—	—	—	—	54,480	62,810	54,480	62,810
Nissan Altima	—	—	—	—	320,628	338,609	320,628	338,609
Nissan Maxima	—	—	—	—	53,254	46,042	53,254	46,042
Nissan Platina	—	—	6,610	13,031	—	—	6,610	13,031
Nissan Sentra	—	—	118,588	159,796	—	—	118,588	159,796
Nissan Tsuru	—	—	84,212	76,564	—	—	84,212	76,564
Nissan Versa	—	—	183,231	190,268	—	—	183,231	190,268
Renault Clio	—	—	8,818	9,034	—	—	8,818	9,034
NISSAN TOTAL	—	—	401,459	448,693	373,882	384,651	775,341	833,344
Pontiac Vibe	—	—	—	—	70,843	49,367	70,843	49,367
Toyota Corolla	—	—	—	—	149,349	200,189	149,349	200,189
NUMMI TOTAL	—	—	—	—	220,192	249,556	220,192	249,556
Subaru Legacy	—	—	—	—	73,489	84,960	73,489	84,960
Toyota Camry	—	—	—	—	91,671	37,972	91,671	37,972
SUBARU TOTAL	—	—	—	—	165,160	122,932	165,160	122,932
Toyota Avalon	—	—	—	—	51,563	76,219	51,563	76,219
Toyota Camry	—	—	—	—	382,433	409,946	382,433	409,946
Toyota Corolla	132,543	159,297	—	—	—	—	132,543	159,297
Toyota Matrix	81,369	65,378	—	—	—	—	81,369	65,378
Toyota Solara	—	—	—	—	17,692	28,487	17,692	28,487
TOYOTA TOTAL	213,912	224,675	—	—	451,688	514,652	665,600	739,327
Volkswagen Beetle	—	—	37,893	40,124	—	—	37,893	40,124
Volkswagen Beetle Cabrio	—	—	17,100	26,752	—	—	17,100	26,752
Volkswagen Bora	—	—	24,245	26,507	—	—	24,245	26,507
Volkswagen Jetta	—	—	369,858	316,183	—	—	369,858	316,183
VOLKSWAGEN TOTAL	—	—	449,096	409,566	—	—	449,096	409,566
TOTAL CARS	1,195,436	1,342,133	1,217,458	1,209,097	3,776,641	3,924,268	6,189,535	6,475,498

SOURCE: *Ward's AutoInfoBank.*

N. America Truck Production by Model

NORTH AMERICA TRUCK PRODUCTION BY MODEL

	Canada		Mexico		United States		North America	
	2008	2007	2008	2007	2008	2007	2008	2007
Hummer H2	—	—	—	—	6,881	13,630	6,881	13,630
AM GENERAL TOTAL	**—**	**—**	**—**	**—**	**6,881**	**13,630**	**6,881**	**13,630**
BMW X5	—	—	—	—	123,271	129,440	123,271	129,440
BMW X6	—	—	—	—	37,697	—	37,697	
BMW TOTAL	**—**	**—**	**—**	**—**	**160,968**	**129,440**	**160,968**	**129,440**
Chevrolet Equinox	82,242	105,260	—	—	—	—	82,242	105,260
Pontiac Torrent	30,815	41,478	—	—	—	—	30,815	41,478
Suzuki XL7	12,397	31,403	—	—	—	—	12,397	31,403
CAMI TOTAL	**125,454**	**178,141**	**—**	**—**	**—**	**—**	**125,454**	**178,141**
Aspen	—	—	—	—	24,546	28,384	24,546	28,384
Pacifica	—	48,722	—	—	—	—	—	48,722
PT Cruiser	—	—	57,938	102,922	—	—	57,938	102,922
Town & Country	134,392	117,794	—	—	12,993	24,160	147,385	141,954
Chrysler Total	**134,392**	**166,516**	**57,938**	**102,922**	**37,539**	**52,544**	**229,869**	**321,982**
Caravan	111,915	95,055	—	—	58,302	114,080	170,217	209,135
Dakota	—	—	—	—	27,614	55,884	27,614	55,884
Durango	—	—	—	—	26,437	48,399	26,437	48,399
Journey	—	—	124,709	—	—	—	124,709	—
Nitro	—	—	—	—	38,974	113,793	38,974	113,793
Ram Pickup	—	—	97,140	169,301	184,376	241,424	281,516	410,725
Dodge Total	**111,915**	**95,055**	**221,849**	**169,301**	**335,703**	**573,580**	**669,467**	**837,936**
Commander	—	—	—	—	19,263	58,773	19,263	58,773
Compass	—	—	—	—	45,590	67,603	45,590	67,603
Grand Cherokee	—	—	—	—	72,931	127,518	72,931	127,518
Liberty	—	—	—	—	81,603	107,402	81,603	107,402
Patriot	—	—	—	—	90,432	102,027	90,432	102,027
Wrangler	—	—	—	—	52,153	62,436	52,153	62,436
Wrangler Unlimited	—	—	—	—	75,754	94,280	75,754	94,280
Jeep Total	**—**	**—**	**—**	**—**	**437,726**	**620,039**	**437,726**	**620,039**
Mitsubishi Raider	—	—	—	—	4,513	3,812	4,513	3,812
Volkswagen Routan	22,035	—	—	—	—	—	22,035	—
CHRYSLER TOTAL	**268,342**	**261,571**	**279,787**	**272,223**	**815,481**	**1,249,975**	**1,363,610**	**1,783,769**
Chassis	—	—	—	—	3,829	10,191	3,829	10,191
Econoline	—	—	—	—	126,640	179,918	126,640	179,918
Edge	129,064	175,870	—	—	—	—	129,064	175,870
Escape	—	—	—	—	208,624	209,774	208,624	209,774
Expedition	—	—	—	—	54,179	107,035	54,179	107,035
Explorer	—	—	—	—	87,433	162,575	87,433	162,575
F-Series	—	—	34,280	38,019	517,805	795,204	552,085	833,223
Flex	38,049	—	—	—	—	—	38,049	—
Freestyle	—	—	—	—	—	11,564	—	11,564
Ranger	—	—	—	—	89,000	97,753	89,000	97,753
Taurus X	—	—	—	—	21,276	29,508	21,276	29,508
Ford Total	**167,113**	**175,870**	**34,280**	**38,019**	**1,108,786**	**1,603,522**	**1,310,179**	**1,817,411**
Mark LT	—	—	—	—	4,823	9,311	4,823	9,311
MKX	31,747	49,556	—	—	—	—	31,747	49,556
Navigator	—	—	—	—	13,490	26,161	13,490	26,161
Lincoln Total	**31,747**	**49,556**	**—**	**—**	**18,313**	**35,472**	**50,060**	**85,028**
Mariner	—	—	—	—	33,554	34,786	33,554	34,786
Mountaineer	—	—	—	—	10,172	24,102	10,172	24,102
Mercury Total	**—**	**—**	**—**	**—**	**43,726**	**58,888**	**43,726**	**58,888**
Mazda Pickup	—	—	—	—	4,320	6,393	4,320	6,393
Mazda Tribute	—	—	—	—	15,907	23,785	15,907	23,785
FORD TOTAL	**198,860**	**225,426**	**34,280**	**38,019**	**1,191,052**	**1,728,060**	**1,424,192**	**1,991,505**
Enclave	—	—	—	—	62,785	38,971	62,785	38,971
Rainier	—	—	—	—	—	2,561	—	2,561
Rendezvous	—	—	—	5	—	—	—	5
Terraza	—	—	—	—	—	3,144	—	3,144
Buick Total	**—**	**—**	**—**	**5**	**62,785**	**44,676**	**62,785**	**44,681**
Escalade	—	—	—	—	26,170	39,169	26,170	39,169
Escalade ESV	—	—	—	—	10,748	15,144	10,748	15,144
Escalade EXT	—	—	4,622	7,544	—	—	4,622	7,544
SRX	—	—	—	—	17,021	24,474	17,021	24,474
Cadillac Total	**—**	**—**	**4,622**	**7,544**	**53,939**	**78,787**	**58,561**	**86,331**
Avalanche	—	—	29,205	57,661	—	—	29,205	57,661
Captiva Sport	—	—	18,406	—	—	—	18,406	—
Colorado	—	—	—	—	57,290	85,400	57,290	85,400
Express	—	—	—	—	95,019	123,441	95,019	123,441
HHR	—	—	110,854	106,874	—	—	110,854	106,874
Kodiak	—	—	1,440	2,794	8,013	11,901	9,453	14,695
Silverado	67,582	218,898	109,941	82,498	245,174	445,508	422,697	746,904
Suburban	—	—	13,631	58,394	35,166	25,715	48,797	84,109
Tahoe	—	—	—	—	101,202	167,324	101,202	167,324
Tiltmaster	—	—	—	—	414	1,024	414	1,024
TrailBlazer	—	—	—	—	71,490	148,658	71,490	148,658
Traverse	—	—	—	—	43,293	—	43,293	—

N. America Truck Production by Model

NORTH AMERICA TRUCK PRODUCTION BY MODEL - continued

	Canada		Mexico		United States		North America	
	2008	2007	2008	2007	2008	2007	2008	2007
Uplander	—	—	—	—	63,588	87,139	63,588	87,139
Chevrolet Total	**67,582**	**218,898**	**283,477**	**308,221**	**720,649**	**1,096,110**	**1,071,708**	**1,623,229**
Acadia	—	—	—	—	92,903	103,059	92,903	103,059
Canyon	—	—	—	—	17,032	23,210	17,032	23,210
Envoy	—	—	—	—	27,405	49,539	27,405	49,539
Forward	—	—	—	—	586	1,275	586	1,275
Savana	—	—	—	—	29,068	31,019	29,068	31,019
Sierra	36,839	97,184	38,079	21,931	94,172	149,973	169,090	269,088
Topkick	—	—	—	—	13,586	15,210	13,586	15,210
Yukon	—	—	—	—	53,308	77,886	53,308	77,886
Yukon XL	—	—	—	—	31,875	42,848	31,875	42,848
GMC Total	**36,839**	**97,184**	**38,079**	**21,931**	**359,935**	**494,019**	**434,853**	**613,134**
Hummer H3	—	—	—	—	15,507	49,242	15,507	49,242
Hummer H3T	—	—	—	—	3,707	—	3,707	—
Hummer Total	**—**	**—**	**—**	**—**	**19,214**	**49,242**	**19,214**	**49,242**
Ascender	—	—	—	—	310	2,502	310	2,502
i-Series	—	—	—	—	701	4,027	701	4,027
Isuzu NPR	—	—	—	—	1,427	2,701	1,427	2,701
Isuzu Truck	—	—	—	—	552	620	552	620
Isuzu Total	**—**	**—**	**—**	**—**	**2,990**	**9,850**	**2,990**	**9,850**
Pontiac Montana SV6	—	—	—	—	20,430	19,977	20,430	19,977
Outlook	—	—	—	—	22,448	47,531	22,448	47,531
Relay	—	—	—	—	—	5	—	5
Vue	—	—	88,706	64,283	—	16,929	88,706	81,212
Saturn Total	**—**	**—**	**88,706**	**64,283**	**22,448**	**64,465**	**111,154**	**128,748**
Saab 9-7X	—	—	—	—	4,159	5,476	4,159	5,476
GM TOTAL	**104,421**	**316,082**	**414,884**	**401,984**	**1,266,549**	**1,862,602**	**1,785,854**	**2,580,668**
Acura MDX	55,776	68,706	—	—	—	—	55,776	68,706
Acura RDX	—	—	—	—	20,960	25,319	20,960	25,319
Honda CR-V	—	—	51,247	10,905	110,821	48,867	162,068	59,772
Honda Element	—	—	—	—	19,608	37,576	19,608	37,576
Honda Odyssey	—	—	—	—	161,219	196,043	161,219	196,043
Honda Pilot	—	16,867	—	—	121,516	118,101	121,516	134,968
Honda Ridgeline	25,251	55,150	—	—	—	—	25,251	55,150
HONDA TOTAL	**81,027**	**140,723**	**51,247**	**10,905**	**434,124**	**425,906**	**566,398**	**577,534**
HYUNDAI TOTAL (Santa Fe)	**—**	**—**	**—**	**—**	**84,454**	**116,985**	**84,454**	**116,985**
Mercedes GL	—	—	—	—	34,958	39,308	34,958	39,308
Mercedes M-Class	—	—	—	—	96,395	114,039	96,395	114,039
Mercedes R-Class	—	—	—	—	21,208	21,009	21,208	21,009
MERCEDES TOTAL	**—**	**—**	**—**	**—**	**152,561**	**174,356**	**152,561**	**174,356**
MITSUBISHI TOTAL (Endeavor)	**—**	**—**	**—**	**—**	**4,538**	**15,922**	**4,538**	**15,922**
Infiniti QX56	—	—	—	—	8,522	12,346	8,522	12,346
Nissan Armada	—	—	—	—	21,138	35,359	21,138	35,359
Nissan Chassis	—	—	27,673	24,392	—	—	27,673	24,392
Nissan Frontier	—	—	—	—	38,793	63,123	38,793	63,123
Nissan Pathfinder	—	—	—	—	28,644	70,422	28,644	70,422
Nissan Pickup	—	—	20,315	25,203	—	—	20,315	25,203
Nissan Quest	—	—	—	—	17,151	21,406	17,151	21,406
Nissan Titan	—	—	—	—	25,037	69,850	25,037	69,850
Nissan Xterra	—	—	—	—	30,065	46,505	30,065	46,505
Suzuki Equator	—	—	—	—	1,000	—	1,000	—
NISSAN TOTAL	**—**	**—**	**47,988**	**49,595**	**170,350**	**319,011**	**218,338**	**368,606**
Toyota Tacoma	—	—	—	—	121,820	158,325	121,820	158,325
NUMMI TOTAL	**—**	**—**	**—**	**—**	**121,820**	**158,325**	**121,820**	**158,325**
SUBARU TOTAL (Tribeca)	**—**	**—**	**—**	**—**	**18,108**	**24,217**	**18,108**	**24,217**
Hino Truck	—	—	—	—	3,062	6,230	3,062	6,230
Lexus RX350	69,630	78,074	—	—	—	—	69,630	78,074
Toyota RAV4	3,852	—	—	—	—	—	3,852	—
Toyota Sequoia	—	—	—	—	37,098	23,488	37,098	23,488
Toyota Sienna	—	—	—	—	135,989	159,453	135,989	159,453
Toyota Tacoma	—	—	50,085	34,100	—	—	50,085	34,100
Toyota Tundra	—	—	—	—	125,263	240,101	125,263	240,101
Toyota Venza	—	—	—	—	6,348	—	6,348	—
TOYOTA TOTAL	**73,482**	**78,074**	**50,085**	**34,100**	**307,760**	**429,272**	**431,327**	**541,446**
Blue Diamond	—	—	8,670	13,174	—	—	8,670	13,174
Dina Camiones	—	—	118	—	—	—	118	—
Freightliner	11,460	17,156	29,871	30,766	52,239	62,866	93,570	110,788
International	15,986	9,410	17,980	19,371	40,087	39,278	74,053	68,059
Kenworth	7,773	10,074	13,611	14,224	18,729	21,624	40,113	45,922
Peterbilt	—	—	—	—	17,794	20,974	17,794	20,974
Scania Heavy Truck	—	--	4	112	—	—	4	112
Volkswagen	—	--	1,706	1,563	—	—	1,706	1,563
Volvo Truck	—	--	255	112	32,868	34,757	33,123	34,869
Other	—	--	—	--	87	842	87	842
TOTAL TRUCKS	**886,805**	**1,236,657**	**950,486**	**886,148**	**4,896,450**	**6,828,042**	**6,733,741**	**8,950,847**

SOURCE: *Ward's AutoInfoBank.*

U.S. Factory Sales of Trucks and Buses by Gross Vehicle Weight Rating

U.S. FACTORY SALES OF TRUCKS AND BUSES BY GROSS VEHICLE WEIGHT RATING

| | Gross Vehicle Weight Rating (Pounds) | | | | | | | | |
	6,000 & Less	6,001- 10,000	10,001- 14,000	14,001- 16,000	16,001- 19,500	19,501- 26,000	26,001- 33,000	33,001 & Over	Total
U.S. TOTAL									
2008	2,317,625	1,655,766	99,692	21,420	27,558	27,977	44,943	127,880	4,322,861
2007	3,232,324	2,504,072	156,610	35,293	34,478	46,158	54,761	137,016	6,200,712
2006	3,459,190	2,381,970	115,140	31,471	33,757	68,069	78,754	274,480	6,442,831
2005	4,059,286	2,585,660	146,809	36,812	37,359	55,666	71,305	253,840	7,246,737
2004	4,176,947	2,767,305	136,229	36,203	26,058	67,252	61,918	194,827	7,466,739
2003	4,238,125	2,503,395	116,416	26,888	20,086	46,211	56,225	136,083	7,143,429
2002	4,279,792	2,274,661	121,867	29,277	15,913	40,507	62,070	139,633	6,963,720
2001	3,915,731	1,968,010	66,787	29,876	22,616	35,815	69,749	115,002	6,223,586
2000	4,533,600	1,973,801	100,293	48,572	25,137	36,874	106,750	197,451	7,022,478
1999	4,876,534	1,891,397	116,868	44,250	19,699	25,528	122,411	248,332	7,345,019
1998	4,458,970	1,431,110	147,839	33,513	17,441	19,850	116,412	210,050	6,435,185
1997	4,377,340	1,366,899	47,022	32,286	4,056	16,687	128,245	180,282	6,152,817
1996	4,073,778	1,344,826	38,525	32,912	4,127	12,379	106,657	162,526	5,775,730
1995	3,742,739	1,583,878	901	37,073	1,549	16,369	125,703	205,257	5,713,469
1994	3,811,837	1,478,854	848	29,585	550	13,559	115,334	189,708	5,640,275
1993	3,488,278	1,124,106	—	8,149	—	21,943	93,939	158,809	4,895,224
1992	2,978,214	850,876	—	7,193	2	21,993	81,601	122,123	4,062,002
1991	2,533,904	658,425	—	3,820	56	19,498	77,850	93,950	3,387,503
1990	2,574,071	906,423	—	789	1,726	38,123	87,107	116,966	3,725,205
1989	2,657,084	1,130,606	11	146	4,593	37,788	90,440	141,282	4,061,950
1988	2,704,891	1,105,069	—	182	5,618	55,840	97,771	151,203	4,120,574
U.S DOMESTIC									
2008	1,975,203	1,392,987	92,105	19,680	25,311	26,929	39,315	97,015	3,668,545
2007	2,745,028	2,185,881	146,794	32,162	31,123	45,195	50,747	102,614	5,339,544
2006	3,005,776	2,125,307	111,461	29,255	30,804	66,753	73,039	231,418	5,673,813
2005	3,569,546	2,333,147	142,116	33,926	33,446	54,557	65,524	213,873	6,446,135
2004	3,795,422	2,530,711	131,889	33,870	23,702	65,869	56,579	164,711	6,802,753
2003	3,818,750	2,300,058	112,745	24,960	18,304	45,515	50,927	114,990	6,486,249
2002	3,827,782	2,073,553	117,927	26,986	14,279	39,607	56,691	120,409	6,277,234
2001	3,511,326	1,794,251	61,168	27,038	20,216	34,905	64,454	99,422	5,612,780
2000	4,070,026	1,757,683	97,697	35,407	22,602	35,752	100,175	171,565	6,290,907
1999	4,453,332	1,723,012	112,349	37,328	17,542	24,362	113,147	218,041	6,699,113
1998	4,053,521	1,303,786	141,781	29,629	15,779	18,989	105,874	177,852	5,847,211
1997	3,894,222	1,236,119	44,893	28,428	3,931	15,609	116,922	149,183	5,489,307
1996	3,699,385	1,225,792	37,559	30,309	4,056	11,717	97,720	141,941	5,248,479
1995	3,405,062	1,458,713	780	35,427	1,471	15,046	114,194	180,652	5,211,345
1994	3,475,044	1,353,576	848	28,437	533	12,123	102,745	165,375	5,138,681
1993	3,187,731	1,031,829	—	7,630	—	19,277	84,779	140,247	4,471,493
1992	2,711,172	785,198	—	6,612	2	19,160	71,899	108,003	3,702,046
1991	2,281,761	594,435	—	3,547	28	16,536	69,703	83,875	3,049,885
1990	2,383,892	848,690	—	693	1,644	34,141	78,553	107,025	3,454,638
1989	2,447,962	1,057,077	11	54	4,234	32,721	81,971	127,880	3,751,910
1988	2,496,648	1,020,515	—	86	5,238	49,670	87,994	135,163	3,795,314

* Reporting firms do not represent the entire industry.
SOURCE: *Ward's Automotive Group.*

U.S. FACTORY SALES OF TRUCKS AND BUSES BY GROSS VEHICLE WEIGHT RATING, 1988-2008

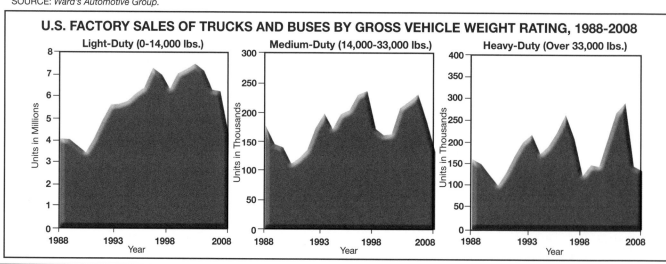

U.S. Factory Sales of Diesel Trucks and Vehicle Factory Sales from U.S. and Canadian Plants

U.S. FACTORY SALES OF DIESEL TRUCKS BY GROSS VEHICLE WEIGHT RATING

| | Gross Vehicle Weight Rating (Pounds) | | | | | | | | |
	6,000 & Less	6,001- 10,000	10,001- 14,000	14,001- 16,000	16,001- 19,500	19,501- 26,000	26,001- 33,000	33,001 & Over	Total
U.S. TOTAL									
2008	1,126	213,647	44,000	17,320	25,441	16,238	22,588	127,549	467,909
2007	1,292	260,435	66,575	27,631	31,665	24,170	27,592	136,839	576,199
2006	1,598	240,289	78,943	23,817	30,935	51,224	46,103	274,459	747,368
2005	2,258	246,744	100,773	27,158	34,457	40,869	39,820	253,828	745,907
2004	2,241	253,504	93,426	25,546	23,901	50,985	33,201	194,827	677,631
2003	2,445	256,122	79,054	19,865	18,518	35,633	26,393	136,083	574,113
2000	2,580	279,224	50,571	30,223	23,422	19,807	72,509	197,451	675,787
1995	5,995	225,968	150	25,241	1,346	11,403	93,237	205,254	568,594
1990	449	102,051	—	81	51	12,567	61,010	116,931	293,140
1985	15,447	132,871	5,870	—	—	16,537	57,238	132,429	360,392
1980	72,501	4,973	—	—	—	15,268	34,544	116,860	244,146
U.S DOMESTIC									
2008	81	164,700	42,539	15,674	23,267	15,626	18,689	96,899	377,475
2007	105	207,668	64,365	24,632	28,425	23,645	24,836	102,570	476,246
2006	135	194,968	76,322	21,707	28,109	50,372	41,881	231,397	644,891
2005	192	204,413	97,427	24,431	30,692	39,939	36,183	213,861	647,138
2004	231	212,652	90,331	23,305	21,660	49,803	29,287	164,711	591,980
2003	255	213,969	76,437	18,040	16,771	35,003	23,477	114,990	498,942
2000	271	221,830	48,911	26,997	20,921	18,812	68,678	171,565	577,985
1995	4,579	191,758	92	23,913	1,272	10,597	84,213	180,652	497,076
1990	337	94,030	—	55	51	11,458	53,957	107,002	266,890
1985	9,663	123,882	5,870	—	—	14,253	50,492	120,311	324,471
1980	68,868	4,397	—	—	—	12,337	30,958	98,002	214,562

* Reporting firms do not represent the entire industry.
SOURCE: *Ward's Automotive Group.*

U.S. AND CANADA VEHICLE FACTORY SALES

| | U.S. Plants | | | | Canadian Plants | | | |
	U.S Total	Exports to Canada	Other Exports	U.S. Domestic	Canada Total	Exports to U.S.	Other Exports	Canada Domestic
CARS								
2008	3,776,641	NA	NA	NA	1,195,436	NA	NA	NA
2007	3,924,268	NA	NA	NA	1,342,133	NA	NA	NA
2006	4,366,996	NA	NA	NA	1,427,582	NA	NA	NA
2005	4,321,272	NA	NA	NA	1,406,777	NA	NA	NA
2004	4,229,625	NA	NA	NA	1,400,129	NA	NA	NA
2003	4,510,469	NA	NA	NA	1,340,175	NA	NA	NA
2000	5,504,385	285,348	236,589	4,982,448	1,151,889	1,063,547	12,617	75,725
1995	6,309,839	265,594	256,422	5,787,820	1,028,970	912,939	22,128	93,903
1990	6,049,749	416,459	131,419	5,501,871	901,903	795,621	3,725	102,557
1985	8,002,259	635,546	29,978	7,336,735	1,068,420	878,052	5,878	184,490
1980	6,400,026	488,857	70,864	5,840,305	827,124	539,239	86,297	201,588
TRUCKS AND BUSES								
2008	4,322,861	296,702	357,614	3,668,545	684,183	555,449	24,896	103,838
2007	6,200,712	374,739	486,429	5,339,544	861,711	746,417	13,004	102,290
2006	6,442,831	388,689	380,329	5,673,813	713,960	626,986	9,841	77,133
2005	7,246,737	424,819	375,783	6,446,135	830,683	747,926	7,558	75,199
2004	7,466,739	419,384	244,602	6,802,753	923,873	837,521	8,542	77,810
2003	7,143,429	411,539	245,641	6,486,249	917,240	806,830	8,648	101,762
2000	7,022,478	410,698	320,873	6,290,907	1,161,653	954,641	8,899	198,114
1995	5,713,469	318,470	183,654	5,211,345	1,004,717	871,134	5,180	128,403
1990	3,725,205	207,559	63,008	3,454,638	8,124,697	660,176	26,441	125,850
1985	3,464,327	197,903	32,828	3,233,596	853,974	677,998	7,706	168,270
1980	1,667,283	86,420	117,055	1,463,808	525,968	290,529	47,228	188,211

NA - Not available.
* Reporting firms do not represent the entire industry.
SOURCE: *Ward's Automotive Group.*

Car Production by Make and State

U.S. CAR PRODUCTION BY STATE AND PLANT, 2008

State/City	Model	Units	Percent	State/City	Model	Units	Percent
ALABAMA		**152,588**	**4.0**		**Total AutoAlliance**	**167,490**	**4.4**
Montgomery	Hyundai Sonata	152,588	4.0	Detroit	Dodge Viper	1,545	—
	Total Hyundai	**152,588**	**4.0**	Sterling Heights	Chrysler Sebring Convertible	25,592	0.7
CALIFORNIA		**220,192**	**5.8**		Chrysler Sebring Sedan	53,664	1.4
Fremont	Pontiac Vibe	70,843	1.9		Dodge Avenger	82,247	2.2
	Toyota Corolla	149,349	4.0		**Total Chrysler**	**163,048**	**4.3**
	Total NUMMI	**220,192**	**5.8**	Wayne	Ford Focus	236,612	6.3
DELAWARE		**18,873**	**0.5**		**Total Ford**	**236,612**	**6.3**
Wilmington	Opel GT	3,128	0.1	Hamtramck	Buick Lucerne	53,301	1.4
	Pontiac Solstice	6,843	0.2		Cadillac DTS	32,558	0.9
	Saturn Sky	8,902	0.2	Lansing Grand River	Cadillac CTS	86,333	2.3
	Total General Motors	**18,873**	**0.5**		Cadillac STS	14,796	0.4
ILLINOIS		**263,981**	**7.0**	Orion	Chevrolet Malibu	93,271	2.5
Belvidere	Dodge Caliber	127,499	3.4		Pontiac G6	157,154	4.2
	Total Chrysler	**127,499**	**3.4**		**Total General Motors**	**437,413**	**11.6**
Chicago	Ford Taurus	46,546	1.2	**MISSISSIPPI**		**161,031**	**4.3**
	Lincoln MKS	23,388	0.6	Canton	Nissan Altima	161,031	4.3
	Mercury Sable	12,068	0.3		**Total Nissan**	**161,031**	**4.3**
	Total Ford	**82,002**	**2.2**	**OHIO**		**854,209**	**22.6**
Normal	Mitsubishi Eclipse	15,944	0.4	Lordstown	Chevrolet Cobalt	250,002	6.6
	Mitsubishi Galant	38,536	1.0		Pontiac G5	58,013	1.5
	Total Mitsubishi	**54,480**	**1.4**		**Total General Motors**	**308,015**	**8.2**
INDIANA		**172,011**	**4.6**	East Liberty	Honda Civic	107,454	2.8
Greensburg	Honda Civic	6,851	0.2	Marysville	Acura TL	57,207	1.5
	Total Honda	**6,851**	**0.2**		Honda Accord	381,533	10.1
Lafayette	Subaru Legacy	73,489	1.9		**Total Honda**	**546,194**	**14.5**
	Toyota Camry	91,671	2.4	**SOUTH CAROLINA**		**9,771**	**0.3**
	Total Subaru	**165,160**	**4.4**	Spartanburg	BMW Z4	9,771	0.3
KANSAS		**222,535**	**5.9**		**Total BMW**	**9,771**	**0.3**
Fairfax	Chevrolet Malibu	158,025	4.2	**TENNESSEE**		**212,851**	**5.6**
	Saturn Aura	64,510	1.7	Smyrna	Nissan Altima	159,597	4.2
	Total General Motors	**222,535**	**5.9**		Nissan Maxima	53,254	1.4
KENTUCKY		**484,036**	**12.8**		**Total Nissan**	**212,851**	**5.6**
Bowling Green	Cadillac XLR	1,451	—				
	Chevrolet Corvette	30,897	0.8	**TOTAL U.S. CARS**		**3,776,641**	**100.0**
	Total General Motors	**32,348**	**0.9**				
Georgetown	Toyota Avalon	51,563	1.4				
	Toyota Camry	382,433	10.1				
	Toyota Solara	17,692	0.5				
	Total Toyota	**451,688**	**12.0**				
MICHIGAN		**1,004,563**	**26.6**				
Flat Rock	Ford Mustang	92,345	2.4				
	Mazda6	75,145	2.0				

TOP STATES IN CALENDAR 2008 U.S. PRODUCTION

Rank	Cars	Rank	Trucks
1. Michigan	1,004,563	1. Michigan	848,091
2. Ohio	854,209	2. Missouri	680,424
3. Kentucky	484,036	3. Ohio	629,877
4. Illinois	263,981	4. Alabama	519,750
5. Kansas	222,535	5. Indiana	423,241

SOURCE: Ward's AutoInfoBank.

Truck Production by Make and State

U.S. TRUCK PRODUCTION BY STATE AND PLANT, 2008

State/City	Model	Units	Percent
ALABAMA		**519,750**	**10.6**
Lincoln	Honda Odyssey	161,219	3.3
	Honda Pilot	121,516	2.5
	Total Honda	**282,735**	**5.8**
Montgomery	Hyundai Santa Fe	84,454	1.7
	Total Hyundai	**84,454**	**1.7**
Vance	Mercedes GL	34,958	0.7
	Mercedes M-Class	96,395	2.0
	Mercedes R-Class	21,208	0.4
	Total Mercedes	**152,561**	**3.1**
CALIFORNIA		**121,820**	**2.5**
Fremont	Toyota Tacoma	121,820	2.5
	Total NUMMI	**121,820**	**2.5**
DELAWARE		**50,983**	**1.0**
Newark	Chrysler Aspen	24,546	0.5
	Dodge Durango	26,437	0.5
	Total Chrysler	**50,983**	**1.0**
GEORGIA		**84,018**	**1.7**
Doraville	Chevrolet Uplander	63,588	1.3
	Pontiac Montana SV6	20,430	0.4
	Total General Motors	**84,018**	**1.7**
ILLINOIS		**161,836**	**3.3**
Belvidere	Jeep Compass	45,590	0.9
	Jeep Patriot	90,432	1.8
	Total Chrysler	**136,022**	**2.8**
Chicago	Ford Taurus X	21,276	0.4
	Total Ford	**21,276**	**0.4**
Normal	Mitsubishi Endeavor	4,538	0.1
	Total Mitsubishi	**4,538**	**0.1**
INDIANA		**423,241**	**8.6**
Mishawaka	Hummer H2	6,881	0.1
	Total AM General	**6,881**	**0.1**
Fort Wayne	Chevrolet Silverado	140,495	2.9
	GMC Sierra	49,457	1.0
	Total General Motors	**189,952**	**3.9**
Lafayette	Subaru Tribeca	18,108	0.4
	Total Subaru	**18,108**	**0.4**
Princeton	Toyota Sequoia	37,098	0.8
	Toyota Sienna	135,989	2.8
	Toyota Tundra	35,213	0.7
	Total Toyota	**208,300**	**4.3**
KENTUCKY		**298,430**	**6.1**
Kentucky Truck	Ford F-SuperDuty	194,477	4.0
Louisville	Ford Explorer	87,433	1.8
	Mercury Mountaineer	10,172	0.2
	Total Ford	**292,082**	**6.0**
Georgetown	Toyota Venza	6,348	0.1
	Total Toyota	**6,348**	**0.1**
LOUISIANA		**94,237**	**1.9**
Shreveport	Chevrolet Colorado	57,290	1.2
	GMC Canyon	17,032	0.3
	Hummer H3	15,507	0.3
	Hummter H3T	3,707	0.1
	Isuzu i-Series	701	--
	Total General Motors	**94,237**	**1.9**
MICHIGAN		**848,091**	**17.3**
Detroit	Jeep Commander	19,263	0.4
	Jeep Grand Cherokee	72,931	1.5
Warren	Dodge Dakota	27,614	0.6
	Dodge Ram Pickup	104,023	2.1
	Mitsubishi Raider	4,513	0.1
	Total Chrysler	**228,344**	**4.7**
Dearborn Truck	Ford F-Series	176,724	3.6
	Lincoln Mark LT	4,823	0.1
Detroit	Ford Chassis	3,829	0.1
Wayne	Ford Expedition	54,179	1.1
	Lincoln Navigator	13,490	0.3
	Total Ford	**253,045**	**5.2**
Flint 1	Chevrolet Silverado	48,469	1.0
	GMC Sierra	24,224	0.5
Flint 3	Chevrolet Kodiak	8,013	0.2
	GMC Topkick	13,586	0.3
	Isuzu Truck	552	--
Lansing Delta	Buick Enclave	62,785	1.3
	GMC Acadia	92,903	1.9
	Saturn Outlook	22,448	0.5
Lansing Grand River	Cadillac SRX	17,021	0.3
Pontiac East	Chevrolet Silverado	56,210	1.1
	GMC Sierra	20,491	0.4
	Total General Motors	**366,702**	**7.5**
MINNESOTA		**93,320**	**1.9**
Twin Cities	Ford Ranger	89,000	1.8
	Mazda Pickup	4,320	0.1
	Total Ford	**93,320**	**1.9**
MISSISSIPPI		**71,848**	**1.5**
Canton	Infiniti QX56	8,522	0.2
	Nissan Armada	21,138	0.4
	Nissan Quest	17,151	0.4
	Nissan Titan	25,037	0.5
	Total Nissan	**71,848**	**1.5**
MISSOURI		**680,424**	**13.9**
St. Louis North	Dodge Ram Pickup	80,353	1.6
St. Louis South	Chrysler Town & Country	12,993	0.3
	Dodge Caravan	58,302	1.2
	Total Chrysler	**151,648**	**3.1**
Kansas City 1	Ford Escape	208,624	4.3
	Mazda Tribute	15,907	0.3
	Mercury Mariner	33,554	0.7
Kansas City 2	Ford F-Series	146,604	3.0
	Total Ford	**404,689**	**8.3**
Wentzville	Chevrolet Express	95,019	1.9
	GMC Savana	29,068	0.6
	Total General Motors	**124,087**	**2.5**
OHIO		**629,877**	**12.9**
Toledo North	Dodge Nitro	38,974	0.8
	Jeep Liberty	81,603	1.7
Toledo South	Jeep Wrangler	52,153	1.1
	Jeep Wrangler Unlimited	75,754	1.5
	Total Chrysler	**248,484**	**5.1**
Avon Lake	Ford Econoline	126,640	2.6
	Total Ford	**126,640**	**2.6**
Moraine	Chevrolet TrailBlazer	71,490	1.5
	GMC Envoy	27,405	0.6
	Isuzu Ascender	310	--
	Saab 9-7X	4,159	0.1
	Total General Motors	**103,364**	**2.1**
East Liberty	Honda CR-V	110,821	2.3
	Honda Element	19,608	0.4
Marysville	Acura RDX	20,960	0.4
	Total Honda	**151,389**	**3.1**
SOUTH CAROLINA		**160,968**	**3.3**
Spartanburg	BMW X5	123,271	2.5
	BMW X6	37,697	0.8
	Total BMW	**160,968**	**3.3**
TENNESSEE		**141,795**	**2.9**
Spring Hill	Chevrolet Traverse	43,293	0.9
	Total General Motors	**43,293**	**0.9**
Smyrna	Nissan Frontier	38,793	0.8
	Nissan Pathfinder	28,644	0.6
	Nissan Xterra	30,065	0.6
	Suzuki Equator	1,000	--
	Total Nissan	**98,502**	**2.0**
TEXAS		**252,885**	**5.2**
Arlington	Cadillac Escalade	26,170	0.5
	Cadillac Escalade ESV	10,748	0.2
	Chevrolet Suburban	17,035	0.3
	Chevrolet Tahoe	72,110	1.5
	GMC Yukon	27,597	0.6
	GMC Yukon XL	9,175	0.2
	Total General Motors	**162,835**	**3.3**
San Antonio	Toyota Tundra	90,050	1.8
	Total Toyota	**90,050**	**1.8**
WISCONSIN		**98,061**	**2.0**
Janesville 1	Chevrolet Suburban	18,131	0.4
	Chevrolet Tahoe	29,092	0.6
	GMC Yukon	25,711	0.5
	GMC Yukon XL	22,700	0.5
Janesville 3	Chevrolet Tiltmaster	414	--
	GMC Forward	586	--
	Isuzu NPR	1,427	--
	Total General Motors	**98,061**	**2.0**
	Other Medium/Heavy Truck	**164,866**	**3.4**
TOTAL TRUCKS		**4,896,450**	**100.0**

SOURCE: *Ward's AutoInfoBank.*

Factory Installations of Selected Equipment

FACTORY INSTALLATIONS OF SELECTED EQUIPMENT BY MODEL YEAR

	2008		2007		2006		2005	
	Units (000)	% of Total	Units (000)	% of Total	Units (000)	% of Total	Units (000)	% of Total
CARS								
Automatic Transmission	5,597	91.7	5,253	90.4	5,362	91.4	5,251	90.4
5-Speed Transmission	375	6.2	408	7.0	392	6.7	441	7.6
6-Speed Transmission	128	2.1	154	2.6	113	1.9	82	1.4
All-Wheel Drive	158	2.6	159	2.7	145	2.5	184	3.2
4-Cylinder Engine	3,481	57.1	3,059	52.6	2,846	48.5	3,110	53.5
6-Cylinder Engine	1,840	30.2	2,015	34.6	2,277	38.8	2,275	39.1
8-Cylinder Engine	341	5.6	419	7.2	596	10.2	428	7.4
Traction Control	2,559	41.9	2,332	40.1	2,191	37.3	1,699	29.2
Antilock Brakes	4,743	77.7	4,186	72.0	4,006	68.3	3,448	59.3
Power Door Locks	5,895	96.6	5,544	95.3	5,607	95.6	5,400	92.9
Power Seats, 4 or 6 way	2,857	46.8	2,676	46.0	3,136	53.5	2,903	49.9
Memory Seats	394	6.5	365	6.3	491	8.4	451	7.8
Power Windows	5,885	96.5	5,564	95.7	5,603	95.5	5,356	92.1
Sun Roof	1,580	25.9	1,499	25.8	1,593	27.2	1,461	25.1
Side Airbags	4,521	74.1	3,633	62.5	2,768	47.2	1,947	33.5
Side Curtain Airbags	4,934	80.9	3,846	66.1	2,371	40.4	1,443	24.8
Navigation System	274	4.5	216	3.7	236	4.0	68	1.2
Keyless Remote	5,605	91.9	5,278	90.8	5,275	89.9	5,228	89.9
Air Conditioning,Automatic Temp. Control	1,263	20.7	1,256	21.6	1,495	25.5	1,556	26.8
Air Conditioning, Manual Temp. Control	4,796	78.6	4,517	77.7	4,394	74.9	4,257	73.2
Limited-Slip Differential	262	4.3	270	4.6	243	4.1	195	3.3
Styled Wheels	3,737	61.3	3,675	63.2	3,749	63.9	3,488	60.0
Adjustable Steering Column	6,100	100.0	5,752	98.9	5,803	98.9	5,708	98.2
Automatic Headlamp	3,430	56.2	2,968	51.0	2,744	46.8	2,560	44.0
Cruise Control	5,662	92.8	5,278	90.8	5,493	93.6	5,229	89.9
LIGHT TRUCKS (0-10,000 lbs. G.V.W.R.)								
AutomaticTransmission	6,860	97.8	7,373	96.5	6,235	96.6	8,024	95.8
Four Wheel Antilock Brakes	6,690	95.3	7,158	93.7	5,980	92.7	7,523	89.8
Rear Antilock Brakes	203	2.9	247	3.2	162	2.5	329	3.9
Keyless Entry	6,135	87.4	6,533	85.5	5,205	80.7	7,015	83.7
Anti-Theft Device	6,808	97.0	7,149	93.6	5,460	84.6	6,899	82.3
Side Airbag	3,471	49.5	2,396	31.4	1,301	20.2	1,705	20.4
Four-Wheel Drive	3,411	48.6	3,565	46.7	3,125	48.4	4,053	48.4
Diesel Engine	459	6.5	392	5.1	564	8.8	517	6.2
4-Cylinder Gasoline Engine	706	10.1	754	9.9	451	7.0	424	5.1
5-Cylinder Gasoline Engine	88	1.3	112	1.5	215	3.3	144	1.7
6-Cylinder Gasoline Engine	3,261	47.6	3,461	45.3	2,846	43.8	4,216	50.4
8-Cylinder Gasoline Engine	2,487	40.6	3,275	42.9	2,888	44.9	3,539	42.2
10-Cylinder Gasoline Engine	29	0.4	35	0.5	51	0.9	54	0.7
Air Conditioning	2,284	98.7	7,619	99.8	6,432	99.7	8,370	99.9
Cruise Control	6,422	91.5	6,856	89.8	5,744	89.0	7,554	90.2
Limited-Slip Differential	2,049	29.2	2,413	31.6	2,060	31.9	2,881	34.4

* Based on production in the United States, Canada and Mexico for the United States market.
SOURCE: Ward's Automotive Group.

Recreation Vehicle Shipments

U.S. RECREATION VEHICLE SHIPMENTS BY TYPE

| | | Travel Trailers | | Folding | | Motor Homes | | | Multi-use |
| | | | | | | Type A | Type B | Type C | |
Year	Total All Types	Conven-tional	Fifth Wheel[1]	Camping Trailers	Truck Campers	Conven-tional	Van Campers[2]	Chopped Vans[3]	Van Con-versions
2008	237,000	128,100	57,000	18,900	4,700	14,900	1,900	11,500	NA
2007	353,500	180,200	81,500	28,800	7,500	32,900	3,100	19,500	NA
2006	416,800	203,600	88,800	34,000	8,200	32,700	3,000	20,200	26,300
2005	419,500	196,600	84,800	32,800	8,800	37,900	2,600	20,900	35,100
2004	412,100	163,600	91,000	34,100	9,600	46,300	2,500	23,000	42,000
2003	377,800	139,800	74,600	35,700	8,800	41,500	2,100	18,300	57,000
2002	378,700	129,700	66,100	44,800	10,000	39,600	2,800	18,000	67,700
2001	321,000	102,200	54,700	40,800	9,900	33,400	2,600	13,200	64,200
2000	418,300	114,500	62,300	51,300	11,100	41,000	3,400	16,500	118,200
1999	473,800	117,500	60,500	60,100	11,500	49,400	3,600	18,600	152,600
1998	441,300	98,600	56,500	63,300	10,800	42,900	3,600	17,000	148,600
1997	438,800	78,800	52,800	57,600	10,300	37,600	3,800	13,600	184,300
1996	466,800	75,400	48,500	57,300	11,000	36,500	4,100	14,700	219,300
1995	475,200	75,300	45,900	61,100	11,900	33,000	4,100	15,700	228,200
1994	518,800	79,100	48,900	61,700	11,400	37,300	3,500	17,300	259,600
1993	420,200	69,700	43,900	51,900	10,900	31,900	3,000	16,500	192,400
1992	382,700	63,600	38,900	43,300	10,600	27,300	2,900	16,800	179,300
1991	293,700	49,300	28,300	33,900	9,600	23,500	3,500	15,200	130,400
1990	347,300	52,500	27,900	30,700	9,700	29,000	5,900	17,400	174,200
1989	388,300	53,500	29,400	33,900	9,900	35,400	5,000	20,800	200,400
1988	420,000	58,300	31,300	42,300	11,000	41,500	5,200	26,200	204,200
1987	393,600	59,100	27,100	41,600	10,100	40,800	6,600	26,400	181,900
1986	371,700	55,100	23,100	36,500	7,400	33,300	6,200	28,200	181,900
1985	351,700	54,700	20,700	35,900	6,900	33,600	6,700	28,400	164,800
1984	391,000	65,600	19,600	40,900	7,600	42,100	7,100	32,800	175,300

(1) To be towed by pickup truck with fifth-wheel hitch mounted on the truck bed.
(2) Panel-type trucks with interior converted to living area.
(3) Chopped Vans: Mini - unit over 8' high attaches to van chassis of 6,500 lbs. GVWR or more; Low Profile - unit less than 8' high attaches to van chassis of 6,500 lbs. GVWR or more: Compact - unit attaches to van chassis less than 6,500 lbs. GVWR.
SOURCE: Recreation Vehicle Industry Assn.

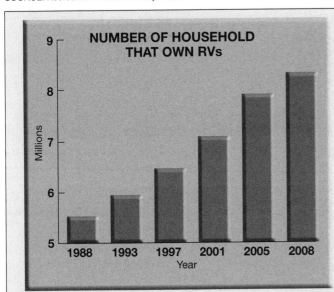

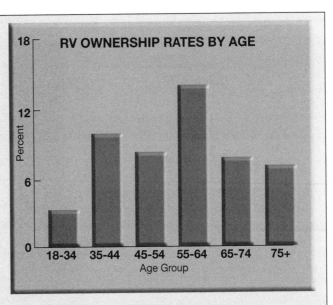

SOURCE: Recreation Vehicle Industry Association. Permission for further use must be obtained from the Recreation Vehicle Industry Association.

World Vehicle Production by Country

WORLD VEHICLE PRODUCTION IN MAJOR COUNTRIES, 2008

Region/Country	Cars	Commercial Vehicles	Total
North America			
Canada	1,195,436	886,805	2,082,241
Mexico	1,217,458	950,486	2,167,944
United States	3,776,641	4,896,450	8,673,091
Total	**6,189,535**	**6,733,741**	**12,923,276**
Western Europe			
Austria	125,436	25,441	150,877
Belgium	680,149	44,367	724,516
France	2,144,744	422,816	2,567,560
Germany	5,532,032	513,698	6,045,730
Italy	659,221	364,553	1,023,774
Netherlands	59,223	73,271	132,494
Portugal	132,242	42,913	175,155
Spain	2,013,861	527,783	2,541,644
Sweden	252,287	46,310	298,597
United Kingdom	1,447,777	201,716	1,649,493
Total	**13,046,972**	**2,262,868**	**15,309,840**
Eastern/Central Europe			
Czech Republic	933,312	12,510	945,822
Hungary	342,359	3,696	346,055
Poland	840,000	104,500	944,500
Russia	1,468,579	325,914	1,794,493
Turkey	621,567	525,543	1,147,110
Other	1,387,864	54,190	1,442,054
Total	**5,593,681**	**1,026,353**	**6,620,034**
Asia/Pacific			
Australia	285,590	38,528	324,118
China	6,340,596	3,165,973	9,506,569
India	1,506,539	809,093	2,315,632
Japan	9,916,149	1,647,480	11,563,629
South Africa	321,124	241,841	562,965
South Korea	2,435,616	1,391,066	3,826,682
Taiwan	138,709	44,260	182,969
Other	1,289,873	1,156,781	2,446,654
Total	**22,234,196**	**8,495,022**	**30,729,218**
South America			
Argentina	399,577	197,509	597,086
Brazil	2,561,496	658,979	3,220,475
Total	**2,961,073**	**856,488**	**3,817,561**
Total Vehicles	**50,025,457**	**19,374,472**	**69,399,929**

NOTE: North America excludes buses. Table excludes smaller non-reporting countries.
SOURCE: Compiled by Ward's from various industry sources.

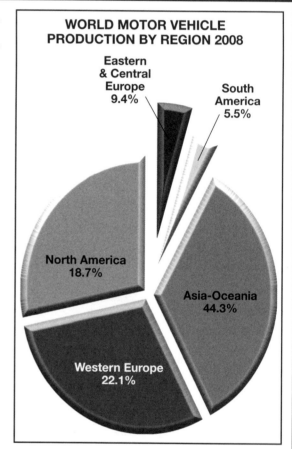

WORLD MOTOR VEHICLE PRODUCTION BY REGION 2008

- Eastern & Central Europe 9.4%
- South America 5.5%
- North America 18.7%
- Asia-Oceania 44.3%
- Western Europe 22.1%

WORLD VEHICLE PRODUCTION (In Thousands)

Year	United States	Canada	U.S. & Canada Total	Western Europe	Japan	Other	World Total	Percent of World Total United States	Percent of World Total U.S. & Canada
2008	8,673	2,082	10,755	15,310	11,564	31,771	69,400	12.5	15.5
2007	10,752	2,579	13,331	16,892	11,596	30,245	72,064	14.9	18.5
2006	11,260	2,571	13,831	16,540	11,484	26,706	68,561	16.4	20.2
2005	11,947	2,688	14,635	16,806	10,780	23,550	65,771	18.2	22.3
2004	11,988	2,712	14,700	17,195	10,512	21,310	63,717	18.8	23.1
2003	12,116	2,553	14,669	17,148	10,286	18,379	60,482	20.0	24.3
2002	12,280	2,629	14,909	16,907	10,258	16,806	58,880	20.9	25.3
2000	12,771	2,962	15,732	16,749	10,145	14,801	57,427	22.2	27.4
1995	11,985	2,408	14,393	17,045	10,196	8,349	49,983	24.0	28.8
1990	9,783	1,928	11,711	18,866	13,487	4,496	48,554	20.1	24.1
1985	11,653	1,933	13,586	16,113	12,271	2,939	44,909	25.9	30.3
1980	8,010	1,324	9,334	15,496	11,043	2,692	38,565	20.8	24.2
1975	8,987	1,385	10,372	13,581	6,942	2,211	33,106	27.1	31.3
1970	8,284	1,160	9,444	13,049	5,289	1,637	29,419	28.2	32.1
1965	11,138	847	11,985	9,576	1,876	834	24,271	45.9	49.4
1960	7,905	398	8,303	6,837	482	866	16,488	47.9	50.4
1955	9,204	452	9,656	3,741	68	163	13,628	67.5	70.9
1950	8,006	388	8,394	1,991	32	160	10,577	75.7	79.4

SOURCE: Ward's Automotive Group.

World Vehicle Production by Manufacturer

WORLD VEHICLE PRODUCTION BY MANUFACTURER BY RANK, 2007

Manufacturer	Cars	Light Trucks	Heavy Trucks	Buses	Total
General Motors	6,259,520	3,055,575	33,042	1,681	9,349,818
Toyota	7,211,474	1,108,333	129,107	85,776	8,534,690
Volkswagen	5,964,004	256,777	39,600	7,510	6,267,891
Ford	3,565,626	2,586,284	95,596	—	6,247,506
Hyundai-Kia	3,578,374	148,043	159,237	101,401	3,987,055
Honda	3,868,546	43,268	—	—	3,911,814
Peugeot Citroen	3,024,863	432,522	—	—	3,457,385
Nissan	2,650,813	641,734	131,429	7,422	3,431,398
Fiat-Iveco	1,990,715	536,578	127,542	24,616	2,679,451
Renault-Dacia-Samsung	2,276,044	392,996	—	—	2,669,040
Suzuki-Maruti	2,284,139	312,177	—	—	2,596,316
Chrysler	754,855	1,779,269	4,500	—	2,538,624
Daimler	1,335,226	257,350	438,954	65,447	2,096,977
BMW	1,541,503	—	—	—	1,541,503
Mitsubishi	1,100,528	304,273	7,174	—	1,411,975
Mazda	1,165,660	117,779	3,291	—	1,286,730
Daihatsu	711,595	130,968	13,608	—	856,171
Avtovaz	735,897	—	—	—	735,897
FAW	690,712	—	—	—	690,712
Tata	243,251	170,230	157,781	16,896	588,158
Fuji-Subaru	512,606	72,422	—	—	585,028
Chana	543,787	—	—	—	543,787
Isuzu	—	49,810	478,535	3,668	532,013
Beijing AIG	454,272	—	—	—	454,272
Dongfeng	437,035	—	—	—	437,035
Chery Auto	427,882	—	—	—	427,882
Others	189,057	69,935	85,036	24,700	368,728
SAIC	313,002	—	—	—	313,002
Brilliance	293,588	—	—	—	293,588
GAZ	39,138	179,596	30,105	—	248,839
Volvo Truck	—	14,825	210,446	10,753	236,024
Harbin Hafei	231,488	—	—	—	231,488
Geely	216,774	—	—	—	216,774
Anhui Jianghuai	209,880	—	—	—	209,880
Mahindra & Mahindra	104,441	64,115	—	—	168,556
PACCAR-DAF	—	—	126,960	—	126,960
Great Wall	122,605	—	—	—	122,605
Jiangxi Changhe	112,083	—	—	—	112,083
Porsche	107,170	—	—	—	107,170
Hino	—	4,586	97,323	4,984	106,893
BYD	100,376	—	—	—	100,376
China National	100,202	—	—	—	100,202
MAN	—	—	92,485	5,956	98,441
Navistar	—	—	70,839	15,919	86,758
Fujian	84,138	—	—	—	84,138
Scania	—	—	71,017	7,314	78,331
UAZ	31,869	40,293	—	—	72,162
Shannxi Auto	68,160	—	—	—	68,160
Shangdong Kaima	65,790	—	--	—	65,790

SOURCE: OICA

U.S. Retail Sales of Cars and Trucks

U.S. VEHICLE SALES

Year	Cars			Trucks			Total Vehicles		
	Domestic	Import	Total	Domestic	Import	Total	Domestic	Import	Total
2008	4,535	2,278	6,813	5,573	1,107	6,680	10,108	3,385	13,493
2007	5,253	2,365	7,618	7,434	1,408	8,842	12,687	3,773	16,460
2006	5,476	2,345	7,821	7,859	1,369	9,228	13,335	3,714	17,049
2005	5,533	2,187	7,720	8,488	1,237	9,725	14,021	3,424	17,444
2004	5,396	2,149	7,545	8,484	1,269	9,753	13,880	3,418	17,299
2003	5,527	2,083	7,610	8,111	1,246	9,357	13,638	3,329	16,967
2002	5,878	2,226	8,103	7,952	1,084	9,035	13,830	3,309	17,139
2001	6,325	2,098	8,423	8,048	1,002	9,050	14,373	3,100	17,472
2000	6,831	2,016	8,847	8,092	873	8,965	14,923	2,889	17,812
1999	6,979	1,719	8,698	7,922	795	8,716	14,901	2,513	17,415
1998	6,762	1,380	8,142	7,151	674	7,826	13,913	2,054	15,967
1997	6,917	1,355	8,272	6,632	593	7,226	13,549	1,949	15,498
1996	7,255	1,272	8,527	6,478	452	6,929	13,732	1,724	15,456
1995	7,129	1,506	8,635	6,064	417	6,481	13,193	1,923	15,116
1994	7,255	1,735	8,991	5,996	425	6,421	13,251	2,160	15,411
1993	6,742	1,776	8,518	5,287	394	5,681	12,029	2,170	14,199
1992	6,286	1,927	8,213	4,482	423	4,904	10,768	2,350	13,117
1991	6,162	2,023	8,185	3,814	550	4,365	9,976	2,574	12,550
1990	6,919	2,384	9,303	4,217	630	4,846	11,136	3,014	14,149
1989	7,098	2,680	9,779	4,405	661	5,067	11,503	3,342	14,845
1988	7,543	3,004	10,547	4,511	734	5,245	12,054	3,737	15,792
1987	7,085	3,107	10,192	4,059	942	5,001	11,144	4,049	15,193
1986	8,215	3,189	11,404	3,930	989	4,919	12,145	4,178	16,323
1985	8,205	2,775	10,979	3,905	841	4,746	12,110	3,615	15,725
1984	7,952	2,372	10,324	3,480	679	4,159	11,432	3,051	14,483
1983	6,795	2,353	9,148	2,663	500	3,163	9,458	2,853	12,312
1982	5,757	2,200	7,956	2,146	436	2,582	7,902	2,636	10,538
1981	6,181	2,308	8,489	1,821	468	2,289	8,001	2,777	10,778
1980	6,580	2,369	8,949	2,015	480	2,494	8,594	2,849	11,444
1979	8,341	2,332	10,673	3,010	470	3,480	11,351	2,802	14,153
1978	9,312	2,002	11,314	3,773	336	4,109	13,085	2,338	15,423
1977	9,109	2,074	11,183	3,352	323	3,675	12,461	2,397	14,859
1976	8,611	1,499	10,110	2,944	237	3,181	11,555	1,736	13,291
1975	7,053	1,571	8,624	2,249	229	2,478	9,302	1,800	11,103
1974	7,454	1,399	8,853	2,512	176	2,688	9,966	1,575	11,541
1973	9,676	1,748	11,424	2,916	233	3,148	12,592	1,981	14,572
1972	9,327	1,614	10,940	2,486	143	2,629	11,813	1,757	13,569
1971	8,681	1,561	10,242	2,011	85	2,096	10,692	1,646	12,338
1970	7,119	1,280	8,400	1,746	65	1,811	8,865	1,345	10,211
1969	8,464	1,118	9,582	1,936	34	1,970	10,400	1,152	11,552
1968	8,625	1,031	9,656	1,807	24	1,831	10,432	1,055	11,487
1967	7,568	769	8,337	1,524	21	1,545	9,092	790	9,882
1966	8,377	651	9,028	1,619	17	1,636	9,996	668	10,664
1965	8,763	569	9,332	1,539	14	1,553	10,302	583	10,885
1964	7,617	484	8,101	1,351	42	1,393	8,968	526	9,494
1963	7,334	386	7,720	1,230	40	1,270	8,564	426	8,990
1961	5,556	379	5,935	908	29	937	6,464	408	6,872
1959	5,486	614	6,100	928	37	965	6,414	651	7,065
1957	5,826	207	6,033	878	16	894	6,704	223	6,927
1955	7,408	58	7,466	1,012	3	1,015	8,420	61	8,481
1953	5,775	33	5,808	965	NA	965	6,740	33	6,773
1951	5,143	21	5,164	1,111	NA	1,111	6,254	21	6,275
1942-1950	NA	NA	NA	NA	NA	NA	NA	NA	NA
1941	3,763	NA	3,763	902	NA	902	4,665	NA	4,665
1939	2,724	NA	2,724	521	NA	521	3,245	NA	3,245
1937	3,508	NA	3,508	645	NA	645	4,153	NA	4,153

NOTE: Data are in thousands of units. NA is not available.

U.S. Retail Sales of Cars by Model

U.S. SALES OF CARS BY MODEL

Model	2008	2007	2006	2005	2004
1-Series*	12,018	—	—	—	—
3-Series*	112,464	142,490	120,180	106,950	106,549
5-Series*	45,915	54,142	56,756	52,722	45,584
6-Series*	6,533	9,033	9,322	9,934	8,198
7-Series*	12,276	14,773	17,796	18,165	16,155
Z4	5,879	10,097	12,284	10,045	13,654
Z8*	—	—	5	17	110
BMW Total	**195,085**	**230,535**	**216,343**	**197,833**	**190,250**
Mini Cooper*	54,077	42,045	39,171	40,820	36,032
BMW TOTAL	**249,162**	**272,580**	**255,514**	**238,653**	**226,282**
300M	—	—	—	—	5,110
300 Series	62,352	120,636	143,647	144,048	107,820
Concorde	—	—	—	203	4,223
Crossfire*	2,021	8,774	8,216	14,665	14,969
PT Cruiser Convertible	1,094	10,978	12,502	17,852	15,996
Sebring Convertible	27,437	21,599	18,457	35,766	36,434
Sebring Coupe	—	—	856	4,877	10,410
Sebring Sedan	44,226	71,531	50,044	49,678	57,250
Chrysler Total	**137,130**	**233,518**	**233,722**	**267,089**	**252,212**
Avenger	61,963	83,804	—	—	—
Caliber	84,158	101,079	92,224	—	—
Challenger	17,423	—	—	—	—
Charger	97,367	119,289	114,201	44,804	—
Intrepid	—	—	—	285	7,880
Magnum	6,912	30,256	40,095	52,487	39,217
Neon	—	—	17,239	113,332	113,476
Stratus Coupe	—	—	400	7,973	19,752
Stratus Sedan	—	1,478	50,993	91,688	79,017
Viper	1,172	435	1,455	1,652	1,782
Dodge Total	**268,995**	**336,341**	**316,607**	**312,221**	**261,124**
CHRYSLER TOTAL	**406,125**	**569,859**	**550,329**	**579,310**	**513,336**
C-Class*	72,471	63,701	50,187	60,658	69,251
CL*	2,733	3,672	1,312	1,320	2,683
CLK*	10,844	15,009	16,415	18,227	22,556
CLS*	5,775	7,906	10,763	14,835	—
E-Class*	38,576	48,950	50,195	50,383	58,954
S-Class*	17,787	26,081	30,886	16,036	20,460
SL*	5,464	6,126	8,462	10,080	12,885
SLK*	4,941	7,270	10,410	11,278	7,360
Mercedes Total	**158,591**	**178,715**	**178,630**	**182,817**	**194,149**
Fortwo*	24,622	—	—	—	—
Smart Total	**24,622**	**—**	**—**	**—**	**—**
DAIMLER TOTAL	**183,213**	**178,715**	**178,630**	**182,817**	**194,149**
Crown Victoria	48,557	60,901	62,976	63,939	70,816
Escort	—	—	—	—	1,210
Five Hundred	—	35,146	84,218	107,932	14,106
Focus	195,823	173,213	177,006	184,825	208,339
Ford GT	—	231	1,919	1,302	144
Fusion	147,569	149,552	142,502	16,983	—
Mustang	91,251	134,626	166,530	160,975	129,858
Taurus	52,667	33,032	174,803	196,919	248,148

U.S. Retail Sales of Cars by Model

U.S. SALES OF CARS BY MODEL — continued

Model	2008	2007	2006	2005	2004
Thunderbird	—	—	469	9,548	11,998
Ford Total	**535,867**	**586,701**	**810,423**	**742,423**	**684,619**
Lincoln LS	—	—	8,797	19,109	27,066
MKS	12,982	—	—	—	—
MKZ	30,117	34,363	11,176	—	—
Town Car	15,653	26,739	39,295	47,122	51,908
Zephyr	—	—	21,938	4,985	—
Lincoln Total	**58,752**	**61,102**	**81,206**	**71,216**	**78,974**
Grand Marquis	29,766	50,664	54,688	64,716	79,329
Milan	31,393	37,244	35,853	5,321	—
Montego	—	10,755	22,332	27,007	2,974
Sable	16,187	10,366	—	24,149	42,737
Mercury Total	**77,346**	**109,029**	**112,873**	**121,193**	**125,040**
30*	4,299	2,090	—	—	—
40*	9,687	18,141	24,566	24,241	25,540
50*	1,856	2,850	4,138	5,671	2,509
60*	8,966	18,511	25,753	24,695	27,835
70*	8,787	8,310	9,549	8,832	14,551
80*	11,038	12,347	5,469	10,181	13,390
Volvo Total	**44,633**	**62,249**	**69,475**	**73,620**	**83,825**
FORD TOTAL	**716,598**	**819,081**	**1,073,977**	**1,008,452**	**972,458**
Century	—	5	83	6,504	67,264
LaCrosse	36,873	47,747	71,072	92,669	10,995
LeSabre	—	121	2,313	75,369	114,157
Lucerne	54,930	82,923	96,515	8,821	—
Park Ave	—	26	51	2,175	17,138
Regal	—	—	30	602	13,775
Buick Total	**91,803**	**130,822**	**170,064**	**186,140**	**223,329**
CTS	58,774	57,029	54,846	61,512	57,211
Deville	—	71	807	38,661	68,195
DTS	30,479	51,469	58,224	23,322	—
Eldorado	—	—	—	—	7
Seville	—	—	9	137	3,386
STS	14,790	20,873	25,676	33,497	9,484
XLR	1,250	1,750	3,203	3,730	3,665
Cadillac Total	**105,293**	**131,192**	**142,765**	**160,859**	**141,948**
Aveo*	55,360	67,028	58,244	68,085	56,642
Camaro	—	—	—	—	127
Cavalier	—	57	355	18,960	195,275
Classic	—	17	18	42,358	88,211
Cobalt	188,045	200,620	211,449	212,667	4,959
Corvette	26,971	33,685	36,518	32,489	35,276
Impala	265,840	311,128	289,868	246,481	290,259
Malibu	178,253	128,312	163,853	203,503	179,806
Monte Carlo	711	15,784	34,113	33,562	57,679
Prizm	—	—	—	—	5
Chevrolet Total	**715,180**	**756,631**	**794,418**	**858,105**	**908,239**
Alero	—	—	67	1,382	20,156
Aurora	—	—	—	18	206
Intrigue	—	—	—	—	55
Oldsmobile Total	**—**	**—**	**67**	**1,400**	**20,417**
Bonneville	—	130	1,160	10,037	29,852

U.S. Retail Sales of Cars by Model

U.S. SALES OF CARS BY MODEL — continued

Model	2008	2007	2006	2005	2004
Firebird	—	—	—	—	109
G5	25,439	27,928	7,902	—	—
G6	140,240	150,001	157,644	124,844	16,185
G8*	15,002	—	—	—	—
Grand Am	—	99	828	31,613	133,707
Grand Prix	8,636	87,622	108,634	122,398	131,551
GTO*	52	4,200	11,268	11,590	13,569
Solstice	10,739	16,779	19,710	5,445	—
Sunfire	—	39	853	25,114	36,095
Vibe	46,551	37,170	45,221	64,271	58,894
Pontiac Total	**246,659**	**323,968**	**353,220**	**395,312**	**419,962**
9-2X*	3	118	1,435	5,940	1,788
9-3*	15,167	22,979	24,134	24,108	27,322
9-5*	2,538	4,357	4,991	6,023	9,049
Saab Total	**17,708**	**27,454**	**30,560**	**36,071**	**38,159**
Astra*	11,968	—	—	—	—
Aura	59,380	59,964	19,746	—	—
Ion	315	47,873	102,042	100,891	104,044
Saturn L	—	2	20	5,036	19,453
Sky	9,162	11,263	8,671	—	—
Saturn Total	**80,825**	**119,102**	**130,479**	**105,927**	**123,497**
GM TOTAL	**1,257,468**	**1,489,169**	**1,621,573**	**1,743,814**	**1,875,551**
CL	—	—	—	1	283
NSX*	—	2	58	206	178
RL*	4,517	6,262	11,501	17,572	8,753
RSX*	1	296	16,996	20,809	21,940
TL	46,766	58,545	71,348	78,218	77,895
TSX*	31,998	33,037	38,035	34,856	30,365
Acura Total	**83,282**	**98,142**	**137,938**	**151,662**	**139,414**
Accord	309,461	355,767	323,079	350,257	352,925
Accord*	63,328	36,464	31,362	19,036	33,845
Civic	305,509	292,192	272,899	263,833	274,540
Civic*	33,780	38,903	43,739	44,582	34,656
FCX*	11	10	—	6	6
Fit*	79,794	56,432	27,934	—	—
Insight*	—	3	728	666	583
S2000*	2,538	4,302	6,271	7,780	7,320
Honda Total	**794,421**	**784,073**	**706,012**	**686,160**	**703,875**
HONDA TOTAL	**877,703**	**882,215**	**843,950**	**837,822**	**843,289**
Accent*	50,431	36,055	34,735	41,012	43,258
Azera*	14,461	21,948	24,057	500	—
Elantra*	94,720	85,724	98,853	116,336	112,892
Genesis*	6,167	—	—	—	—
Sonata	117,357	145,568	149,463	65,747	—
Sonata*	—	—	50	64,618	107,189
Tiburon*	9,111	14,073	17,382	20,600	20,125
XG350*	—	—	2,776	17,145	16,630
HYUNDAI TOTAL	**292,247**	**303,368**	**327,316**	**325,958**	**300,094**
Amanti*	3,614	5,522	9,594	18,668	19,894
Optima*	44,904	40,901	38,408	41,349	53,492
Rio*	36,532	33,370	28,388	30,290	38,518
Spectra*	68,465	73,474	72,557	56,088	44,004

U.S. Retail Sales
of Cars by Model

U.S. SALES OF CARS BY MODEL — continued

Model	2008	2007	2006	2005	2004
KIA TOTAL	153,515	153,267	148,947	146,395	155,908
Mazda3*	109,957	120,291	94,437	97,388	76,080
Mazda6	52,590	57,575	66,203	71,447	72,148
Mazda 626	—	—	—	2	15
Millenia*	—	—	—	—	18
MX-5 Miata*	10,977	15,075	16,897	9,801	9,356
Protégé*	—	—	—	—	6,371
RX-8*	3,368	5,767	9,344	14,673	23,690
MAZDA TOTAL	176,892	198,708	186,881	193,311	187,678
Diamante*	—	—	—	160	4,379
Eclipse	20,107	27,292	33,003	24,487	19,361
Galant	26,941	26,491	27,673	33,976	43,491
Lancer*	27,861	31,376	23,167	27,849	41,706
MITSUBISHI TOTAL	74,909	85,159	83,843	86,472	108,937
G20*	—	—	—	—	1
G35*	64,181	71,811	60,745	68,728	71,177
I35*	—	—	—	1,044	11,637
M35/45*	15,618	21,885	25,658	24,000	2,090
Q45*	—	22	393	1,129	1,972
Infiniti Total	79,799	93,718	86,796	94,901	86,877
350Z*	10,337	18,957	24,635	27,278	30,690
Altima	269,668	284,762	232,457	255,371	235,889
GT-R*	1,730	—	—	—	—
Maxima	47,072	52,574	69,763	75,425	76,340
Maxima*	—	—	—	—	27
Sentra	99,797	106,522	117,922	119,489	106,934
Versa	85,182	79,443	22,044	—	—
Nissan Total	513,786	542,258	466,821	477,563	449,880
NISSAN TOTAL	593,585	635,976	553,617	572,464	536,757
Boxster*	2,982	3,622	4,503	7,879	3,513
Carrera GT*	—	4	85	340	189
Cayman*	3,513	6,027	7,025	—	—
Porsche 911*	8,324	12,493	12,045	10,107	9,654
PORSCHE TOTAL	14,819	22,146	23,658	18,326	13,356
Impreza*	49,098	46,333	41,148	33,637	32,209
Legacy	66,876	78,428	84,442	87,788	89,453
SUBARU TOTAL	115,974	124,761	125,590	121,425	121,662
Aerio*	80	1,531	8,769	7,967	9,439
Forenza*	20,796	42,113	48,579	41,394	24,796
SX4*	29,483	15,209	3,453	—	—
Verona*	3	315	2,302	8,411	12,874
SUZUKI TOTAL	50,362	59,168	63,103	57,772	47,109
Jaguar S-Type*	904	3,524	5,875	8,897	10,975
Jaguar Vanden Plas*	853	1,512	1,614	2,676	2,445
Jaguar X-Type*	431	3,198	5,214	10,941	21,542
Jaguar XF*	8,578	—	—	—	—
Jaguar XJ6/8*	1,471	2,638	3,078	4,930	6,990
Jaguar XJR*	128	324	335	698	1,117
Jaguar XK8*	2,459	4,487	4,567	2,282	2,806
TATA TOTAL	14,824	15,683	20,683	30,424	45,875
ES330*	—	—	15,390	67,577	75,916
ES350*	64,135	82,867	60,597	—	—
GS300/350*	13,876	21,314	23,665	27,807	6,914

U.S. Retail Sales of Cars by Model

U.S. SALES OF CARS BY MODEL — continued

Model	2008	2007	2006	2005	2004
GS430/450/460*	1,883	2,067	3,725	5,650	1,348
IS250/350*	49,432	54,933	54,267	11,018	—
IS300*	—	—	—	4,771	9,972
LS430/460/600*	20,255	35,226	19,546	26,043	32,272
SC430*	1,986	3,927	5,847	8,360	9,708
Lexus Total	**151,567**	**200,334**	**183,037**	**151,226**	**136,130**
tC*	40,980	63,852	79,125	74,415	28,062
xA*	39	9,547	32,603	28,033	24,184
xB*	45,220	45,834	61,306	54,037	47,013
xD*	27,665	10,948	—	—	—
Scion Total	**113,904**	**130,181**	**173,034**	**156,485**	**99,259**
Avalon	42,790	72,945	88,938	95,318	36,460
Camry	428,841	418,757	362,961	402,887	402,063
Camry*	7,776	54,351	85,484	28,816	24,927
Celica*	1	4	14	3,113	8,710
Corolla/Matrix	252,877	348,016	335,054	330,782	306,510
Corolla*	98,130	23,374	52,334	10,508	26,651
Echo*	—	3	16	1,544	3,899
MR2 Spyder*	1	—	5	780	2,621
Prius*	158,884	181,221	106,971	107,897	53,991
Yaris*	102,328	84,799	70,308	—	—
Toyota Total	**1,091,628**	**1,183,470**	**1,102,085**	**981,645**	**865,832**
TOYOTA TOTAL	**1,357,099**	**1,513,985**	**1,458,156**	**1,289,356**	**1,101,221**
A3*	4,759	6,354	8,040	5,389	—
A4*	36,930	35,606	40,230	37,516	33,438
A4 Cabrio*	4,709	6,975	6,599	6,938	7,394
A5*	4,120	—	—	—	—
A6*	11,406	11,239	15,819	18,074	14,455
A8*	2,433	3,059	4,686	5,430	5,943
R8*	900	241	—	—	—
RS6*	—	—	—	—	450
S4*	1,705	2,830	3,033	4,468	6,336
S5*	2,162	625	—	—	—
S6*	550	762	397	—	—
S8*	392	767	352	—	—
TT*	4,486	4,355	954	2,822	5,275
Audi Total	**74,552**	**72,813**	**80,110**	**80,637**	**73,291**
Beetle	15,520	17,155	18,166	17,003	21,025
Beetle Cabrio	10,957	13,866	16,944	19,336	21,132
CC*	2,105	—	—	—	—
EOS*	12,837	12,744	3,394	—	—
Golf*	12,232	14,643	17,089	15,690	24,669
Jetta	97,461	98,951	103,331	104,063	91,790
Passat*	30,034	37,183	54,208	49,233	67,640
Phaeton*	—	17	235	820	1,939
Rabbit*	23,176	27,201	11,610	—	—
VW Cabriolet	—	—	—	—	1
Volkswagen Total	**204,322**	**221,760**	**224,977**	**206,145**	**228,196**
VOLKSWAGEN TOTAL	**278,874**	**294,573**	**305,087**	**286,782**	**301,487**
TOTAL CARS	**6,813,369**	**7,618,413**	**7,820,854**	**7,719,553**	**7,545,149**

*Units imported from outside North America.
SOURCE: Ward's AutoInfoBank.

U.S. Retail Sales of Cars by Source, Market Class and Purchasing Sector

U.S. SALES OF CARS BY SOURCE

Year	Domestic	Imports From Japan	From Germany	From Other Countries	Total Imports	U.S. Total	Import Percent Total	Japan	Germany
2008	4,535,098	1,141,768	506,736	629,767	2,278,271	6,813,369	33.4	16.8	7.4
2007	5,253,350	1,183,144	567,287	614,632	2,365,063	7,618,413	31.0	15.5	7.4
2006	5,476,090	1,154,455	560,726	629,583	2,344,764	7,820,854	30.0	14.8	7.2
2005	5,533,020	922,934	534,286	729,313	2,186,533	7,719,553	28.3	12.0	6.9
2004	5,396,090	810,004	541,940	797,115	2,149,059	7,545,149	28.5	10.7	7.2
2003	5,527,430	830,355	543,823	708,873	2,083,051	7,610,481	27.4	10.9	7.1
2002	5,877,645	930,253	546,654	748,677	2,225,584	8,103,229	27.5	11.5	6.7
2001	6,324,996	836,685	522,659	738,285	2,097,629	8,422,625	24.9	9.9	6.2
2000	6,830,505	862,780	516,614	636,726	2,016,120	8,846,625	22.8	9.8	5.8
1999	6,979,357	757,568	466,870	494,489	1,718,927	8,698,284	19.8	8.7	5.4
1998	6,761,940	691,162	366,724	321,895	1,379,781	8,141,721	16.9	8.5	4.5
1997	6,916,769	726,104	297,028	332,173	1,355,305	8,272,074	16.4	8.8	3.6
1996	7,254,557	726,940	237,009	308,247	1,272,196	8,526,753	14.9	8.5	2.8
1995	7,128,707	981,506	207,482	317,269	1,506,257	8,634,964	17.4	11.4	2.4
1994	7,255,303	1,239,450	192,275	303,489	1,735,214	8,990,517	19.3	13.8	2.1
1993	6,741,667	1,328,445	186,177	261,570	1,776,192	8,517,859	20.9	15.6	2.2
1992	6,285,916	1,451,766	200,851	274,580	1,927,197	8,213,113	23.5	17.7	2.4
1991	6,161,573	1,500,239	192,713	330,454	2,023,406	8,184,979	24.7	18.3	2.4
1990	6,918,869	1,719,384	263,263	401,699	2,384,346	9,303,215	25.6	18.5	2.8
1989	7,098,098	1,897,957	246,206	536,256	2,680,419	9,778,517	27.4	19.4	2.5
1988	7,543,116	2,022,602	280,097	700,993	3,003,692	10,546,808	28.5	19.2	2.7
1987	7,085,279	2,114,224	337,232	655,142	3,106,598	10,191,877	30.5	20.7	3.3
1986	8,215,017	2,339,503	431,433	418,286	3,189,222	11,404,239	28.0	20.5	3.8
1985	8,204,670	2,170,898	407,684	195,935	2,774,517	10,979,187	25.3	19.8	3.7

SOURCE: *Ward's AutoInfoBank.*

U.S. CAR SALES BY SEGMENT

Year	Small	Middle	Large	Luxury	Total
2008	36.9	41.3	6.8	15.1	100.0
2007	33.3	41.6	9.0	16.1	100.0
2006	32.2	41.4	10.1	16.3	100.0
2005	31.2	42.0	10.2	16.6	100.0
2004	30.5	44.6	7.9	17.0	100.0
2003	30.9	45.5	6.3	17.3	100.0
2002	30.4	46.1	6.1	17.4	100.0
2001	30.6	46.1	6.4	16.8	100.0
2000	29.8	46.1	7.0	17.1	100.0
1999	25.2	50.8	7.6	16.5	100.0
1998	24.1	51.7	8.2	16.0	100.0

SOURCE: Ward's AutoInfoBank.

U.S. CAR SALES BY SECTOR

Year	Units by Consuming Sector (000) Consumer	Business	Government	Total	% of Total Sales Consumer	Business
2008	3,684	2,808	321	6,813	54.1	41.2
2007	4,088	3,250	280	7,618	53.7	42.7
2006	4,298	3,236	287	7,821	55.0	41.4
2005	4,308	3,143	269	7,720	55.8	40.7
2004	4,251	3,061	233	7,545	56.3	40.6
2003	4,341	3,074	195	7,610	57.0	40.4
2002	4,524	3,373	206	8,103	55.8	41.6
2001	4,632	3,568	223	8,423	55.0	42.4
2000	4,680	3,949	218	8,847	52.9	44.6
1999	4,366	4,155	175	8,697	50.2	47.8
1998	3,988	3,992	161	8,142	49.0	49.0
1997	3,910	4,216	147	8,273	47.3	51.0
1996	4,079	4,273	176	8,527	47.8	50.1
1995	4,351	4,186	151	8,687	50.1	48.2
1994	4,600	4,268	124	8,991	51.2	47.5
1993	4,657	3,748	113	8,518	54.7	44.0
1992	4,566	3,529	119	8,214	55.6	43.0
1991	4,424	3,648	103	8,175	54.1	44.6
1990	5,677	3,477	147	9,301	61.0	37.4
1989	6,288	3,362	127	9,777	64.3	34.4
1988	6,746	3,669	131	10,546	64.0	34.8

SOURCE: U.S. Department of Commerce, Bureau of Economic Analysis.

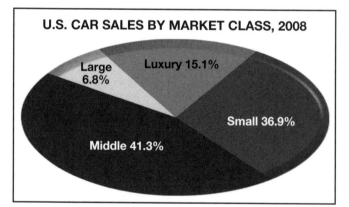

U.S. CAR SALES BY MARKET CLASS, 2008

Large 6.8%
Luxury 15.1%
Small 36.9%
Middle 41.3%

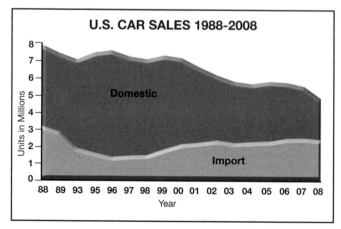

U.S. CAR SALES 1988-2008

Domestic
Import

U.S. Light Truck Sales by Segment

U.S. LIGHT TRUCK SALES BY SEGMENT

	2008	2007	2006	2005	2004
BMW X3*	17,622	28,058	31,291	30,769	34,604
BMW X5	31,858	35,202	26,798	37,598	35,225
BMW X6	4,548	—	—	—	—
BMW Total	**54,028**	**63,260**	**58,089**	**68,367**	**69,829**
Chrysler Pacifica	7,345	53,947	78,243	85,557	92,363
Chrysler PT Cruiser	49,816	88,607	126,148	115,888	99,959
Dodge Journey	47,097	—	—	—	—
Jeep Compass	25,349	39,491	18,579	—	—
Jeep Patriot	55,654	40,434	—	—	—
Chrysler Total	**185,261**	**222,479**	**222,970**	**201,445**	**192,322**
Ford Edge	110,798	130,125	2,201	—	—
Ford Escape	156,544	165,596	157,395	165,122	183,430
Ford Flex	14,457	—	—	—	—
Ford Freestyle	—	23,765	58,602	76,739	8,509
Ford Taurus X	23,112	18,345	—	—	—
Lincoln MKX	29,076	37,953	859	—	—
Mercury Mariner	32,306	34,844	33,941	34,099	7,171
Volvo XC70*	9,489	12,628	13,132	13,991	16,059
Volvo XC90*	18,980	31,336	33,200	35,976	39,183
Ford Total	**394,762**	**454,592**	**299,330**	**325,927**	**254,352**
Buick Enclave	44,706	29,286	—	—	—
Buick Rendezvous	27	15,295	45,954	60,589	60,039
Cadillac SRX	16,156	22,543	22,043	22,999	30,019
Chevrolet Equinox	67,447	89,552	113,888	130,542	84,024
Chevrolet HHR	96,053	105,175	101,298	41,011	—
Chevrolet Traverse	9,456	—	—	—	—
GMC Acadia	66,440	72,765	480	—	—
Pontiac Aztek	—	25	347	5,020	20,588
Pontiac Torrent	20,625	32,644	43,174	10,303	—
Saturn Outlook	25,340	34,748	144	—	—
Saturn Vue	81,676	84,767	88,581	91,972	86,957
GM Total	**427,926**	**486,800**	**415,909**	**362,436**	**281,627**
Acura MDX	45,377	58,606	54,121	57,948	59,505
Acura RDX	15,845	23,356	9,164	—	—
Honda CRV	90,480	26,130	—	—	—
Honda CRV*	106,799	193,030	170,028	150,219	149,281
Honda Element	26,447	35,218	51,829	56,262	59,927
Honda Pilot	96,746	117,146	152,154	143,353	128,158
Honda Total	**381,694**	**453,486**	**437,296**	**407,782**	**396,871**
Hyundai Santa Fe	70,994	92,421	45,898	—	—
Hyundai Santa Fe*	—	—	18,033	68,006	111,447
Hyundai Tucson*	19,027	41,476	52,067	61,048	7,074
Hyundai Veracruz*	11,004	12,589	—	—	—
Hyundai Total	**101,025**	**146,486**	**115,998**	**129,054**	**118,521**
Kia Rondo*	28,645	26,020	594	—	—
Kia Sportage*	32,754	49,393	37,071	28,982	—
Kia Total	**61,399**	**75,413**	**37,665**	**28,982**	**—**
Mazda5*	22,021	13,718	17,109	4,761	—
Mazda CX-7*	26,811	41,659	22,325	—	—
Mazda CX-9*	26,100	25,566	—	—	—
Mazda Tribute	10,806	13,680	26,785	36,761	41,078
Mazda Total	**85,738**	**94,623**	**66,219**	**41,522**	**41,078**
Mercedes GL-Class	23,328	26,396	18,776	—	—
Mercedes M-Class	34,320	33,879	31,632	27,504	—
Mercedes R-Class	7,733	13,031	18,168	4,959	—
Mercedes Total	**65,381**	**73,306**	**68,576**	**32,463**	**—**
Mitsubishi Endeavor	5,938	11,886	14,017	20,994	22,433
Mitsubishi Outlander*	13,471	23,285	11,493	11,848	18,104
Mitsubishi Total	**19,409**	**35,171**	**25,510**	**32,842**	**40,537**
Infiniti EX*	12,873	305	—	—	—
Infiniti FX*	12,660	20,727	22,656	26,786	30,964
Nissan Murano*	71,401	76,358	81,362	74,454	62,057
Nissan Rogue*	73,053	17,808	—	—	—
Nissan Total	**169,987**	**115,198**	**104,018**	**101,240**	**93,021**
Porsche Total (Cayenne)*	**11,216**	**12,547**	**10,569**	**13,607**	**18,117**
Subaru Forester*	60,748	44,530	51,258	53,541	58,424
Subaru Tribeca	10,975	16,790	18,614	14,797	—
Subaru Total	**71,723**	**61,320**	**69,872**	**68,338**	**58,424**
Suzuki Total (XL7)	**22,554**	**22,722**	**684**	**—**	**—**
Land Rover LR2*	5,618	9,205	—	—	—
Tata Total	**5,618**	**9,205**	**—**	**—**	**—**
Lexus RX	63,610	74,351	75,508	67,589	61,350
Lexus RX*	20,571	28,989	32,840	41,186	45,181
Toyota Highlander*	104,661	127,878	129,794	137,409	133,077
Toyota RAV4*	137,020	172,752	152,047	70,518	70,314
Toyota Venza	1,474	—	—	—	—
Toyota Total	**327,336**	**403,970**	**390,189**	**316,702**	**309,922**
Audi Allroad*	—	—	3	2,429	4,626

U.S. Light Truck Sales by Segment

U.S. LIGHT TRUCK SALES BY SEGMENT — continued

	2008	2007	2006	2005	2004
Audi Q7*	13,209	20,695	10,003	—	—
Volkswagen Tiguan*	8,664	—	—	—	—
Volkswagen Touareg*	6,755	8,812	10,163	18,050	27,706
Volkswagen Total	**28,628**	**29,507**	**20,169**	**20,479**	**32,332**
CROSS UTILITY TOTAL	**2,413,685**	**2,760,085**	**2,343,063**	**2,151,186**	**1,906,953**
Chrysler Aspen	22,254	28,788	7,656	—	—
Dodge Durango	21,420	45,503	70,606	115,439	137,148
Dodge Nitro	36,368	74,825	16,990	—	—
Jeep Commander	27,694	63,027	88,497	17,048	—
Jeep Grand Cherokee	73,678	120,937	139,148	213,584	182,313
Jeep Liberty	66,911	92,105	133,557	166,883	167,376
Jeep Wrangler	84,615	119,243	80,271	79,017	77,550
Chrysler Total	**332,940**	**544,428**	**536,725**	**591,971**	**564,387**
Ford Excursion	—	—	965	16,283	20,010
Ford Expedition	55,123	90,287	87,203	114,137	159,846
Ford Explorer	78,439	137,817	179,229	239,788	339,333
Lincoln Aviator	—	—	1,711	15,873	23,644
Lincoln Navigator	14,836	24,050	23,947	25,844	36,398
Mercury Mountaineer	10,596	23,849	29,567	32,491	43,916
Ford Total	**158,994**	**276,003**	**322,622**	**444,416**	**623,147**
Buick Rainier	117	4,819	12,691	15,271	24,134
Cadillac Escalade	23,947	36,654	39,017	29,876	36,994
Cadillac Escalade ESV	11,054	16,370	16,170	13,502	15,618
Chevrolet S Blazer	—	7	114	4,936	32,950
Chevrolet Suburban	54,058	83,673	77,211	87,011	119,545
Chevrolet Tahoe	91,578	146,256	161,491	152,305	186,161
Chevrolet Tracker	—	—	11	474	14,898
Chevrolet TrailBlazer	74,878	134,626	174,797	244,150	283,484
GMC Envoy	23,876	48,586	74,452	107,862	134,897
GMC Yukon	39,064	63,428	71,476	73,458	86,571
GMC Yukon XL	26,404	45,303	45,413	53,652	65,917
Hummer H1	17	125	365	374	447
Hummer H2	6,095	12,431	17,107	23,213	28,898
Hummer H3	20,681	43,430	54,052	33,140	—
Hummer H3T	692	—	—	—	—
Oldsmobile Bravada	—	—	19	327	1,973
Saab 9-7X	3,660	5,257	5,789	2,272	—
GM Total	**376,121**	**640,965**	**750,175**	**841,823**	**1,032,487**
Isuzu Ascender	1,760	2,948	4,857	7,585	7,686
Isuzu Axiom	—	8	124	1,319	3,153
Isuzu Rodeo	—	4	129	2,380	16,331
Isuzu Trooper*	—	—	7	4	18
Isuzu Total	**1,760**	**2,960**	**5,117**	**11,288**	**27,188**
Kia Borrego*	1,869	—	—	—	—
Kia Sorento*	29,699	36,300	50,672	47,610	52,878
Kia Sportage*	—	—	—	27	120
Kia Total	**31,568**	**36,300**	**50,672**	**47,637**	**52,998**
Mercedes G-Class*	931	1,152	587	1,334	1,491
Mercedes M-Class	—	—	—	7,455	25,681
Mercedes Total	**931**	**1,152**	**587**	**8,789**	**27,172**
Mitsubishi Montero*	4	401	1,610	2,778	5,181
Mitsubishi Montero Sport*	—	—	—	758	6,954
Mitsubishi Total	**4**	**401**	**1,610**	**3,536**	**12,135**
Infiniti QX4*	—	—	—	3	10
Infiniti QX56	7,657	12,288	11,694	14,711	13,136
Nissan Armada	15,685	31,632	32,864	39,508	37,275
Nissan Pathfinder	33,555	63,056	73,120	74,964	11,983
Nissan Pathfinder*	—	—	4	1,192	26,136
Nissan Xterra	33,579	51,355	62,325	72,447	66,690
Nissan Total	**90,476**	**158,331**	**180,007**	**202,825**	**155,230**
Suzuki Vitara	—	—	8	233	3,476
Suzuki Vitara*	11,936	19,540	26,931	8,624	4,860
Suzuki XL7*	—	454	10,264	15,472	18,501
Suzuki Total	**11,936**	**19,994**	**37,203**	**24,329**	**26,837**
Land Rover Discovery*	—	—	1	817	13,083
Land Rover Freelander*	—	1	42	2,141	5,430
Land Rover LR3*	4,039	11,039	16,930	19,346	3,447
Land Rover Range Rover*	8,393	12,316	12,044	13,430	13,546
Land Rover Range Rover Sport*	11,668	16,989	18,757	10,441	—
Tata Total	**24,100**	**40,345**	**47,774**	**46,175**	**35,506**
Lexus GX*	16,424	23,035	25,454	34,339	35,420
Lexus LX*	7,915	2,468	5,595	8,555	9,846
Toyota 4Runner*	47,878	87,718	103,086	103,830	114,212
Toyota FJ Cruiser*	28,668	55,170	56,225	—	—
Toyota Land Cruiser*	3,801	3,251	3,376	4,870	6,778
Toyota Sequoia	30,693	23,273	34,315	45,904	58,114
Toyota Total	**135,379**	**194,915**	**228,051**	**197,498**	**224,370**
SPORT UTILITY TOTAL	**1,164,209**	**1,915,794**	**2,160,543**	**2,420,287**	**2,781,457**

U.S. Light Truck Sales by Segment

U.S. LIGHT TRUCK SALES BY SEGMENT — continued

	2008	2007	2006	2005	2004
Chrysler Town & Country	118,563	138,151	159,105	180,759	142,523
Chrysler Voyager	—	—	—	—	1,834
Dodge Caravan	123,749	176,150	211,140	226,771	242,307
Dodge Ram Van	—	—	321	7,180	
Dodge Sprinter Van*	14,600	16,586	21,961	19,662	10,232
Chrysler Total	**256,912**	**330,887**	**392,206**	**427,513**	**404,076**
Ford Econoline	124,596	168,722	180,457	179,543	171,017
Ford Freestar	—	2,390	50,125	77,585	100,622
Ford Windstar	—	—	—	—	2,950
Mercury Monterey	—	700	4,467	8,166	17,407
Ford Total	**124,596**	**171,812**	**235,049**	**265,294**	**291,996**
Buick Terraza	544	5,569	11,948	20,288	2,137
Chevrolet Astro	—	25	386	19,215	34,564
Chevrolet Express	86,986	114,730	123,195	127,585	114,562
Chevrolet Uplander	40,456	69,885	58,699	72,980	3,948
Chevrolet Venture	—	25	196	7,029	66,522
GMC Safari	—	13	56	3,436	8,345
GMC Savana	22,437	25,706	29,973	34,765	41,702
Oldsmobile Silhouette	—	—	10	139	6,461
Pontiac Montana	—	26	388	3,732	31,411
Pontiac Montana SV6	64	1,359	13,100	23,439	2,218
Saturn Relay	163	1,474	7,171	15,758	1,563
GM Total	**150,650**	**218,812**	**245,122**	**328,366**	**313,433**
Honda Total (Odyssey)	**135,493**	**173,046**	**177,919**	**174,275**	**154,238**
Hyundai Total (Entourage)*	**8,470**	**17,155**	**12,206**	—	
Kia Total (Sedona)*	**26,915**	**40,493**	**57,018**	**52,837**	**61,149**
Mazda Total (MPV)*	—	**122**	**11,600**	**17,634**	**24,860**
Nissan Total (Quest)	**18,252**	**28,590**	**31,905**	**40,357**	**46,430**
Toyota Total (Sienna)	**115,944**	**138,162**	**163,269**	**161,380**	**159,119**
Volkswagen Eurovan*	—	—	—	—	209
Volkswagen Routan	3,387	—	—	—	
Volkswagen Total	**3,387**	—	—	—	**209**
VAN TOTAL	**840,619**	**1,119,079**	**1,326,294**	**1,467,656**	**1,455,510**
Dodge Dakota	26,044	50,702	76,098	104,051	105,614
Dodge Ram Pickup	240,454	357,707	364,177	400,543	426,289
Chrysler Total	**266,498**	**408,409**	**440,275**	**504,594**	**531,903**
Ford F-Series	476,469	633,949	744,996	854,878	891,482
Ford Ranger	65,872	72,711	92,420	120,958	156,322
Lincoln Mark LT	4,631	8,382	12,753	10,274	
Ford Total	**546,972**	**715,042**	**850,169**	**986,110**	**1,047,804**
Cadillac Escalade EXT	4,709	7,967	7,019	7,766	9,638
Chevrolet Avalanche	35,003	55,550	57,076	63,186	80,566
Chevrolet Colorado	54,346	75,716	93,876	128,359	117,475
Chevrolet S10 Pickup	—	—	4	149	10,014
Chevrolet Silverado	465,065	618,257	636,069	705,980	680,663
Chevrolet SSR	13	244	3,803	8,107	9,648
GMC Canyon	14,974	20,888	23,979	34,845	27,193
GMC Sierra	168,544	208,243	210,736	229,488	213,736
GMC Sonoma	—	—	—	66	3,303
GM Total	**742,654**	**986,865**	**1,032,562**	**1,177,946**	**1,152,236**
Honda Total (Ridgeline)	**33,875**	**42,795**	**50,193**	**42,593**	—
Isuzu Total (i-Series)	**2,998**	**4,138**	**3,497**	**889**	—
Mazda Total (Pickup)	**1,319**	**2,657**	**4,086**	**5,872**	**10,266**
Mitsubishi Total (Raider)	**2,935**	**8,262**	**7,595**	**1,145**	—
Nissan Frontier	44,997	64,397	77,510	72,838	70,703
Nissan Titan	34,053	65,746	72,192	86,945	83,848
Nissan Total	**79,050**	**130,143**	**149,702**	**159,783**	**154,551**
Subaru Total (Baja)	**2**	**1,127**	**5,241**	**6,239**	**7,316**
Suzuki Total (Equator)	**13**	—	—	—	
Toyota Tacoma	144,655	173,238	178,351	168,831	152,933
Toyota Tundra	137,249	196,555	124,508	126,529	112,484
Toyota Total	**281,904**	**369,793**	**302,859**	**295,360**	**265,417**
PICKUP TOTAL	**1,958,220**	**2,669,231**	**2,846,179**	**3,180,531**	**3,169,493**
Freightliner	—	—	—	14	270
General Motors	657	936	855	1,031	952
General Motors*	384	1,003	1,358	1,383	1,072
International	704	—	—	—	—
Isuzu Truck	1,034	1,153	1,270	1,465	1,457
Isuzu Truck*	1,534	3,197	3,659	3,702	3,535
Mitsubishi Fuso*	202	52	93	670	720
Nissan Diesel*	112	279	232	276	352
Sterling*	12	—	—	—	
COMMERCIAL CHASSIS TOTAL	**4,639**	**6,620**	**7,467**	**8,541**	**8,358**
TOTAL LIGHT TRUCKS	**6,381,372**	**8,470,809**	**8,683,546**	**9,228,201**	**9,321,771**

*Units imported from outside North America.
SOURCE: Ward's AutoInfoBank.

U.S. Retail Sales of Trucks by Manufacturer, Gross Vehicle Weight Rating, and Source

U.S. TRUCK SALES BY GVW CLASS AND SOURCE, 2008

	Gross Vehicle Weight Rating (Pounds)								
	6,000 & Less	6,001- 10,000	10,001- 14,000	14,001- 16,000	16,001- 19,500	19,501- 26,000	26,001- 33,000	33,001 & Over	Total
DOMESTIC*									
BMW	36,406	—	—	—	—	—	—	—	36,406
Chrysler	742,883	254,490	29,638	—	5,386	—	—	—	1,032,397
Ford	521,200	615,516	60,139	18,437	17,699	6,767	3,551	—	1,243,309
Freightliner/Sterling/Western Star	—	—	—	3,568	1,456	9,174	16,611	42,639	73,448
General Motors	687,390	969,443	41,175	5,110	10,629	1,614	5,163	—	1,720,524
Hino	—	—	—	165	145	3,478	1,129	—	4,917
Honda	444,263	—	—	—	—	—	—	—	444,263
Hyundai	70,994	—	—	—	—	—	—	—	70,994
International	—	95	609	2,564	894	15,736	15,828	32,399	68,125
Isuzu	4,758	—	1,034	1,127	—	413	106	—	7,438
Kenworth	—	—	—	—	150	828	2,732	15,855	19,565
Mack	—	—	—	—	—	—	—	11,794	11,794
Mazda	12,125	—	—	—	—	—	—	—	12,125
Mercedes-Benz	65,381	—	—	—	—	—	—	—	65,381
Mitsubishi	8,873	—	—	—	—	—	—	—	8,873
Nissan	153,725	34,053	—	—	—	—	—	—	187,778
Peterbilt	—	—	—	—	130	182	3,480	17,613	21,405
Subaru	10,977	—	—	—	—	—	—	—	10,977
Suzuki	22,567	—	—	—	—	—	—	—	22,567
Toyota	493,782	—	—	—	—	—	—	—	493,782
Volkswagen	3,387	—	—	—	—	—	—	—	3,387
Volvo Truck	—	—	—	—	—	—	—	13,061	13,061
Other Domestic	—	—	—	—	—	—	—	112	112
Total Domestic	**3,278,711**	**1,873,597**	**132,595**	**30,971**	**36,489**	**38,192**	**48,600**	**133,473**	**5,572,628**
IMPORT									
BMW	17,622	—	—	—	—	—	—	—	17,622
Chrysler	—	14,600	—	—	—	—	—	—	14,600
General Motors	—	—	384	1,449	863	—	—	—	2,696
Honda	106,799	—	—	—	—	—	—	—	106,799
Hyundai	38,501	—	—	—	—	—	—	—	38,501
Isuzu	—	—	1,534	2,475	2,036	—	—	—	6,045
Kia	119,882	—	—	—	—	—	—	—	119,882
Land Rover	29,718	—	—	—	—	—	—	—	29,718
Mazda	74,932	—	—	—	—	—	—	—	74,932
Mercedes-Benz	931	—	—	—	—	—	—	—	931
Mitsubishi	13,475	—	—	—	—	—	—	—	13,475
Mitsubishi Fuso	—	—	202	933	493	623	87	—	2,338
Nissan	169,987	—	—	—	—	—	—	—	169,987
Nissan Diesel	—	—	112	191	307	582	193	—	1,385
Porsche	11,216	—	—	—	—	—	—	—	11,216
Sterling	—	—	12	355	112	—	—	—	479
Subaru	60,748	—	—	—	—	—	—	—	60,748
Suzuki	11,936	—	—	—	—	—	—	—	11,936
Toyota	366,781	—	—	—	—	—	—	—	366,781
Volkswagen	28,628	—	—	—	—	—	—	—	28,628
Volvo (Ford)	28,469	—	—	—	—	—	—	—	28,469
Total Import	**1,079,625**	**14,600**	**2,244**	**5,403**	**3,811**	**1,205**	**280**	**—**	**1,107,168**
Total Trucks	**4,358,336**	**1,888,197**	**134,839**	**36,374**	**40,300**	**39,397**	**48,880**	**133,473**	**6,679,796**

*Units produced in the United States, Canada and Mexico.
SOURCE: *Ward's AutoInfoBank.*

U.S. Retail Sales of Trucks by Gross Vehicle Weight Rating and Body Type

U.S. LIGHT TRUCK SALES BY GVWR AND BODY TYPE

GVWR/Body type	2008	2007	2006	2005	2004
0-6,000 Lbs.					
Utility	3,211,387	4,075,748	3,890,851	3,887,647	3,820,113
Mini Van	592,000	793,335	970,708	1,105,780	1,110,817
Passenger Carrier	3,670	1,939	2,228	3,841	4,395
Van	20,800	35,065	33,498	32,359	30,803
Compact Pickup	392,735	516,875	616,653	694,942	670,787
Conventional Pickup	137,744	259,372	581,610	808,730	781,606
Total 0-6,000 lbs.	**4,358,336**	**5,682,334**	**6,095,548**	**6,533,299**	**6,418,521**
6,001-10,000 Lbs.					
Utility	370,507	607,973	619,409	691,218	877,488
Passenger Carrier	40,060	50,397	53,955	53,478	47,736
Van	129,688	170,677	192,360	200,923	195,624
Van Cutaway	54,496	67,666	73,545	71,275	66,135
Conventional Pickup	1,293,446	1,725,866	1,498,885	1,511,152	1,608,988
Total 6,001-10,000 lbs.	**1,888,197**	**2,622,579**	**2,438,154**	**2,528,046**	**2,795,971**
10,001 - 14,000 lbs.					
Conventional Pickup	130,278	159,151	142,012	157,941	98,474
Other Body Types	4,561	6,745	7,832	8,915	8,805
Total 10,001 - 14,000 lbs.	**134,839**	**165,896**	**149,844**	**166,856**	**107,279**
Total Light Trucks	**6,381,372**	**8,470,809**	**8,683,546**	**9,228,201**	**9,321,771**

SOURCE: *Ward's AutoInfoBank.*

U.S. SALES OF DOMESTIC AND IMPORTED TRUCKS

	Domestic				Imports				
	Gross Vehicle Weight Rating								
Year	0-14,000 lbs.	14,001-33,000 lbs.	33,001 lbs. & Over	Total Domestic	From Japan	From Germany	From Other Countries	Total Imports	Total U.S. Sales
2008	5,284,903	154,252	133,473	5,572,628	764,204	41,235	301,729	1,107,168	6,679,796
2007	7,082,724	199,977	150,965	7,433,666	906,935	37,945	463,356	1,408,236	8,841,902
2006	7,336,796	237,949	284,008	7,858,753	878,020	42,696	448,658	1,369,374	9,228,127
2005	8,012,886	221,830	252,792	8,487,508	721,659	53,748	461,861	1,237,268	9,724,776
2004	8,075,513	205,451	203,197	8,484,161	774,203	60,890	434,170	1,269,263	9,753,424
2003	7,801,392	167,565	141,964	8,110,921	840,084	41,829	364,127	1,246,040	9,356,961
2002	7,646,764	159,128	146,031	7,951,923	812,433	12,680	258,387	1,083,500	9,035,423
2001	7,718,464	189,573	139,591	8,047,628	813,389	11,957	176,779	1,002,125	9,049,753
2000	7,650,805	229,836	211,502	8,092,143	759,836	3,747	109,322	872,905	8,965,048
1999	7,420,031	239,562	262,316	7,921,909	707,866	3,395	83,274	794,535	8,716,444
1998	6,745,284	196,321	209,483	7,151,088	621,187	1,742	51,549	674,478	7,825,566
1997	6,270,164	183,767	178,551	6,632,482	546,564	1,792	44,948	593,304	7,225,786
1996	6,131,673	176,140	170,009	6,477,822	415,959	995	34,583	451,537	6,929,359
1995	5,690,903	171,948	201,303	6,064,154	385,558	1,460	30,189	417,207	6,481,361
1994	5,658,302	151,897	185,696	5,995,895	406,014	4,675	14,273	424,962	6,420,857

SOURCE: Ward's AutoInfoBank.

Annual and Monthly Records
for U.S. Production and Sales

RECORD U.S. PRODUCTION YEARS

Cars		Trucks	
Year	Units	Year	Units
1973	9,660,821	2004	7,730,729
1965	9,329,104	2005	7,625,381
1977	9,211,411	2003	7,576,559
1978	9,173,606	1999	7,387,029
1968	8,843,031	2002	7,260,805
1972	8,821,737	2000	7,231,497
1966	8,598,917	2006	6,893,281

RECORD U.S. SALES YEARS

Cars		Trucks	
Year	Units	Year	Units
1973	11,423,851	2004	9,753,424
1986	11,404,239	2005	9,724,776
1978	11,314,079	2003	9,356,961
1977	11,183,412	2006	9,228,127
1985	10,979,187	2001	9,049,753
1972	10,940,482	2002	9,035,423
1979	10,672,768	2000	8,965,048

RECORD U.S. PRODUCTION BY MONTH

Month	Year	Units
	Cars	
January	1973	917,273
February	1973	856,117
March	1965	963,101
April	1978	870,689
May	1973	941,019
June	1977	949,440
July	1965	740,576
August	1950	684,970
September	1972	758,578
October	1973	951,434
November	1965	913,146
December	1964	866,632
	Trucks	
January	2003	632,322
February	2004	674,210
March	2004	783,795
April	2004	688,282
May	2000	707,996
June	2005	702,460
July	2003	425,176
August	2005	727,641
September	2005	716,791
October	2003	751,813
November	2004	619,700
December	2003	590,003

RECORD U.S. SALES BY MONTH

Month	Year	Units
	Cars	
January	1973	874,084
February	1973	918,681
March	1973	1,140,386
April	1978	1,043,341
May	1978	1,159,996
June	1978	1,138,504
July	1973	958,270
August	1986	1,000,658
September	1987	1,217,171
October	1972	1,068,400
November	1972	1,029,689
December	1987	995,415
	Trucks	
January	2004	654,205
February	2000	770,224
March	2005	891,509
April	2005	822,115
May	2004	915,670
June	2005	1,009,319
July	2005	1,129,149
August	2003	918,029
September	2004	859,127
October	2001	939,731
November	2001	744,961
December	2004	925,190

U.S. PRODUCTION MILESTONES

Cars		Trucks		Total Vehicles	
Year	Units	Year	Units	Year	Units
2003	500 millionth	2005	200 millionth	2001	600 millionth
1994	400 millionth	1998	150 millionth	1992	500 millionth
1986	350 millionth	1988	100 millionth	1982	400 millionth
1979	300 millionth	1971	50 millionth	1972	300 millionth
1973	250 millionth	1965	40 millionth	1962	200 millionth
1967	200 millionth	1957	30 millionth	1955	150 millionth
1952	100 millionth	1949	20 millionth	1948	100 millionth
1935	50 millionth	1938	10 millionth	1931	50 millionth
1925	25 millionth	1929	5 millionth	1920	10 millionth
1920	10 millionth	1920	1 millionth	1912	1 millionth
1912	1 millionth	1915	100,000th	1906	100,000th

SOURCE: Ward's Automotive Group

Top Selling Vehicles and Automotive Color Popularity

TOP 20 SELLING CARS IN THE U.S.

2008		2007		2006	
Toyota Camry	436,617	Toyota Camry	473,108	Toyota Camry	448,445
Honda Accord	372,789	Honda Accord	392,231	Toyota Corolla/Matrix	387,388
Toyota Corolla/Matrix	351,007	Toyota Corolla/Matrix	371,390	Honda Accord	354,441
Honda Civic	339,289	Honda Civic	331,095	Honda Civic	316,638
Nissan Altima	269,668	Chevrolet Impala	311,128	Chevrolet Impala	289,868
Chevrolet Impala	265,840	Nissan Altima	284,762	Nissan Altima	232,457
Ford Focus	195,823	Chevrolet Cobalt	200,620	Chevrolet Cobalt	211,449
Chevrolet Cobalt	188,045	Toyota Prius	181,221	Ford Focus	177,006
Chevrolet Malibu	178,253	Ford Focus	173,213	Ford Taurus	174,803
Toyota Prius	158,884	Pontiac G6	150,001	Ford Mustang	166,530
Ford Fusion	147,569	Ford Fusion	149,552	Chevrolet Malibu	163,853
Pontiac G6	140,240	Hyundai Sonata	145,568	Pontiac G6	157,644
Hyundai Sonata	117,357	BMW 3 Series	142,490	Hyundai Sonata	149,513
BMW 3 Series	112,464	Ford Mustang	134,626	Chrysler 300 Series	143,647
Mazda3	109,957	Chevrolet Malibu	128,312	Ford Fusion	142,502
Toyota Yaris	102,328	Chrysler 300 Series	120,636	BMW 3 Series	120,180
Nissan Sentra	99,797	Mazda3	120,291	Nissan Sentra	117,922
Volkswagen Jetta	97,461	Dodge Charger	119,289	Dodge Charger	114,201
Dodge Charger	97,367	Nissan Sentra	106,522	Pontiac Grand Prix	108,634
Hyundai Elantra	94,720	Dodge Caliber	101,079	Toyota Prius	106,971

TOP 20 SELLING LIGHT TRUCKS IN THE U.S.

2008		2007		2006	
Ford F-Series	476,469	Ford F-Series	633,949	Ford F-Series	744,996
Chevrolet Silverado	465,065	Chevrolet Silverado	618,257	Chevrolet Silverado	636,069
Dodge Ram Pickup	240,454	Dodge Ram Pickup	357,707	Dodge Ram Pickup	364,177
Honda CR-V	197,279	Honda CR-V	219,160	Dodge Caravan	211,140
GMC Sierra	168,544	GMC Sierra	208,243	GMC Sierra	210,736
Ford Escape	156,544	Toyota Tundra	196,555	Ford Econoline	180,457
Toyota Tacoma	144,655	Dodge Caravan	176,150	Ford Explorer	179,229
Toyota Tundra	137,249	Toyota Tacoma	173,238	Toyota Tacoma	178,351
Toyota RAV4	137,020	Honda Odyssey	173,046	Honda Odyssey	177,919
Honda Odyssey	135,493	Toyota RAV4	172,752	Chevrolet TrailBlazer	174,797
Ford Econoline	124,596	Ford Econoline	168,722	Honda CR-V	170,028
Dodge Caravan	123,749	Ford Escape	165,596	Toyota Sienna	163,269
Chrysler Town & Country	118,563	Chevrolet Tahoe	146,256	Chevrolet Tahoe	161,491
Toyota Sienna	115,944	Toyota Sienna	138,162	Chrysler Town & Country	159,105
Ford Edge	110,798	Chrysler Town & Country	138,151	Ford Escape	157,395
Toyota Highlander	104,661	Ford Explorer	137,817	Honda Pilot	152,154
Honda Pilot	96,746	Chevrolet TrailBlazer	134,626	Toyota RAV4	152,047
Chevrolet HHR	96,053	Ford Edge	130,125	Jeep Grand Cherokee	139,148
Chevrolet Tahoe	91,578	Toyota Highlander	127,878	Jeep Liberty	133,557
Chevrolet Express	86,986	Jeep Grand Cherokee	120,937	Toyota Highlander	129,794

SOURCE: *Ward's AutoInfoBank.*

AUTOMOTIVE PAINT COLOR POPULARITY BY VEHICLE TYPE, 2008 MODEL YEAR

Luxury Cars		Full Size/Intermediate Cars		Compact/Sports Cars		Light Trucks	
Color	Percent	Color	Percent	Color	Percent	Color	Percent
Black/Black Effect	26%	Silver	20%	Silver	20%	White/White Pearl	30%
White/White Pearl	23%	Blue	18%	Black/Black Effect	18%	Black/Black Effect	17%
Silver	12%	White/White Pearl	16%	Gray	17%	Red	14%
Red	10%	Black/Black Effect	13%	Blue	15%	Silver	12%
Gray	9%	Gray	12%	Red	12%	Gray	11%
Blue	8%	Red	8%	White/White Pearl	10%	Blue	8%
Beige/Brown	6%	Beige/Brown	8%	Yellow/Gold	2%	Beige/Brown	3%
Yellow/Gold	5%	Green	5%	Beige/Brown	4%	Green	3%
Green	1%	Yellow/Gold	1%	Green	2%	Yellow/Gold	3%
Other	1%	Other	1%	Other	1%	Other	1%

SOURCE: Du Pont Automotive Products.

Canada Vehicle Sales and Registrations

CANADA VEHICLE SALES BY SOURCE

Year	Cars			Commercial Vehicles			Total Vehicles
	Domestic[1]	Imports	Total	Domestic[1]	Imports	Total	
2008	547,321	325,399	872,720	664,145	136,657	800,802	1,673,522
2007	552,838	288,747	841,585	723,401	125,359	848,760	1,690,345
2006	578,491	280,335	858,826	674,514	132,668	807,182	1,666,008
2005	572,202	275,234	847,436	668,342	114,364	782,706	1,630,142
2004	545,767	275,783	821,550	649,525	103,728	753,253	1,574,803
2003	603,444	261,545	864,989	654,112	105,949	760,061	1,625,050
2002	651,703	282,354	934,057	700,427	97,339	797,766	1,731,823
2001	620,162	248,026	868,188	651,952	77,735	729,687	1,597,875
2000	640,916	208,216	849,132	673,631	63,320	736,951	1,586,083
1999	620,233	186,207	806,440	676,107	57,832	733,939	1,540,379
1998	590,041	150,775	740,816	629,720	56,056	685,776	1,426,592
1997	628,739	109,816	738,555	628,124	56,315	684,439	1,422,994
1996	572,001	88,803	660,804	516,288	25,302	541,590	1,202,394
1995	554,878	116,103	670,981	470,147	23,470	493,617	1,164,598
1994	584,985	165,343	750,328	478,826	27,828	506,654	1,256,982
1993	511,611	229,257	740,868	407,864	41,850	449,714	1,190,582
1992	511,220	289,107	800,327	369,896	54,155	424,051	1,224,378
1991	576,480	299,308	875,788	346,332	62,529	408,861	1,284,649
1990	588,944	299,037	887,981	358,098	68,132	426,230	1,314,211
1989	669,040	321,779	990,819	419,065	68,662	487,727	1,478,546
1988	738,388	314,649	1,053,037	456,016	52,419	508,435	1,561,472
1987	716,575	348,239	1,064,814	414,617	48,557	463,174	1,527,988
1986	756,265	331,314	1,087,579	370,148	54,361	424,509	1,512,088
1985	794,511	338,592	1,133,103	344,939	50,982	395,921	1,529,024
1984	724,932	246,278	971,210	273,604	38,688	312,292	1,283,502
1983	625,088	218,230	843,318	192,609	45,161	237,770	1,081,088
1982	489,435	224,046	713,481	166,986	40,435	207,421	920,902
1981	646,942	257,253	904,195	250,775	35,912	286,687	1,190,882

(1) Units produced in the United States, Canada and Mexico.
SOURCE: *Ward's AutoInfoBank*.

CANADA TOTAL REGISTRATIONS BY PROVINCE, 2008

Province	Total Vehicle Registrations by Weight			
	less than 9,000 lbs.	over 9,000 lbs.	Buses	Total
Alberta	2,558,244	218,949	14,764	2,791,957
British Columbia	2,548,212	143,082	9,563	2,700,857
Manitoba	659,493	29,032	3,851	692,376
New Brunswick	484,797	12,031	3,032	499,860
Newfoundland	281,656	7,836	1,254	290,746
Northwest Territories	22,068	2,241	138	24,447
Nova Scotia	539,006	17,087	1,879	557,972
Nunavut	3,310	413	21	3,744
Ontario	7,176,013	218,980	28,164	7,423,157
Prince Edward Island	79,134	4,233	108	83,475
Quebec	4,525,950	96,827	17,245	4,640,022
Saskatchewan	708,247	68,838	3,793	780,878
Yukon Territory	26,800	3,460	345	30,605
Total	**19,612,930**	**823,009**	**84,157**	**20,520,096**

SOURCE: Statistics Canada.

CANADA TOTAL REGISTRATIONS

Year	Cars (000)	Commercial Vehicles (000)	Total (000)
2008	19,613	907	20,520
2007	19,199	872	20,071
2006	18,739	841	19,580
2005	18,124	786	18,910
2004	17,920	745	18,665
2003	17,755	741	18,496
2002	17,544	723	18,267
2001	17,055	728	17,783
2000	16,832	739	17,571
1999	16,538	2,679	19,217
1998	13,887	3,694	17,581
1997	13,487	3,591	17,078
1996	13,217	3,644	16,861
1994	13,122	3,466	16,588
1992	12,781	3,413	16,194
1990	12,622	3,931	16,553
1988	12,086	3,766	15,852
1986	11,586	3,213	14,799

NOTE: Beginning in 2000, data excludes farm tractors and off-road vehicles. SOURCE: Statistics Canada.

Canada Vehicle Sales

CANADA VEHICLE SALES BY MODEL

Model	2008	2007	2006	2005	2004
1-Series*	2,212	—	—	—	—
3-Series*	11,754	13,102	10,721	8,800	7,727
5-Series*	2,042	2,651	2,577	2,541	2,002
6-Series*	286	371	433	365	478
7-Series*	424	467	542	645	605
Z4	249	390	492	417	521
Z8*	—	—	1	2	5
BMW Total	**16,967**	**16,981**	**14,766**	**12,770**	**11,338**
Mini Cooper*	4,905	3,703	3,410	3,401	2,800
BMW TOTAL	**21,872**	**20,684**	**18,176**	**16,171**	**14,138**
300M	—	—	—	91	407
300 Series	7,443	10,210	13,316	14,564	10,073
Concorde	—	—	—	—	833
Crossfire*	119	75	574	738	763
Intrepid	—	—	—	370	2,648
PT Cruiser Convertible	19	739	1,509	1,878	1,235
Sebring Convertible	2,404	1,325	1,081	1,449	1,591
Sebring Sedan	7,600	8,250	10,165	15,160	15,444
Chrysler Total	**17,585**	**20,599**	**26,645**	**34,250**	**32,994**
Avenger	7,873	7,067	—	—	—
Caliber	19,544	18,553	19,524	—	—
Challenger	1,631	—	—	—	—
Charger	6,675	7,858	7,440	2,919	—
Dodge SX 2.0	—	—	1,847	15,064	14,876
Magnum	585	2,494	4,547	5,114	2,137
Viper	157	27	93	138	115
Dodge Total	**36,465**	**35,999**	**33,451**	**23,235**	**17,128**
CHRYSLER TOTAL	**54,050**	**56,598**	**60,096**	**57,485**	**50,122**
B-Class*	3,207	3,035	2,723	817	—
C-Class*	7,966	5,066	4,603	4,844	6,295
E-Class*	2,161	2,267	1,841	2,244	2,151
S-Class*	1,026	1,320	1,205	455	785
SL-Class*	398	286	345	416	599
SLK*	519	—	—	—	—
SLR*	11	11	7	28	10
Maybach*	5	6	8	6	7
Mercedes Total	**15,293**	**11,991**	**10,732**	**8,810**	**9,847**
Smart Fortwo*	3,749	2,433	3,023	4,080	915
DAIMLER TOTAL	**19,042**	**14,424**	**13,755**	**12,890**	**10,762**
Crown Victoria	2,938	2,809	3,315	3,311	3,326
Five Hundred	—	1,045	3,659	5,276	730
Focus	23,654	24,013	27,718	26,861	28,391
Ford GT	—	95	245	—	—
Fusion	13,326	15,882	17,370	694	—
Mustang	6,261	7,987	9,150	10,045	6,968
Taurus	2,064	1,513	6,691	7,870	12,724
Thunderbird	—	—	—	105	218
Ford Total	**48,243**	**53,344**	**68,148**	**54,162**	**52,357**
Lincoln LS	—	—	234	700	1,100
MKS	615	—	—	—	—
MKZ	1,358	1,585	527	—	—
Town Car	652	883	1,107	1,265	1,548
Zephyr	—	—	1,205	270	—
Lincoln Total	**2,625**	**2,468**	**3,073**	**2,235**	**2,648**
Mercury Total (Grand Marquis)	**305**	**335**	**336**	**691**	**1,375**
30*	1,142	1,143	—	—	—
40*	683	1,099	1,431	2,030	1,711
50*	353	606	717	1,009	456
60*	541	1,425	1,978	2,205	2,886
70*	551	719	1,109	1,047	1,180
80*	243	543	248	376	520
Volvo Total	**3,513**	**5,535**	**5,483**	**6,667**	**6,753**
FORD TOTAL	**54,686**	**61,682**	**77,040**	**63,755**	**63,133**
Allure	9,200	8,741	11,072	14,408	1,414
Century	—	—	5	1,161	7,151
Lesabre	—	—	25	1,233	2,583
Lucerne	2,872	2,948	4,042	343	—
Park Ave	—	—	2	34	150
Regal	—	—	2	10	1,285
Buick Total	**12,072**	**11,689**	**15,148**	**17,189**	**12,583**
CTS	4,223	3,839	3,946	4,154	2,079
Deville	—	6	30	486	1,363
DTS	704	959	1,308	586	—
Seville	—	—	3	15	263
STS	279	505	659	810	202
XLR	30	59	81	133	154
Cadillac Total	**5,236**	**5,368**	**6,027**	**6,184**	**4,061**
Aveo	121	—	—	—	—

Canada Vehicle Sales

CANADA VEHICLE SALES BY MODEL — continued

Model	2008	2007	2006	2005	2004
Aveo*	10,532	11,082	10,315	12,863	13,712
Camaro	—	—	—	6	7
Cavalier	—	—	4	7,122	29,229
Cobalt	33,754	32,613	31,729	26,405	178
Corvette	596	787	992	1,185	680
Epica*	6	46	635	1,837	6,089
Impala	14,913	16,326	21,486	18,474	20,876
Malibu	17,596	9,857	18,097	17,871	15,062
Monte Carlo	37	802	1,548	1,341	2,216
Optra*	76	4,148	6,654	12,345	16,853
Chevrolet Total	**77,631**	**75,661**	**91,460**	**99,449**	**104,902**
Alero	—	—	5	144	7,461
Aurora	—	—	—	4	52
Intrigue	—	—	—	—	2
Oldsmobile Total	**—**	**—**	**5**	**148**	**7,515**
Bonneville	—	1	26	295	705
Firebird	—	—	—	15	4
G5	26,436	25,211	9,810	—	—
G6	13,640	11,848	18,559	14,038	2,556
G8*	691	—	—	—	—
Grand Am	—	2	17	9,438	17,082
Grand Prix	333	13,086	8,234	10,171	12,289
Pursuit	—	—	15,741	16,289	215
Solstice	899	1,816	1,889	517	—
Sunfire	—	—	—	16,256	33,724
Vibe	17,335	12,915	11,444	11,363	10,025
Wave	106	—	—	—	—
Wave*	8,426	8,711	8,019	9,045	1,440
Pontiac Total	**67,866**	**73,590**	**73,739**	**87,427**	**78,040**
9-2X*	1	19	357	493	168
9-3*	1,254	1,575	1,568	1,150	1,308
9-5*	197	327	444	478	388
Saab Total	**1,452**	**1,921**	**2,369**	**2,121**	**1,864**
Astra*	7,536	1	—	—	—
Aura	2,587	3,165	762	—	—
Ion	445	13,932	12,984	14,154	12,323
Saturn L	—	1	1	259	1,091
Saturn S	—	—	—	5	69
Sky	409	613	360	—	—
Saturn Total	**10,977**	**17,712**	**14,107**	**14,418**	**13,483**
GM TOTAL	**175,234**	**185,941**	**202,855**	**226,936**	**222,448**
CL	—	—	—	7	73
CSX	2,998	3,729	5,186	—	—
EL	—	—	—	5,192	5,010
NSX*	—	—	—	1	6
RL*	157	158	233	475	333
RSX*	5	12	1,755	2,886	3,342
TL	4,019	3,995	4,694	5,280	5,801
TSX*	3,118	2,104	2,816	3,918	3,797
Acura Total	**10,297**	**9,998**	**14,684**	**17,759**	**18,362**
Accord	22,623	22,102	20,165	24,115	25,814
Civic	70,270	68,470	67,996	67,570	60,889
Civic*	2,193	2,368	2,032	936	1,236
Fit*	14,836	13,507	10,634	—	—
Insight*	1	2	21	5	9
Prelude*	—	—	—	—	2
S2000*	65	123	146	212	250
Honda Total	**109,988**	**106,572**	**100,994**	**92,838**	**88,200**
HONDA TOTAL	**120,285**	**116,570**	**115,678**	**110,597**	**106,562**
Accent*	29,751	16,390	17,784	15,679	19,172
Azera*	369	762	837	—	—
Elantra*	11,814	14,327	12,228	16,101	15,375
Genesis*	342	—	—	—	—
Sonata	9,320	8,633	6,272	1,939	—
Sonata*	978	2,401	6,194	6,236	6,974
Tiburon*	1,996	1,429	1,231	1,459	2,155
XG350*	—	—	95	534	625
HYUNDAI TOTAL	**54,570**	**43,942**	**44,641**	**41,948**	**44,301**
Amanti*	158	142	710	884	946
Magentis*	1,975	2,021	2,025	1,862	2,041
Rio*	9,742	7,236	7,297	6,926	8,311
Spectra*	5,030	6,602	6,677	6,865	5,826
KIA TOTAL	**16,905**	**16,001**	**16,709**	**16,537**	**17,124**
Mazda3*	50,317	48,236	47,933	50,713	42,680
Mazda6	6,561	8,451	9,971	11,738	10,213

Canada Vehicle Sales

CANADA VEHICLE SALES BY MODEL — continued

Model	2008	2007	2006	2005	2004
MX-5 Miata*	1,407	1,814	1,582	857	1,146
Protégé*	—	—	—	—	4,292
RX-8*	543	659	1,029	1,663	2,118
MAZDA TOTAL	**58,828**	**59,160**	**60,515**	**64,971**	**60,449**
Diamante*	—	—	—	101	84
Eclipse	1,675	1,951	2,097	1,257	993
Galant	902	553	705	971	931
Lancer*	9,157	7,192	4,433	4,009	5,406
MITSUBISHI TOTAL	**11,734**	**9,696**	**7,235**	**6,338**	**7,414**
G35*	4,286	4,908	3,992	4,711	4,954
I35*	—	—	—	3	113
M35/45*	410	550	1,083	1,111	31
Q45*	—	—	7	31	44
Infiniti Total	**4,696**	**5,458**	**5,082**	**5,856**	**5,142**
350Z*	311	469	624	700	983
Altima	16,676	17,126	13,997	17,037	18,508
GT-R*	137	—	—	—	—
Maxima	1,475	1,304	2,940	3,566	5,209
Sentra	11,000	8,563	8,656	12,206	12,744
Versa	21,845	21,940	6,727	—	—
Nissan Total	**51,444**	**49,402**	**32,944**	**33,509**	**37,444**
NISSAN TOTAL	**56,140**	**54,860**	**38,026**	**39,365**	**42,586**
Boxster*	272	282	347	448	215
Carrera GT*	—	—	4	15	11
Cayman*	169	222	288	—	—
Porsche 911*	463	660	657	546	573
PORSCHE TOTAL	**904**	**1,164**	**1,296**	**1,009**	**799**
Impreza*	8,555	7,480	6,155	5,617	5,533
Legacy	4,089	4,919	5,345	5,881	6,493
SUBARU TOTAL	**12,644**	**12,399**	**11,500**	**11,498**	**12,026**
Aerio*	1	303	2,186	3,009	3,172
Swift+*	1,828	2,593	2,671	2,698	3,068
SX4*	7,833	4,424	1,601	—	—
Verona*	—	—	200	236	626
SUZUKI TOTAL	**9,662**	**7,320**	**6,658**	**5,943**	**6,866**
Jaguar S-Type*	32	132	199	281	416
Jaguar X-Type*	80	208	351	586	886
Jaguar XF*	536	—	—	—	—
Jaguar XJ6/8*	133	156	193	250	358
Jaguar XK8*	148	242	200	83	91
TATA TOTAL	**929**	**738**	**943**	**1,200**	**1,751**
ES330*	—	—	501	2,385	2,123
ES350*	3,634	4,251	2,603	—	—
GS300/350*	474	569	534	668	24
GS430/460*	37	27	91	156	37
IS250/350*	3,600	2,792	2,713	521	—
IS300*	—	—	—	340	448
LS430/460*	311	588	269	229	309
SC430*	80	109	159	212	246
Lexus Total	**8,136**	**8,336**	**6,870**	**4,511**	**3,187**
Avalon	380	1,010	1,408	2,115	187
Camry	24,814	28,785	27,325	20,063	21,965
Camry*	2	173	1,740	315	593
Celica*	—	—	21	413	1,027
Corolla	57,736	40,474	44,182	46,533	44,563
Echo*	—	—	381	26,711	31,252
Matrix	23,549	21,369	23,536	24,048	20,017
Prius*	4,458	2,585	2,003	1,956	1,951
Yaris*	40,602	34,424	34,202	6,177	—
Toyota Total	**151,541**	**128,820**	**134,798**	**128,331**	**121,555**
TOYOTA TOTAL	**159,677**	**137,156**	**141,668**	**132,842**	**124,742**
A3*	1,351	1,175	1,531	1,065	—
A4*	4,480	4,334	4,655	4,494	5,650
A5*	400	35	—	—	—
A6*	795	769	1,026	1,022	843
A8*	161	234	273	250	290
R8*	155	34	—	—	—
TT*	660	414	111	199	321
Audi Total	**8,002**	**6,995**	**7,596**	**7,030**	**7,104**
Beetle	869	928	826	697	872
Beetle Cabrio	737	779	778	808	909
EOS*	1,121	1,013	376	—	—
Golf*	10,665	9,453	7,249	5,316	6,875
Jetta	13,915	14,665	19,251	18,202	15,826
Passat*	2,589	3,093	3,716	5,864	4,648

Canada Vehicle Sales

CANADA VEHICLE SALES BY MODEL — continued

Model	2008	2007	2006	2005	2004
Phaeton*	—	—	7	34	93
Rabbit*	7,660	6,324	2,236	—	—
Volkswagen Total	37,556	36,255	34,439	30,921	29,223
VOLKSWAGEN TOTAL	45,558	43,250	42,035	37,951	36,327
TOTAL CARS	872,720	841,585	858,826	847,436	821,550
X3*	2,296	2,975	3,096	2,930	2,304
X5	3,255	4,075	2,158	2,450	2,956
X6	726	—	—	—	—
BMW TOTAL	6,277	7,050	5,254	5,380	5,260
Aspen	1,719	1,535	383	—	—
Pacifica	290	2,016	3,876	3,944	5,159
PT Cruiser	2,615	5,058	8,516	7,827	8,005
Town & Country	4,865	1,531	623	602	850
Chrysler Total	9,489	10,140	13,398	12,373	14,014
Caravan	39,780	55,041	61,901	65,002	63,559
Dakota	4,982	8,425	8,004	9,949	12,466
Durango	1,115	1,634	3,836	4,310	6,394
Journey	11,817	—	—	—	—
Nitro	5,831	8,793	1,692	—	—
Ram Pickup	41,320	42,296	39,837	37,483	37,709
Sprinter Van*	2,486	2,068	2,475	1,952	1,081
Dodge Total	107,331	118,257	117,745	118,696	121,209
Commander	793	1,147	3,359	477	—
Compass	9,423	10,229	2,504	—	—
Grand Cherokee	7,617	8,078	7,075	9,166	7,454
Liberty	6,904	8,776	11,286	13,282	13,543
Patriot	13,836	9,629	—	—	—
Wrangler	12,137	9,834	5,090	5,378	4,524
Jeep Total	50,710	47,693	29,314	28,303	25,521
CHRYSLER TOTAL	167,530	176,090	160,457	159,372	160,744
G-Class*	21	83	217	384	674
GL-Class	1,135	863	467	—	—
M-Class	3,525	2,689	2,172	2,251	1,823
R-Class	394	488	956	265	—
Mercedes Total	5,075	4,123	3,812	2,900	2,497
Mitsubishi Fuso Light-Duty*	21	2	2	37	41
Sterling Light-Duty*	14	—	—	—	—
DAIMLER TOTAL	5,110	4,125	3,814	2,937	2,538
Econoline	8,383	9,639	11,932	13,840	14,047
Edge	11,834	10,349	161	—	—
Escape	32,898	31,643	25,542	23,493	20,360
Excursion	—	—	—	484	426
Expedition	1,557	2,217	2,528	2,413	2,992
Explorer	4,486	7,583	9,234	10,439	14,266
Flex	2,134	—	—	—	—
Freestar	—	883	11,692	15,608	22,078
Freestyle	—	2,848	5,200	6,141	487
F-Series Light-Duty	65,430	70,406	69,501	65,897	68,009
Ranger	24,211	23,386	17,198	10,775	8,775
Taurus X	3,106	1,267	—	—	—
Ford Total	154,039	160,221	152,988	149,090	151,440
Aviator	—	—	—	664	1,072
Mark LT	493	701	685	467	—
MKX	2,218	2,531	53	—	—
Navigator	384	961	968	1,025	1,102
Lincoln Total	3,095	4,193	1,706	2,156	2,174
XC70*	1,492	1,416	1,859	2,217	1,923
XC90*	1,502	1,923	2,569	2,767	2,459
Volvo Total	2,994	3,339	4,428	4,984	4,382
FORD TOTAL	160,128	167,753	159,122	156,230	157,996
Enclave	4,994	2,557	—	—	—
Rainier	5	74	296	455	937
Rendezvous	5	1,112	5,164	4,840	7,203
Terraza	2	467	1,202	1,667	80
Buick Total	5,006	4,210	6,662	6,962	8,220
Escalade	848	1,083	1,070	714	801
Escalade ESV	208	303	272	226	307
Escalade EXT	270	336	297	221	246
SRX	1,045	1,503	1,589	1,166	1,232
Cadillac Total	2,371	3,225	3,228	2,327	2,586
Astro	—	3	21	2,973	2,915
Avalanche	3,875	4,958	5,371	6,376	7,816
Colorado	4,586	6,239	6,538	6,170	5,848
Equinox	11,946	13,205	15,064	12,984	5,450
Express	5,271	7,237	7,301	6,056	6,626
HHR	4,916	5,026	5,480	1,813	—

Canada Vehicle Sales

CANADA VEHICLE SALES BY MODEL — continued

Model	2008	2007	2006	2005	2004
S Blazer	—	—	3	7,579	3,004
S10 Pickup	—	—	—	4	71
Silverado Light-Duty	34,685	40,066	36,480	37,012	38,005
SSR	7	11	94	177	368
Suburban	1,118	1,460	1,246	1,448	1,650
Tahoe	1,874	2,211	1,879	1,468	1,855
Tracker	—	—	—	15	1,553
TrailBlazer	2,206	2,778	3,429	5,297	6,147
Traverse	263	—	—	—	—
Uplander	16,133	18,999	21,047	21,271	1,193
Venture	—	7	33	2,236	21,376
Chevrolet Total	**86,880**	**102,200**	**103,986**	**112,879**	**103,877**
Acadia	5,844	6,067	—	—	—
Canyon	3,602	4,816	5,382	4,867	4,642
Envoy	2,083	1,962	3,897	6,740	8,270
Forward*	112	410	385	351	292
S Jimmy	—	—	5	6,730	2,701
Safari Van	—	—	25	2,384	2,668
Savana	4,640	7,687	7,238	6,552	6,752
Sierra Light-Duty	34,555	40,606	37,834	38,657	39,391
Sonoma	—	—	—	—	63
Yukon	1,585	2,197	2,443	1,871	2,353
Yukon XL	842	1,218	1,316	1,437	1,722
GMC Total	**53,263**	**64,963**	**58,525**	**69,589**	**68,854**
H1	—	—	—	2	4
H2	131	219	245	368	445
H2 SUT	36	58	76	136	53
H3	583	992	1,681	1,250	—
H3T	62	—	—	—	—
Hummer Total	**812**	**1,269**	**2,002**	**1,756**	**502**
Bravada	—	—	—	3	144
Silhouette	—	—	3	13	584
Oldsmobile Total	**—**	**—**	**3**	**16**	**728**
Aztek	—	—	5	104	525
Montana	—	3	15	2,503	27,730
Montana SV6	14,953	19,169	20,193	20,755	1,343
Torrent	10,465	11,799	13,890	2,083	—
Pontiac Total	**25,418**	**30,971**	**34,103**	**25,445**	**29,598**
Saab Total (9-7X)	**116**	**288**	**271**	**76**	**—**
Outlook	1,739	2,072	—	—	—
Relay	6	227	739	1,348	52
Vue	6,007	5,799	6,187	6,650	6,220
Saturn Total	**7,752**	**8,098**	**6,926**	**7,998**	**6,272**
GM TOTAL	**181,618**	**215,224**	**215,706**	**227,048**	**220,637**
MDX	5,514	6,017	4,257	3,836	4,181
RDX	3,573	4,104	1,415	—	—
Acura Total	**9,087**	**10,121**	**5,672**	**3,836**	**4,181**
CRV	20,488	20,915	3,851	—	—
CRV*	12	65	13,970	15,976	15,388
Element	1,810	1,764	3,099	2,880	3,035
Odyssey	10,125	12,025	13,368	12,573	10,559
Pilot	5,564	4,328	5,359	5,213	4,730
Ridgeline	3,987	4,519	4,988	3,512	—
Honda Total	**41,986**	**43,616**	**44,635**	**40,154**	**33,712**
HONDA TOTAL	**51,073**	**53,737**	**50,307**	**43,990**	**37,893**
Entourage*	1,400	2,383	1,779	—	—
Santa Fe	14,401	15,389	5,038	—	—
Santa Fe*	—	40	6,015	11,519	13,192
Tucson*	8,711	12,008	12,586	11,533	1,173
Veracruz*	1,550	1,243	—	—	—
HYUNDAI TOTAL	**26,062**	**31,063**	**25,418**	**23,052**	**14,365**
NPR	5	—	—	—	—
NPR*	2	—	—	—	—
Rodeo	—	—	—	—	5
Trooper*	—	—	—	—	1
ISUZU TOTAL	**7**	**—**	**—**	**—**	**6**
Borrego*	187	—	—	—	—
Rondo*	9,906	7,682	85	—	—
Sedona*	3,615	3,171	4,085	3,683	4,772
Sorento*	1,398	1,573	2,649	3,246	4,346
Sportage*	5,509	6,393	6,041	4,820	167
KIA TOTAL	**20,615**	**18,819**	**12,860**	**11,749**	**9,285**
CX-7*	3,576	4,729	3,338	—	—
CX-9*	1,725	2,117	—	—	—
Mazda5*	11,944	11,690	8,694	2,552	—
Mazda Pickup	3,464	4,297	2,811	2,256	3,098

Canada Vehicle Sales

CANADA VEHICLE SALES BY MODEL — continued

Model	2008	2007	2006	2005	2004
MPV*	—	—	2,272	2,798	4,863
Tribute	5,437	4,666	3,377	5,290	5,478
MAZDA TOTAL	**26,146**	**27,499**	**20,492**	**12,896**	**13,439**
Endeavor	398	826	821	1,040	1,008
Montero*	—	10	60	117	181
Montero Sport*	—	—	—	—	65
Outlander*	6,507	6,227	2,841	2,896	2,115
MITSUBISHI TOTAL	**6,905**	**7,063**	**3,722**	**4,053**	**3,369**
EX*	2,300				
FX*	1,003	1,094	1,430	1,454	2,319
QX56	160	204	267	362	380
Infiniti Total	**3,463**	**1,298**	**1,697**	**1,816**	**2,699**
Armada	100	153	219	438	613
Frontier	1,608	2,162	2,461	2,288	1,094
Murano*	4,557	4,159	5,062	5,042	6,157
Pathfinder	1,196	1,944	3,027	4,385	353
Pathfinder*	—	—	—	—	3,520
Quest	904	1,341	1,428	2,495	2,944
Rogue*	13,163	2,924	—	—	—
Titan	1,520	1,894	2,441	1,837	1,484
X-Trail*	—	4,579	10,211	10,518	6,602
Xterra	800	1,469	2,183	2,799	1,407
Nissan Total	**23,848**	**20,625**	**27,032**	**29,802**	**24,174**
NISSAN TOTAL	**27,311**	**21,923**	**28,729**	**31,618**	**26,873**
PORSCHE TOTAL (Cayenne)*	**778**	**823**	**572**	**917**	**1,017**
Baja	1	1	51	50	84
Forester*	6,322	3,303	3,737	3,614	4,201
Tribeca	925	801	902	804	—
SUBARU TOTAL	**7,248**	**4,105**	**4,690**	**4,468**	**4,285**
Equator	32	—	—	—	—
Vitara	—	—	—	—	744
Vitara*	3,296	3,331	3,664	1,826	1,065
XL7	452	1,336	217	—	—
XL7*	—	14	619	1,044	1,243
SUZUKI TOTAL	**3,780**	**4,681**	**4,500**	**2,870**	**3,052**
Land Rover Discovery*	—	—	—	38	368
Land Rover Freelander*	—	—	3	312	508
Land Rover LR2*	840	1,054	—	—	—
Land Rover LR3*	544	694	1,134	916	132
Land Rover Range Rover*	244	381	476	423	338
Land Rover Range Rover Sport*	665	834	957	397	—
TATA TOTAL	**2,293**	**2,963**	**2,570**	**2,086**	**1,346**
GX470*	291	342	454	668	730
LX470*	—	45	54	72	94
LX570*	353	—	—	—	—
RX330	—	—	523	3,036	3,513
RX330*	—	—	476	1,821	794
RX350	2,766	2,162	2,152	—	—
RX350*	3,455	2,503	1,472	—	—
Lexus Total	**6,865**	**5,052**	**5,131**	**5,597**	**5,131**
4Runner*	725	1,530	2,213	2,696	3,497
FJ Cruiser*	2,630	4,901	4,919	—	—
Highlander*	6,486	5,052	3,039	4,621	5,334
Land Cruiser*	261	262	136	225	182
RAV4	445	—	—	—	—
RAV4*	20,077	16,329	14,804	6,269	6,991
Sequoia	842	195	377	477	562
Sienna	7,000	9,820	11,579	13,622	17,043
Tacoma	9,673	9,477	9,345	6,388	2,836
Tundra	9,477	11,552	2,569	3,050	3,898
Toyota Total	**57,616**	**59,118**	**48,981**	**37,348**	**40,343**
TOYOTA TOTAL	**64,481**	**64,170**	**54,112**	**42,945**	**45,474**
Allroad*	—	—	7	179	318
Q7*	1,269	1,235	618	—	—
Audi Total	**1,269**	**1,235**	**625**	**179**	**318**
Eurovan*	—	—	—	1	5
Routan	355	—	—	—	—
Tiguan*	1,412	—	—	—	—
Touareg*	703	654	684	802	1,519
Volkswagen Total	**2,470**	**654**	**684**	**803**	**1,524**
VOLKSWAGEN TOTAL	**3,739**	**1,889**	**1,309**	**982**	**1,842**
TOTAL LIGHT TRUCKS	**761,101**	**808,977**	**753,634**	**732,593**	**709,421**
TOTAL LIGHT VEHICLES	**1,633,821**	**1,650,562**	**1,612,460**	**1,580,029**	**1,530,971**
TOTAL MED./HVY. TRUCKS	**39,701**	**39,783**	**53,548**	**50,113**	**43,832**
TOTAL VEHICLES	**1,673,522**	**1,690,345**	**1,666,008**	**1,630,142**	**1,574,803**

Units imported from outside North America. SOURCE: Ward's AutoInfoBank

Mexico Vehicle Sales

MEXICO VEHICLE SALES BY MODEL

Model	2008	2007	2006	2005	2004
1-Series*	1,168	977	1,152	980	215
3-Series	—	—	—	3	39
3-Series*	2,855	3,429	2,726	2,134	1,819
5-Series*	636	755	871	754	785
6-Series*	33	48	73	110	78
7-Series*	63	71	74	87	89
Z4	145	145	253	140	233
BMW Total	**4,900**	**5,425**	**5,149**	**4,208**	**3,258**
Mini Cooper*	2,015	2,070	1,806	1,902	1,750
BMW TOTAL	**6,915**	**7,495**	**6,955**	**6,110**	**5,008**
300M	—	—	—	—	434
300 Series	412	660	1,085	1,140	629
Cirrus Coupe	47	40	23	28	47
Cirrus Sedan	1,012	2,772	2,323	2,207	2,831
Concorde	—	—	—	—	1
Crossfire*	96	40	40	140	360
Neon	—	7	924	10,842	10,512
PT Cruiser Convertible	6	54	137	182	135
Chrysler Total	**1,573**	**3,573**	**4,532**	**14,539**	**14,949**
Atoz*	8,946	12,088	14,872	16,374	15,033
Attitude*	10,901	9,068	11,263	233	—
Avenger	8,091	7,798	—	—	—
Caliber	4,811	6,993	7,906	—	—
Challenger	233	—	—	—	—
Charger	3,283	990	2,135	387	—
Stratus Sedan	10	3,042	12,704	16,123	16,761
Verna*	5	31	877	13,644	17,126
Viper	13	3	12	8	10
Dodge Total	**36,293**	**40,013**	**49,769**	**46,769**	**48,930**
CHRYSLER TOTAL	**37,866**	**43,586**	**54,301**	**61,308**	**63,879**
A-Class*	—	—	2	331	370
B-Class*	469	552	637	346	—
C-Class*	2,901	2,657	1,871	1,925	1,917
CL*	19	34	1	17	79
CLK*	79	98	79	71	81
CLS*	114	144	167	96	19
E-Class*	537	713	717	696	611
S-Class*	94	147	143	111	84
SL*	20	26	27	27	43
SLK*	248	322	327	259	235
Mercedes Total	**4,481**	**4,693**	**3,971**	**3,879**	**3,439**
Forfour*	1	39	207	197	41
Fortwo*	786	515	388	239	222
Roadster*	—	—	2	86	140
Smart Total	**787**	**554**	**597**	**522**	**403**
DAIMLER TOTAL	**5,268**	**5,247**	**4,568**	**4,401**	**3,842**
147*	—	—	—	76	220
156*	—	—	—	52	230
Alfa Romeo Total	**—**	**—**	**—**	**128**	**450**
500*	124	—	—	—	—
Albea*	110	—	—	—	—
Grande Punto*	669	605	69	—	—
Palio Adventurer*	648	1,460	861	3,312	6,048
Panda*	445	330	—	—	—
Stilo*	90	116	28	—	—
Fiat Total	**2,086**	**2,511**	**958**	**3,312**	**6,048**
FIAT TOTAL	**2,086**	**2,511**	**958**	**3,440**	**6,498**
Crown Victoria	205	140	263	200	325
Fiesta*	13,861	18,870	30,022	38,348	25,706
Five Hundred	53	459	1,028	1,607	515
Focus	8,230	6,629	4,496	7,175	6,344
Fusion	5,476	5,853	4,983	1,103	—
Ikon	501	6,865	6,088	9,425	13,028
Ka*	441	2,727	4,645	6,933	11,894
Mondeo*	115	824	2,674	4,668	5,118
Mustang	1,769	2,052	2,952	2,253	1,109
Thunderbird	—	—	—	—	337
Ford Total	**30,651**	**44,419**	**57,151**	**71,712**	**64,376**
LS	—	6	67	268	535
MKS	261	—	—	—	—
MKZ	526	491	326	—	—
Town Car	5	67	117	137	196
Zephyr	—	—	523	298	—
Lincoln Total	**792**	**564**	**1,033**	**703**	**731**
Grand Marquis	—	—	—	—	291
Milan	357	520	93	—	—
Montego	15	83	191	174	—
Sable	—	—	—	18	356
Mercury Total	**372**	**603**	**284**	**192**	**647**
30*	376	346	—	—	—
40*	834	1,112	1,258	1,687	1,528
50*	—	8	23	64	—
60*	50	189	385	451	618
70*	44	106	51	6	14
80*	108	186	17	105	127
Volvo Total	**1,412**	**1,947**	**1,734**	**2,313**	**2,287**

Mexico Vehicle Sales

MEXICO VEHICLE SALES BY MODEL — continued

Model	2008	2007	2006	2005	2004
FORD TOTAL	**33,227**	**47,533**	**60,202**	**74,920**	**68,041**
BLS*	152	204	39	—	—
CTS	658	323	156	236	292
Deville	—	—	—	7	98
STS	31	52	59	81	—
XLR	—	1	5	11	22
Cadillac Total	**841**	**580**	**259**	**335**	**412**
Astra*	2,384	2,654	8,504	15,415	16,591
Aveo	14,083	—	—	—	—
Aveo*	5,788	—	—	—	—
Cavalier	—	—	—	82	1,747
Corsa*	6,277	20,800	33,745	41,968	38,584
Corvette	22	37	37	68	35
Epica*	106	—	—	—	—
Impala	1	6	34	30	60
Joy/Swing	34,748	39,644	43,471	47,050	58,036
Joy/Swing*	—	—	—	—	149
Malibu	5,691	5,988	6,996	7,985	8,149
Meriva*	1,618	3,632	5,284	6,536	7,330
Monza	21,394	19,977	19,638	18,707	20,103
Optra*	16,828	21,798	10,444	—	—
Vectra*	117	589	1,380	2,228	3,403
Chevrolet Total	**109,057**	**115,125**	**129,533**	**140,069**	**154,187**
G3	1,783	—	—	—	—
G3*	5,784	7,520	4,416	—	—
G4	—	—	1,610	1,253	—
G5	2,426	2,592	1,038	—	—
G6	557	595	863	1,130	116
Grand Am	—	—	—	98	244
Matiz*	9,721	9,587	10,488	8,972	7,142
Solstice	377	458	372	139	—
Sunfire	—	—	1	619	1,370
Pontiac Total	**20,648**	**20,752**	**18,788**	**12,211**	**8,872**
9-3*	247	228	349	498	726
9-5*	3	27	48	23	76
Saab Total	**250**	**255**	**397**	**521**	**802**
GM TOTAL	**130,796**	**136,712**	**148,977**	**153,136**	**164,273**
RL*	57	92	125	106	9
TL	397	543	755	642	37
TSX*	546	—	—	—	—
Acura Total	**1,000**	**635**	**880**	**748**	**46**
Accord	11,828	9,572	9,002	9,446	8,303
Civic	13,643	13,319	12,050	10,098	8,042
Fit*	3,327	4,745	4,075	1,374	—
Honda Total	**28,798**	**27,636**	**25,127**	**20,918**	**16,345**
HONDA TOTAL	**29,798**	**28,271**	**26,007**	**21,666**	**16,391**
Mazda3*	9,502	6,939	4,750	534	—
Mazda6	2,241	980	1,003	141	—
MX-5 Miata*	179	261	223	—	—
MAZDA TOTAL	**11,922**	**8,180**	**5,976**	**675**	—
TF*	—	—	—	68	185
ZR*	—	—	—	50	188
ZT*	—	—	—	16	34
MG Total	—	—	—	**134**	**407**
Rover 75*	—	—	—	177	368
MG ROVER TOTAL	—	—	—	**311**	**775**
Eclipse	326	729	768	631	349
Galant	356	572	703	893	913
Lancer*	5,525	7,253	5,092	3,865	2,562
Space Star*	—	—	—	58	500
MITSUBISHI TOTAL	**6,207**	**8,554**	**6,563**	**5,447**	**4,324**
I35*	—	—	—	3	25
Q45*	—	1	12	18	41
Infiniti Total	—	**1**	**12**	**21**	**66**
350Z*	25	40	50	120	170
Almera*	—	1	390	1,404	2,533
Altima	5,213	7,127	6,586	6,802	8,154
Aprio*	12,140	6,374	—	—	—
Maxima*	367	172	486	727	1,004
Micra*	120	501	1,403	2,281	569
Platina	6,288	15,687	35,201	49,572	55,869
Sentra	17,859	22,309	33,930	33,370	29,952
Tiida	24,030	26,424	3,377	—	—
Tsubame	—	—	—	—	222
Tsuru	68,874	63,461	66,243	68,201	68,381
Nissan Total	**134,916**	**142,096**	**147,666**	**162,477**	**166,854**
NISSAN TOTAL	**134,916**	**142,097**	**147,678**	**162,498**	**166,920**
206*	2,970	6,010	9,548	11,121	10,196
207*	1,892	178	—	—	—
307*	1,525	3,255	3,086	3,934	4,144
308*	129	—	—	—	—
406*	—	—	—	41	589
407*	185	447	612	306	—
607*	—	14	23	86	123
Grand Raid*	1,144	1,989	863	—	—
Partner*	1,463	1,694	1,936	1,475	1,256
PEUGEOT TOTAL	**9,308**	**13,587**	**16,068**	**16,963**	**16,308**

Mexico Vehicle Sales

MEXICO VEHICLE SALES BY MODEL — continued

Model	2008	2007	2006	2005	2004
911*	183	165	132	101	86
Boxster*	65	74	197	118	90
Carrera GT*	—	—	—	14	10
Cayman*	93	110	15	—	—
PORSCHE TOTAL	**341**	**349**	**344**	**233**	**186**
Clio	8,098	9,019	10,953	12,037	11,817
Clio*	411	911	241	198	675
Laguna*	5	24	148	196	344
Megane*	2,948	3,429	5,472	7,437	8,238
RENAULT TOTAL	**11,462**	**13,383**	**16,814**	**19,868**	**21,074**
Impreza*	333	116	22	—	—
Legacy	151	147	103	—	—
SUBARU TOTAL	**484**	**263**	**125**	—	—
Aerio*	—	600	1,172	199	—
SX4*	4,675	1,668	227	—	—
SUZUKI TOTAL	**4,675**	**2,268**	**1,399**	**199**	—
Jaguar S-Type*	11	60	105	134	180
Jaguar X-Type*	21	105	176	248	444
Jaguar XF*	175	—	—	—	—
Jaguar XJ*	13	8	21	24	29
Jaguar XK8*	17	26	30	10	6
TATA TOTAL	**237**	**199**	**332**	**416**	**659**
Avanza*	2,825	1,307	—	—	—
Camry	4,980	6,872	7,201	2,768	2,241
Corolla	9,850	9,316	7,963	6,440	4,057
Matrix	1,024	1,033	1,163	1,049	1,422
MR2 Spyder*	—	—	35	231	104
Yaris*	13,357	11,762	9,360	2,288	873
TOYOTA TOTAL	**32,036**	**30,290**	**25,722**	**12,776**	**8,697**
A3*	1,726	1,609	1,590	1,529	1,263
A4*	1,724	1,529	1,738	1,824	1,713
A5*	349	25	—	—	—
A6*	331	468	502	412	403
A8*	37	48	52	49	60
R8*	77	14	—	—	—
RS6*	—	—	—	4	—
TT*	328	435	140	94	157
Audi Total	**4,572**	**4,128**	**4,022**	**3,912**	**3,596**
Altea*	87	241	157	347	—
Cordoba*	3,535	4,552	5,931	6,604	6,922
Ibiza*	8,334	9,573	12,156	12,251	13,389
Leon*	1,077	1,119	1,435	1,329	1,569
Toledo*	29	159	168	393	514
SEAT Total	**13,062**	**15,644**	**19,847**	**20,924**	**22,394**
Beetle	3,657	4,365	3,692	2,993	2,598
Beetle Cabrio	47	51	196	285	250
Bora	23,263	25,104	20,682	17,345	—
Derby*	3,008	4,207	7,045	12,462	15,490
Gol*	2,672	—	—	—	—
Golf*	728	1,129	1,259	1,565	2,468
Jetta	41,783	44,395	40,690	37,817	57,086
Jetta*	—	—	—	—	63
Lupo*	826	1,934	5,293	10,870	10,868
Passat*	1,719	2,072	2,591	1,074	1,344
Pointer*	25,279	28,300	31,962	46,791	62,707
Polo*	33	899	3,090	8,605	10,331
Sedan	—	—	—	10	882
Sport Van*	2,799	3,650	2,320	—	—
Volkswagen Total	**105,814**	**116,106**	**118,820**	**139,817**	**164,087**
VOLKSWAGEN TOTAL	**123,448**	**135,878**	**142,689**	**164,653**	**190,077**
TOTAL CARS	**580,992**	**626,403**	**665,678**	**709,020**	**736,952**
X3*	781	1,187	1,207	1,047	836
X5	1,008	1,220	731	1,012	965
X6	211	—	—	—	—
BMW TOTAL	**2,000**	**2,407**	**1,938**	**2,059**	**1,801**
Aspen	772	982	521	—	—
Pacifica	71	447	779	851	783
PT Cruiser	1,571	2,478	4,277	2,906	2,192
Town & Country	3,154	2,822	3,094	—	—
Voyager	1,394	8,505	10,715	15,153	13,449
Chrysler Total	**6,962**	**15,234**	**19,386**	**18,910**	**16,424**
1000*	1,115	225	—	—	—
Dakota	5,431	4,283	3,913	2,116	—
Durango	2,074	2,880	3,480	3,831	3,593
H100*	6,505	8,008	6,127	3,348	3,337
Journey	10,711	—	—	—	—
Nitro	3,000	6,779	2,250	—	—
Ram Pickup	18,832	18,780	18,866	14,723	10,495
Ram Van	—	—	—	—	294
Dodge Total	**47,668**	**40,955**	**34,636**	**24,018**	**17,719**
Commander	238	558	1,013	176	—
Compass	2,960	4,367	1,535	—	—
Grand Cherokee	2,856	3,250	4,058	3,703	2,343
Liberty	3,726	6,988	12,010	15,065	14,277
Patriot	11,516	10,950	—	—	—
Wrangler	2,345	2,653	1,507	1,173	1,102

Mexico Vehicle Sales

MEXICO VEHICLE SALES BY MODEL — continued

Model	2008	2007	2006	2005	2004
Jeep Total	**23,641**	**28,766**	**20,123**	**20,117**	**17,722**
CHRYSLER TOTAL	**78,271**	**84,955**	**74,145**	**63,045**	**51,865**
Ducato*	182	1	—	—	—
Idea*	507	407	—	—	—
Strada*	429	381	78	—	—
FIAT TOTAL	**1,118**	**789**	**78**	**—**	**—**
Courier*	4,426	4,910	6,089	6,702	6,709
Econoline	1,785	1,800	1,894	2,582	2,455
Ecosport*	9,446	13,909	24,215	27,185	22,785
Edge	3,103	2,710	38	—	—
Escape	12,260	10,857	9,716	9,796	9,664
Excursion	—	15	253	—	162
Expedition	3,135	3,535	3,957	3,611	3,841
Explorer	3,676	3,603	4,837	3,650	4,033
Freestar	8	160	3,307	4,708	5,893
F-Series Light-Duty	37,461	40,030	46,038	44,221	42,175
Ranger	14,826	17,669	16,268	12,521	10,662
Transit*	1,638	215	—	—	—
Windstar	—	—	—	—	1,027
Ford Total	**91,764**	**99,398**	**116,374**	**115,229**	**109,406**
Aviator	—	—	9	563	980
Blackwood	—	—	—	—	29
Mark LT	1,189	1,544	2,083	1,058	—
MKX	513	677	—	—	—
Navigator	465	625	674	595	673
Lincoln Total	**2,167**	**2,846**	**2,766**	**2,216**	**1,682**
Mercury Total (Mariner)	**921**	**1,024**	**1,104**	**1,218**	**333**
XC70*	—	4	7	20	10
XC90*	425	770	976	1,221	1,056
Volvo Total	**425**	**774**	**983**	**1,241**	**1,066**
FORD TOTAL	**95,277**	**104,042**	**121,227**	**119,904**	**112,487**
Escalade	257	325	329	229	273
Escalade ESV	338	379	357	266	263
Escalade EXT	277	395	300	171	157
SRX	2	2	26	81	120
Cadillac Total	**874**	**1,101**	**1,012**	**747**	**813**
Avalanche	1,007	1,915	1,240	389	447
Captiva Sport*	7,615	274	—	—	—
Colorado	4,389	4,462	4,169	3,833	2,620
Equinox	1,876	5,402	6,086	6,611	2,985
Express	2,687	3,349	3,940	3,995	3,268
HHR	1,132	3,254	4,092	954	—
LUV*	—	—	488	4,661	4,238
P Model	—	—	—	210	122
Pickup*	—	—	—	—	47
S-10	—	—	—	—	6
Silverado	27,152	28,246	29,461	33,297	29,287
Sonora	—	16	326	639	692
Suburban	3,583	4,431	4,140	2,991	2,842
Tahoe	2,103	3,249	1,720	—	—
Tiltmaster	—	—	6	—	—
Tornado*	12,704	14,677	15,480	12,350	8,113
Tracker	2,677	5,093	5,775	5,621	3,638
TrailBlazer	195	1,320	2,909	4,014	4,777
Uplander	2,467	3,821	5,249	5,438	158
Venture	—	—	—	313	3,393
Zafira*	1	434	876	1,424	2,274
Chevrolet Total	**69,588**	**79,943**	**85,957**	**86,740**	**68,907**
Acadia	2,601	2,048	—	—	—
Canyon	587	618	184	—	—
Sierra	1,678	1,739	24	—	—
Yukon	1,013	1,268	1,110	—	—
GMC Total	**5,879**	**5,673**	**1,318**	**—**	**—**
H2	84	132	473	533	160
H2 SUT	206	262	—	—	—
H3	1,005	1,472	1,940	500	—
H3T	368	—	—	—	—
Hummer Total	**1,663**	**1,866**	**2,413**	**1,033**	**160**
Aztek	—	—	—	90	362
Montana SV6	329	581	802	450	—
Torrent	1,340	1,969	1,768	1,736	—
Pontiac Total	**1,669**	**2,550**	**2,570**	**2,276**	**362**
GM TOTAL	**79,673**	**91,133**	**93,270**	**90,796**	**70,242**
MDX	743	761	466	282	17
RDX	389	455	285	—	—
Acura Total	**1,132**	**1,216**	**751**	**282**	**17**
CRV	16,929	3,941	—	—	—
CRV*	172	14,134	14,084	11,220	10,059
Odyssey	4,264	4,391	5,414	4,360	1,921
Pilot	3,244	1,937	2,445	1,823	1,342
Ridgeline	725	912	401	—	—
Honda Total	**25,334**	**25,315**	**22,344**	**17,403**	**13,322**
HONDA TOTAL	**26,466**	**26,531**	**23,095**	**17,685**	**13,339**
ISUZU TOTAL (Isuzu Truck)*	**787**	**171**	**—**	**—**	**—**
CX-7	7,014	6,089	868	—	—
CX-9	2,204	1,614	—	—	—

Mexico Vehicle Sales

MEXICO VEHICLE SALES BY MODEL — continued

Model	2008	2007	2006	2005	2004
Mazda5*	857	721	651	96	—
MAZDA TOTAL	**10,075**	**8,424**	**1,519**	**96**	**—**
G-Class*	26	4	10	3	8
GL-Class	183	263	112	—	—
GLK*	162	—	—	—	—
M-Class	636	729	827	662	383
R-Class	40	64	68	4	—
Mercedes Total	**1,047**	**1,060**	**1,017**	**669**	**391**
Sprinter Van*	1,690	2,017	1,464	2,405	2,384
MERCEDES TOTAL	**2,737**	**3,077**	**2,481**	**3,074**	**2,775**
Endeavor	1,219	2,039	3,160	2,821	1,546
Grandis*	489	579	255	—	—
L200*	1,672	—	—	—	—
Montero*	400	188	361	484	532
Montero Sport*	152	518	736	962	989
Outlander*	6,665	5,788	5,676	5,290	3,256
MITSUBISHI TOTAL	**10,597**	**9,112**	**10,188**	**9,557**	**6,323**
Armada	321	445	1,012	1,155	1,263
Cabstar*	1,696	468	—	—	—
Frontier	4,309	5,188	6,051	577	1,830
Murano*	1,307	680	1,319	1,721	2,228
Nissan Chassis	25,782	24,187	25,465	22,504	20,481
Nissan Pickup	16,365	17,092	16,827	15,531	13,726
Pathfinder	826	1,345	2,175	1,559	—
Pathfinder*	—	—	—	—	199
Quest	1,012	1,414	1,488	975	806
Rogue*	4,632	892	—	—	—
Titan	435	830	974	1,269	1,527
Urvan*	11,057	9,852	9,974	8,357	7,156
X-Trail*	9,347	9,567	15,069	18,334	18,077
Xterra	17	64	283	452	640
NISSAN TOTAL	**77,106**	**72,024**	**80,637**	**72,434**	**67,933**
Expert*	62	—	—	—	—
Manager*	146	—	—	—	—
PEUGEOT TOTAL	**208**	**—**	**—**	**—**	**—**
PORSCHE TOTAL (Cayenne)*	**414**	**424**	**288**	**280**	**266**
Kangoo*	3,171	4,391	3,078	3,133	1,536
Koleos*	590	—	—	—	—
Scenic	—	—	—	102	1,236
Scenic*	134	344	382	983	245
Trafic*	703	495	—	—	—
RENAULT TOTAL	**4,598**	**5,230**	**3,460**	**4,218**	**3,017**
Forester*	355	207	61	—	—
Tribeca	237	233	122	—	—
SUBARU TOTAL	**592**	**440**	**183**	**—**	**—**
Vitara*	3,114	3,220	3,014	563	—
XL7	215	212	—	—	—
SUZUKI TOTAL	**3,329**	**3,432**	**3,014**	**563**	**—**
Land Rover Discovery*	—	—	—	1	90
Land Rover Freelander*	—	4	173	297	583
Land Rover LR2*	309	367	—	—	—
Land Rover LR3*	99	179	243	247	63
Land Rover Range Rover*	39	82	73	63	64
Land Rover Range Rover Sport*	279	277	285	108	—
TATA TOTAL	**726**	**909**	**774**	**716**	**800**
4Runner*	172	576	1,390	1,149	809
FJ Cruiser*	2,824	2,032	—	—	—
Hiace*	3,679	3,141	2,778	840	—
Highlander*	1,493	1,293	—	—	—
Hilux	6,162	4,914	2,908	2,461	1,940
Land Cruiser*	148	147	217	166	57
RAV4*	7,491	11,948	14,848	10,462	7,085
Sequoia	267	—	—	—	—
Sienna	4,363	6,580	6,950	7,083	5,288
Tacoma	4,154	4,886	5,275	381	—
Tundra	517	401	—	—	—
TOYOTA TOTAL	**31,270**	**35,918**	**34,366**	**22,542**	**15,179**
Allroad*	—	—	—	—	14
QX7*	666	772	183	—	—
Audi Total	**666**	**772**	**183**	**—**	**14**
SEAT Total (Alhambra)*	**4**	**25**	**52**	**165**	**310**
Crafter*	688	93	—	—	—
Crossfox*	4,953	8,294	6,920	—	—
Eurovan*	3,955	5,299	5,866	5,426	2,191
Pointer Pickup*	2,585	2,167	1,934	2,279	2,252
Routan	114	—	—	—	—
Sharan*	381	593	834	966	1,279
Tiguan*	53	—	—	—	—
Touareg*	857	688	653	593	640
Volkswagen Total	**13,586**	**17,134**	**16,207**	**9,264**	**6,362**
VOLKSWAGEN TOTAL	**14,256**	**17,931**	**16,442**	**9,429**	**6,686**
TOTAL LIGHT TRUCKS	**439,500**	**466,949**	**467,105**	**416,398**	**352,713**
TOTAL LIGHT VEHICLES	**1,020,492**	**1,093,352**	**1,132,783**	**1,125,418**	**1,089,665**
TOTAL MED./HVY. TRUCKS	**48,244**	**50,953**	**44,317**	**36,740**	**29,920**
TOTAL VEHICLES	**1,068,736**	**1,144,305**	**1,177,100**	**1,162,158**	**1,119,585**

*Units imported from outside North America. SOURCE: Ward's AutoInfoBank.

Car, Truck and Bus Registrations by State

U.S. TOTAL VEHICLE REGISTRATIONS BY STATE

State	Cars		Trucks and Buses		Total	
	2007	2006	2007	2006	2007	2006
Alabama	1,976,510	1,795,596	2,701,261	2,834,718	4,677,771	4,630,314
Alaska	240,931	242,487	439,210	432,607	680,141	675,094
Arizona	2,237,693	2,189,979	2,134,342	1,992,353	4,372,035	4,182,332
Arkansas	944,255	958,640	1,066,046	1,035,615	2,010,301	1,994,255
California	20,037,727	19,835,554	13,897,659	13,346,504	33,935,386	33,182,058
Colorado	2,364,782	2,353,017	2,874,925	2,770,560	5,239,707	5,123,577
Connecticut	1,988,569	1,999,809	1,058,761	1,052,143	3,047,330	3,051,952
Delaware	472,688	432,509	378,535	380,679	851,223	813,188
Dist. of Columbia	165,633	168,916	51,888	50,189	217,521	219,105
Florida	7,189,598	7,425,148	9,284,310	8,948,417	16,473,908	16,373,565
Georgia	4,155,154	4,141,179	4,357,357	4,145,275	8,512,511	8,286,454
Hawaii	521,669	538,581	471,448	469,959	993,117	1,008,540
Idaho	525,560	541,487	756,339	733,628	1,281,899	1,275,115
Illinois	5,814,178	5,947,468	3,942,826	3,928,778	9,757,004	9,876,246
Indiana	2,705,681	2,694,901	2,413,037	2,352,503	5,118,718	5,047,404
Iowa	1,727,177	1,744,519	1,633,019	1,601,432	3,360,196	3,345,951
Kansas	879,318	872,878	1,549,746	1,516,314	2,429,064	2,389,192
Kentucky	1,937,195	1,969,142	1,609,425	1,588,980	3,546,620	3,558,122
Louisiana	1,938,195	1,950,372	1,988,546	1,922,372	3,926,741	3,872,744
Maine	569,503	581,797	510,340	490,079	1,079,843	1,071,876
Maryland	2,652,872	2,656,597	1,857,592	1,831,800	4,510,464	4,488,397
Massachusetts	3,276,019	3,310,725	2,090,689	2,074,490	5,366,708	5,385,215
Michigan	4,972,114	4,765,547	3,469,428	3,388,688	8,441,542	8,154,235
Minnesota	2,552,023	2,512,491	2,203,730	2,192,423	4,755,753	4,704,914
Mississippi	1,141,299	1,118,200	866,576	879,381	2,007,875	1,997,581
Missouri	2,675,818	2,715,297	2,241,175	2,241,875	4,916,993	4,957,172
Montana	389,754	447,446	558,774	619,116	948,528	1,066,562
Nebraska	815,731	832,511	923,341	900,622	1,739,072	1,733,133
Nevada	698,622	679,828	725,700	686,729	1,424,322	1,366,557
New Hampshire	643,442	585,455	541,400	474,508	1,184,842	1,059,963
New Jersey	3,827,017	3,692,966	2,420,113	2,265,022	6,247,130	5,957,988
New Mexico	703,057	699,312	896,276	881,508	1,599,333	1,580,820
New York	8,866,591	8,528,457	2,627,922	2,755,439	11,494,513	11,283,896
North Carolina	3,601,669	3,659,926	2,715,479	2,641,510	6,317,148	6,301,436
North Dakota	344,258	345,502	366,279	366,667	710,537	712,169
Ohio	6,362,791	6,438,988	4,485,685	4,389,855	10,848,476	10,828,843
Oklahoma	1,605,813	1,606,517	1,618,840	1,595,314	3,224,653	3,201,831
Oregon	1,462,803	1,427,597	1,625,510	1,553,782	3,088,313	2,981,379
Pennsylvania	5,805,046	5,842,819	4,132,895	4,051,344	9,937,941	9,894,163
Rhode Island	491,229	508,389	305,454	297,159	796,683	805,548
South Carolina	1,940,512	1,964,994	1,580,514	1,488,849	3,521,026	3,453,843
South Dakota	372,633	375,760	492,205	468,224	864,838	843,984
Tennessee	3,020,654	2,878,136	2,319,292	2,213,192	5,339,946	5,091,328
Texas	8,800,325	8,805,316	9,271,823	8,733,072	18,072,148	17,538,388
Utah	1,138,442	1,079,455	1,181,729	1,156,633	2,320,171	2,236,088
Vermont	297,176	309,972	267,791	277,696	564,967	587,668
Virginia	3,958,939	4,031,355	2,654,842	2,604,621	6,613,781	6,635,976
Washington	3,146,178	3,087,818	2,611,765	2,601,679	5,757,943	5,689,497
West Virginia	707,442	734,599	706,025	706,500	1,413,467	1,441,099
Wisconsin	2,645,181	2,639,984	2,372,714	2,331,477	5,017,895	4,971,461
Wyoming	215,911	228,057	436,191	417,135	652,102	645,192
Total	**137,523,377**	**136,893,995**	**113,686,769**	**110,679,415**	**251,210,146**	**247,573,410**

NOTE: Registrations include both privately and publicly owned motor vehicles, except those owned by the military. Colorado data have been estimated by Ward's to compensate for under-reporting by the state.
SOURCE: U.S. Department of Transportation, Federal Highway Administration.

Total Truck Registrations by State

U.S. TOTAL TRUCK REGISTRATIONS BY STATE

State	Privately Owned[1]				Privately and Publicly Owned[2]			
	2007	2006	2005	2004	2007	2006	2005	2004
Alabama	2,664,238	2,798,056	2,746,098	2,777,832	2,692,056	2,825,636	2,773,536	2,804,922
Alaska	426,143	419,421	412,418	393,342	436,538	429,901	420,933	402,473
Arizona	2,109,569	1,967,804	1,826,496	1,697,105	2,129,427	1,987,392	1,845,996	1,716,125
Arkansas	1,046,517	1,015,740	968,617	938,284	1,058,288	1,027,414	980,248	949,756
California	13,529,754	12,986,891	12,494,938	11,797,270	13,839,571	13,289,690	12,793,485	12,090,263
Colorado	2,777,007	2,711,921	2,605,111	2,488,421	2,869,105	2,764,608	2,658,277	2,536,617
Connecticut	1,018,693	1,012,622	991,480	956,016	1,048,170	1,041,651	1,020,152	984,151
Delaware	373,007	375,243	303,489	283,177	376,277	378,512	306,644	286,183
Dist. of Columbia	41,906	40,398	42,318	39,979	48,902	47,300	49,201	46,675
Florida	9,067,890	8,734,922	7,169,898	6,411,148	9,235,703	8,899,488	7,331,572	6,569,344
Georgia	4,258,248	4,049,049	3,760,558	3,569,214	4,335,274	4,123,932	3,833,501	3,639,958
Hawaii	456,250	455,413	415,866	394,039	465,508	464,288	424,462	402,299
Idaho	737,839	714,691	772,647	751,265	752,467	729,861	787,007	765,498
Illinois	3,910,671	3,896,872	3,721,964	3,547,149	3,924,516	3,910,742	3,736,095	3,561,103
Indiana	2,235,341	2,272,452	2,182,951	2,381,601	2,379,986	2,319,932	2,228,561	2,426,148
Iowa	1,595,224	1,562,115	1,516,888	1,448,079	1,625,644	1,593,003	1,547,717	1,478,710
Kansas	1,525,657	1,492,577	1,479,490	1,470,733	1,545,810	1,512,396	1,499,020	1,489,985
Kentucky	1,586,207	1,565,915	1,490,658	1,415,034	1,595,127	1,574,731	1,499,461	1,423,633
Louisiana	1,938,915	1,874,264	1,812,247	1,746,697	1,965,532	1,900,270	1,837,751	1,771,505
Maine	492,473	472,992	469,767	442,856	506,809	486,680	482,786	456,058
Maryland	1,821,056	1,795,444	1,688,827	1,536,240	1,845,553	1,819,645	1,712,870	1,559,831
Massachusetts	2,033,485	2,019,069	1,997,581	1,898,100	2,078,931	2,063,283	2,040,731	1,939,924
Michigan	3,111,479	3,281,456	3,798,849	3,612,504	3,443,138	3,362,440	3,882,319	3,691,719
Minnesota	2,155,069	2,145,214	2,093,861	2,045,692	2,185,608	2,174,813	2,123,525	2,074,212
Mississippi	848,739	852,785	833,473	815,469	856,971	869,860	850,021	831,926
Missouri	2,211,160	2,212,332	2,020,761	2,084,250	2,230,097	2,230,390	2,038,795	2,102,497
Montana	537,052	597,738	554,941	554,941	556,291	616,613	573,151	572,944
Nebraska	894,066	871,612	838,636	819,626	916,305	893,627	859,748	840,220
Nevada	708,543	669,824	659,439	622,065	723,687	684,806	674,385	636,705
New Hampshire	526,484	460,060	508,090	490,694	539,421	472,635	520,123	503,858
New Jersey	2,282,884	2,122,043	2,167,033	2,075,843	2,396,824	2,241,195	2,281,050	2,184,532
New Mexico	868,106	853,675	834,716	820,257	892,850	877,956	858,673	843,606
New York	2,456,181	2,585,454	2,721,530	2,386,073	2,555,438	2,685,424	2,822,198	2,485,851
North Carolina	2,628,306	2,556,073	2,480,104	2,457,555	2,681,079	2,607,790	2,531,239	2,507,792
North Dakota	354,998	355,207	342,453	342,456	363,767	364,080	351,176	351,228
Ohio	4,352,430	4,260,213	4,145,590	4,060,978	4,439,732	4,345,371	4,228,831	4,141,968
Oklahoma	1,545,998	1,523,945	1,722,502	1,448,212	1,599,908	1,576,680	1,774,181	1,498,655
Oregon	1,576,233	1,505,788	1,453,468	1,479,061	1,610,170	1,538,960	1,488,563	1,512,392
Pennsylvania	4,025,119	3,944,750	3,869,660	3,715,893	4,094,385	4,013,315	3,937,829	3,783,195
Rhode Island	298,072	290,141	287,570	268,887	303,723	295,433	293,166	274,397
South Carolina	1,532,754	1,442,316	1,360,592	1,289,654	1,561,650	1,470,771	1,388,594	1,317,008
South Dakota	474,607	451,101	451,933	428,263	489,469	465,580	466,368	442,435
Tennessee	2,237,269	2,130,732	2,068,318	2,070,025	2,299,430	2,193,213	2,128,230	2,127,180
Texas	8,927,904	8,398,776	8,226,834	7,850,587	9,179,573	8,642,899	8,468,172	8,084,417
Utah	1,163,343	1,138,579	1,101,976	1,030,360	1,180,408	1,155,325	1,118,491	1,046,461
Vermont	259,997	270,261	231,346	234,100	265,984	275,951	236,708	240,997
Virginia	2,599,753	2,549,672	2,469,859	2,351,680	2,636,607	2,586,357	2,506,491	2,387,893
Washington	2,555,594	2,546,407	2,483,110	2,447,193	2,599,581	2,590,014	2,526,620	2,489,934
West Virginia	676,312	676,317	621,274	624,361	703,233	703,706	649,178	652,709
Wisconsin	2,307,305	2,267,617	2,100,434	2,051,293	2,357,752	2,317,130	2,149,121	2,098,972
Wyoming	418,277	399,997	397,581	390,195	432,985	414,047	411,346	403,556
Total	**110,180,124**	**107,593,956**	**103,716,240**	**99,251,748**	**112,851,260**	**109,856,736**	**105,948,298**	**101,430,420**

(1) Excludes farm trucks registered in certain states and restricted for use in vicinity of owner's farm.
(2) Includes federal, state, county and municipal vehicles; excludes vehicles owned by military.
SOURCE: U.S. Department of Transportation, Federal Highway Administration.

Truck Registrations by State and Type

U.S. TOTAL TRUCK REGISTRATIONS BY STATE AND TYPE, 2007

State	Pickups	Vans	Sport Utilities	Other Light	Truck Tractors	Other Med./Hvy.	Total
Alabama	1,368,697	305,050	839,053	--	103,353	75,903	2,692,056
Alaska	204,536	51,582	157,218	3,721	4,255	15,226	436,538
Arizona	890,154	324,139	800,923	9,184	33,188	71,839	2,129,427
Arkansas	573,339	127,942	329,479	4,522	20,790	2,216	1,058,288
California	3,997,144	2,393,426	5,186,723	50,186	147,735	2,064,357	13,839,571
Colorado(1)	954,230	341,143	1,288,522	6,211	17,767	261,232	2,869,105
Connecticut	303,215	213,133	491,285	4,912	2,394	33,231	1,048,170
Delaware	47,370	27,773	67,564	2,622	1,404	229,544	376,277
Dist. of Columbia	5,489	9,872	22,873	449	212	10,007	48,902
Florida	1,940,153	1,145,872	2,414,060	23,305	286,024	3,426,289	9,235,703
Georgia	1,643,211	609,280	1,475,265	18,862	88,137	500,519	4,335,274
Hawaii	189,612	85,011	174,739	2,486	1,163	12,497	465,508
Idaho	381,230	77,370	202,063	3,579	21,368	66,857	752,467
Illinois	1,151,095	984,356	1,531,234	16,440	73,396	167,995	3,924,516
Indiana	989,387	493,516	685,552	6,795	62,579	142,157	2,379,986
Iowa	689,573	281,530	363,969	5,301	62,754	222,517	1,625,644
Kansas	630,287	331,223	380,607	8,510	29,090	166,093	1,545,810
Kentucky	780,432	242,005	464,613	6,274	28,139	73,664	1,595,127
Louisiana	1,029,222	217,266	605,498	6,879	39,709	66,958	1,965,532
Maine	235,129	74,972	160,571	2,134	4,038	29,965	506,809
Maryland	543,337	413,158	818,520	9,535	17,891	43,112	1,845,553
Massachusetts	576,594	443,358	976,246	11,016	12,947	58,770	2,078,931
Michigan	1,205,070	800,204	1,235,627	4,792	25,304	172,141	3,443,138
Minnesota	814,132	434,242	672,211	10,911	35,789	218,323	2,185,608
Mississippi	472,807	95,948	247,693	3,957	8,792	27,774	856,971
Missouri	984,801	383,894	697,666	8,961	49,821	104,954	2,230,097
Montana	268,671	52,636	135,131	2,264	19,936	77,653	556,291
Nebraska	386,308	139,920	257,972	3,591	38,851	89,663	916,305
Nevada	255,564	85,889	273,954	2,520	8,439	97,321	723,687
New Hampshire	212,532	91,706	202,839	3,180	5,484	23,680	539,421
New Jersey	482,819	564,183	1,204,691	15,121	14,660	115,350	2,396,824
New Mexico	421,543	96,938	264,840	3,305	13,317	92,907	892,850
New York	532,620	568,248	1,075,762	14,708	7,814	356,286	2,555,438
North Carolina	1,062,144	425,769	906,073	12,106	59,403	215,584	2,681,079
North Dakota	159,875	49,532	84,904	1,271	9,429	58,756	363,767
Ohio	1,564,409	1,023,142	1,507,277	15,920	43,441	285,543	4,439,732
Oklahoma	773,698	187,472	403,893	6,766	12,287	215,792	1,599,908
Oregon	686,835	247,003	520,128	8,317	21,812	126,075	1,610,170
Pennsylvania	1,195,244	807,459	1,622,155	16,279	74,404	378,844	4,094,385
Rhode Island	90,629	61,082	127,294	1,168	3,667	19,883	303,723
South Carolina	653,188	240,805	581,258	7,321	21,317	57,761	1,561,650
South Dakota	198,683	61,815	109,973	1,810	19,947	97,241	489,469
Tennessee	1,017,218	352,712	778,263	12,140	67,537	71,560	2,299,430
Texas	4,182,560	1,123,885	3,282,513	30,827	183,268	376,520	9,179,573
Utah	485,309	160,610	418,017	5,518	47,213	63,741	1,180,408
Vermont	114,412	39,453	96,720	994	3,009	11,396	265,984
Virginia	916,775	488,852	1,063,635	10,873	40,959	115,513	2,636,607
Washington	1,050,316	438,995	910,766	13,502	34,274	151,728	2,599,581
West Virginia	332,596	85,819	220,115	2,063	11,353	51,287	703,233
Wisconsin	860,168	523,556	730,441	8,855	41,460	193,272	2,357,752
Wyoming	228,705	35,168	120,175	2,091	4,480	42,366	432,985
Total	**40,733,067**	**18,859,914**	**39,188,563**	**434,054**	**1,985,799**	**8,646,818**	**112,851,260**

(1) Adjusted to compensate for partial data reporting by state.
NOTE: The registrations given in this table are as reported by the states in most instances, but have been supplemented in some cases by estimates by USDOT based on data from other sources.
SOURCE: U.S. Department of Transportation, Federal Highway Administration.

Private, Commercial and Publicly Owned Trailer Registrations by State

U.S. TRAILER REGISTRATIONS BY STATE, 2007

State	Private and Commercial Trailers[1]				Publicly Owned Trailers			Total Trailers
	Commercial Trailers[2]	Car and Light Farm Trailers[3]	House Trailers[4]	Total	Federal Government	State, County and Municipal	Total	
Alabama	74,914	103,925	13,932	192,771	15	1,193	1,208	193,979
Alaska	12,760	107,926	—	120,686	140	1,974	2,114	122,800
Arizona	113,511	395,017	179,415	687,943	102	4,148	4,250	692,193
Arkansas	69,140	507,292	8,603	585,035	7	280	287	585,322
California	756,955	1,645,346	599,944	3,002,245	393	61,922	62,315	3,064,560
Colorado	51,514	121,100	50,990	223,604	85	2,163	2,248	225,852
Connecticut	85,105	117,411	—	202,516	13	2,950	2,963	205,479
Delaware	44,287	30,906	—	75,193	7	1,012	1,019	76,212
Dist. of Columbia	84	957	—	1,041	160	367	527	1,568
Florida	75,267	1,679,364	—	1,754,631	193	30,775	30,968	1,785,599
Georgia	222,317	695,047	49,055	966,419	136	4,989	5,125	971,544
Hawaii	4,773	27,159	—	31,932	5	1,434	1,439	33,371
Idaho	45,251	72,688	70,901	188,840	63	3,157	3,220	192,060
Illinois	135,247	609,037	143,468	887,752	246	179	425	888,177
Indiana	70,176	334,168	97,113	501,457	42	2,484	2,526	503,983
Iowa	231,011	413,121	82,446	726,578	21	5,087	5,108	731,686
Kansas	86,601	25,014	19,678	131,293	25	969	994	132,287
Kentucky	5,092	37,610	43,464	86,166	64	145	209	86,375
Louisiana	192,175	332,975	8,841	533,991	27	3,327	3,354	537,345
Maine	794,033	119,587	—	913,620	8	2,934	2,942	916,562
Maryland	21,738	269,809	—	291,547	109	434	543	292,090
Massachusetts	25,894	306,678	—	332,572	77	235	312	332,884
Michigan	42,235	100,663	19,493	162,391	90	4,848	4,938	167,329
Minnesota	195,331	842,921	114,210	1,152,462	87	4,067	4,154	1,156,616
Mississippi	32,208	64,131	9,453	105,792	33	1,672	1,705	107,497
Missouri	102,536	505,079	—	607,615	132	484	616	608,231
Montana	28,927	220,406	98,192	347,525	56	2,841	2,897	350,422
Nebraska	109,317	218,383	—	327,700	13	1,276	1,289	328,989
Nevada	11,862	105,232	46,795	163,889	50	1,202	1,252	165,141
New Hampshire	10,674	156,797	—	167,471	4	1,314	1,318	168,789
New Jersey	28,094	406,586	—	434,680	170	122	292	434,972
New Mexico	45,266	26,124	20,239	91,629	147	3,696	3,843	95,472
New York	10,236	665,874	—	676,110	375	10,917	11,292	687,402
North Carolina	90,887	751,140	2,074	844,101	47	8,682	8,729	852,830
North Dakota	32,447	38,896	23,188	94,531	9	1,176	1,185	95,716
Ohio	99,723	541,728	104,677	746,128	132	15,280	15,412	761,540
Oklahoma	184,907	71,909	6,378	263,194	37	2,352	2,389	265,583
Oregon	55,189	105,704	98,017	258,910	104	11,876	11,980	270,890
Pennsylvania	152,489	581,137	278,272	1,011,898	216	4,587	4,803	1,016,701
Rhode Island	6,994	55,201	—	62,195	8	1,106	1,114	63,309
South Carolina	22,544	36,315	153	59,012	34	1,363	1,397	60,409
South Dakota	55,693	56,762	80,322	192,777	32	1,623	1,655	194,432
Tennessee	84,421	32,771	205	117,397	75	400	475	117,872
Texas	285,898	1,794,516	—	2,080,414	191	45,901	46,092	2,126,506
Utah	53,626	95,908	86,734	236,268	79	526	605	236,873
Vermont	95,207	84,844	—	180,051	2	807	809	180,860
Virginia	82,151	168,294	71,958	322,403	64	2,774	2,838	325,241
Washington	63,893	518,877	114,911	697,681	167	2,341	2,508	700,189
West Virginia	109,086	146,090	73,137	328,313	9	3,201	3,210	331,523
Wisconsin	350,660	1,609	63,331	415,600	30	1,735	1,765	417,365
Wyoming	20,091	286,160	34,037	340,288	94	1,341	1,435	341,723
Total	**5,580,437**	**16,632,194**	**2,713,626**	**24,926,257**	**4,425**	**271,668**	**276,093**	**25,202,350**

(1) The completeness of data on trailer registrations varies greatly. Data are reported to the extent available and in some cases are supplemented by estimates of the Federal Highway Administration.
(2) This column includes all commercial type vehicles and semitrailers that are in private or for-hire use.
(3) Several states do not require the registration of light farm or automobile trailers.
(4) Mobile homes and house trailers are shown in this column for states which require them to be registered and are able to segregate them from other trailers. In states where this classification is not available, house trailers are included with light car trailers.
SOURCE: U.S. Department of Transportation, Federal Highway Administration.

Bus Registrations by State

U.S. TOTAL BUS REGISTRATIONS BY STATE, 2007

| State | Private and Commercial | | Publicly Owned | | Total Privately and Publicly Owned | | |
	Commercial Buses[1]	School and Other[2]	Federal	School[3]	Commercial and Federal	School	Total Buses
Alabama	2,565	227	46	6,367	2,611	6,594	9,205
Alaska	1,599	586	88	399	1,687	985	2,672
Arizona	1,151	218	444	3,102	1,595	3,320	4,915
Arkansas	48	1,590	34	6,086	82	7,676	7,758
California	29,237	11,075	549	17,227	29,786	28,302	58,088
Colorado	758	990	50	4,022	808	5,012	5,820
Connecticut	3,068	6,622	14	887	3,082	7,509	10,591
Delaware	463	1,103	7	685	470	1,788	2,258
District of Columbia	2,421	126	323	116	2,744	242	2,986
Florida	3,827	--	244	44,536	4,071	44,536	48,607
Georgia	1,632	3,338	124	16,989	1,756	20,327	22,083
Hawaii	3,432	906	33	1,569	3,465	2,475	5,940
Idaho	672	652	175	2,373	847	3,025	3,872
Illinois	5,561	12,306	100	343	5,661	12,649	18,310
Indiana	4,383	5,076	65	23,527	4,448	28,603	33,051
Iowa	1,202	297	16	5,860	1,218	6,157	7,375
Kansas	344	995	14	2,583	358	3,578	3,936
Kentucky	634	805	186	12,673	820	13,478	14,298
Louisiana	1,151	15,239	29	6,595	1,180	21,834	23,014
Maine	176	359	14	2,982	190	3,341	3,531
Maryland	2,903	3,872	178	5,086	3,081	8,958	12,039
Massachusetts	3,701	7,395	97	565	3,798	7,960	11,758
Michigan	2,431	7,414	91	16,354	2,522	23,768	26,290
Minnesota	2,428	4,875	8	10,811	2,436	15,686	18,122
Mississippi	1,023	2,647	92	5,843	1,115	8,490	9,605
Missouri	818	2,958	42	7,260	860	10,218	11,078
Montana	366	587	22	1,508	388	2,095	2,483
Nebraska	621	747	12	5,656	633	6,403	7,036
Nevada	1,525	191	166	131	1,691	322	2,013
New Hampshire	373	1,216	3	387	376	1,603	1,979
New Jersey	4,576	14,263	67	4,383	4,643	18,646	23,289
New Mexico	451	1,795	362	818	813	2,613	3,426
New York	17,643	10,852	260	43,729	17,903	54,581	72,484
North Carolina	2,651	7,834	65	23,850	2,716	31,684	34,400
North Dakota	161	614	78	1,659	239	2,273	2,512
Ohio	18,790	2,761	99	24,303	18,889	27,064	45,953
Oklahoma	409	1,825	161	16,537	570	18,362	18,932
Oregon	1,906	3,054	82	10,298	1,988	13,352	15,340
Pennsylvania	9,520	20,438	145	8,407	9,665	28,845	38,510
Rhode Island	359	1,358	7	7	366	1,365	1,731
South Carolina	1,085	4,283	38	13,458	1,123	17,741	18,864
South Dakota	396	433	140	1,767	536	2,200	2,736
Tennessee	2,622	1,541	94	15,605	2,716	17,146	19,862
Texas	3,577	15,793	295	72,585	3,872	88,378	92,250
Utah	361	122	45	793	406	915	1,321
Vermont	92	553	5	1,157	97	1,710	1,807
Virginia	2,368	243	287	15,337	2,655	15,580	18,235
Washington	1,069	2,574	232	8,309	1,301	10,883	12,184
West Virginia	717	63	53	1,959	770	2,022	2,792
Wisconsin	1,503	8,561	28	4,870	1,531	13,431	14,962
Wyoming	880	128	12	2,186	892	2,314	3,206
Total	**151,649**	**193,500**	**5,821**	**484,539**	**157,470**	**678,039**	**835,509**

(1) Includes municipally owned transit buses.
(2) In some instances church, industrial and other private buses are included here; and in other instances privately-owned school buses could not be segregated from commercial buses, and are included with the latter.
(3) This column consists primarily of publicly owned school buses but includes a few privately owned school, institutional, and industrial buses registered free or at a reduced rate.
SOURCE: U.S. Department of Transportation, Federal Highway Administration.

School Bus Ownership and Usage by State

U.S. SCHOOL BUS OWNERSHIP AND USAGE BY STATE, 2006-2007 SCHOOL YEAR

	Pupils Transported at Public Expense	Bus Ownership			Total Miles of Service	Total Expenditures for Pupil Transportation
		Publicly Owned	Contractor	Total		
Alabama	366,260	8,882	258	9,140	80,198,280	336,381,102
Alaska	NA	257	828	1,085	NA	56,001,937
Arizona	361,306	8,096	—	8,096	81,848,953	194,714,856
Arkansas	341,573	5,978	250	6,228	256,443	153,000,000
California	926,448	15,999	8,788	24,787	424,053,356	1,345,389,953
Colorado	322,522	5,920	180	6,100	52,246,889	228,059,881
Connecticut	467,168	NA	NA	NA	NA	54,161,766
Delaware	107,500	—	1,250	1,250	23,000,000	81,600,000
Florida	1,033,088	18,998	1,116	20,114	284,322,929	1,086,282,565
Georgia	992,488	17,551	94	17,645	160,673,760	498,000,000
Hawaii	40,000	NA	830	830	30,000	NA
Idaho	102,606	1,923	770	2,693	26,102,311	69,378,079
Illinois	NA	NA	NA	NA	NA	NA
Indiana	738,608	10,542	2,580	13,122	NA	NA
Iowa	231,271	5,379	668	6,047	42,381,788	NA
Kansas	199,379	3,461	1,689	5,150	72,231,634	204,776,395
Kentucky	411,134	9,956	—	9,956	102,000,000	293,896,785
Louisiana	454,746	5,376	2,776	8,152	68,884,920	306,341,288
Maine	160,984	2,099	614	2,713	34,672,583	85,086,212
Maryland	622,817	3,755	3,259	7,014	121,048,128	467,107,765
Massachusetts	604,507	NA	NA	NA	NA	470,113,181
Michigan	NA	16,601	681	17,282	187,003,597	631,875,974
Minnesota	730,055	5,509	8,219	13,728	179,568,421	490,588,493
Mississippi	442,222	6,386	289	6,675	54,761,091	165,762,027
Missouri	561,946	7,447	4,824	12,271	107,550,674	409,087,740
Montana	69,374	1,249	1,480	2,729	18,072,114	61,102,539
Nebraska	64,017	4,059	642	4,701	35,706,835	82,246,049
Nevada	112,319	2,401	—	2,401	32,077,813	NA
New Hampshire	136,541	482	2,181	2,663	NA	65,475,948
New Jersey	747,763	NA	NA	NA	NA	1,105,000,000
New Mexico	185,244	711	159	870	36,977,885	107,889,498
New York	1,942,503	24,439	20,000	44,439	215,321,369	2,246,651,100
North Carolina	776,300	13,909	123	14,032	175,025,679	365,118,927
North Dakota	38,442	NA	NA	NA	21,584,342	37,133,249
Ohio	998,572	17,799	1,523	19,322	171,087,840	860,067,983
Oklahoma	369,311	NA	NA	NA	50,626,533	190,024,449
Oregon	283,040	3,399	2,200	5,599	55,281,208	NA
Pennsylvania	1,376,224	5,304	16,212	21,516	399,621,010	1,270,911,091
Rhode Island	156,454	335	1,356	1,691	NA	NA
South Carolina	352,917	120	60	180	78,145,762	234,574,418
South Dakota	43,731	NA	NA	NA	14,769,078	38,004,188
Tennessee	565,654	NA	1,593	1,593	53,887,140	NA
Texas	1,500,000	NA	NA	NA	341,100,000	1,150,000,000
Utah	174,680	2,283	81	2,364	26,669,047	85,628,294
Vermont	NA	NA	NA	NA	NA	NA
Virginia	929,944	13,580	—	13,580	195,912,921	686,371,426
Washington	483,247	8,586	1,336	9,922	92,337,309	356,461,433
West Virginia	235,483	3,694	NA	3,694	42,481,087	199,733,456
Wisconsin	554,000	2,000	8,000	10,000	NA	NA
Wyoming	32,721	1,694	—	1,694	12,736,856	60,578,869
Total	**22,347,109**	**266,159**	**96,909**	**363,068**	**4,172,257,585**	**16,830,578,916**

NOTE: NA Not available.
SOURCE: Bobit Publishing Company, School Bus Fleet Fact Book.

Government Ownership of Vehicles by State

U.S. GOVERNMENT OWNERSHIP OF VEHICLES BY STATE, 2007

State	Federal[1]				State, County and Municipal[2]				Total Publicly Owned Vehicles
	Cars	Trucks	Buses	Total	Cars	Trucks	Buses	Total	
Alabama	1,723	5,486	46	7,255	15,223	22,332	6,367	43,922	51,177
Alaska	521	3,540	88	4,149	2,181	6,855	399	9,435	13,584
Arizona	2,305	10,291	444	13,040	15,429	9,567	3,102	28,098	41,138
Arkansas	961	3,072	34	4,067	8,897	8,699	6,086	23,682	27,749
California	13,104	49,837	549	63,490	196,043	259,980	17,227	473,250	536,740
Colorado	1,802	9,790	50	11,642	8,739	17,820	4,022	30,581	42,223
Connecticut	913	4,882	14	5,809	10,847	24,595	887	36,329	42,138
Delaware	281	862	7	1,150	6,962	2,408	685	10,055	11,205
Dist. of Columbia	2,626	4,182	323	7,131	1,740	2,814	116	4,670	11,801
Florida	4,886	16,687	244	21,817	109,712	151,126	44,536	305,374	327,191
Georgia	2,570	8,123	124	10,817	27,749	68,903	16,989	113,641	124,458
Hawaii	530	1,924	33	2,487	7,581	7,334	1,569	16,484	18,971
Idaho	684	5,480	175	6,339	5,459	9,148	2,373	16,980	23,319
Illinois	3,622	11,851	100	15,573	72,069	1,994	343	74,406	89,979
Indiana	1,424	4,946	65	6,435	24,771	41,853	23,132	89,756	96,191
Iowa	712	3,666	16	4,394	11,811	26,754	5,860	44,425	48,819
Kansas	822	3,531	14	4,367	7,408	16,622	2,583	26,613	30,980
Kentucky	1,633	4,866	186	6,685	24,711	4,054	12,673	41,438	48,123
Louisiana	1,674	5,385	29	7,088	52,936	21,232	6,595	80,763	87,851
Maine	442	1,347	14	1,803	5,767	12,989	2,982	21,738	23,541
Maryland	2,652	7,638	178	10,468	11,479	16,859	5,086	33,424	43,892
Massachusetts	2,739	7,624	97	10,460	18,064	37,822	565	56,451	66,911
Michigan	2,692	9,730	91	12,513	47,603	72,135	16,354	136,092	148,605
Minnesota	1,545	6,085	8	7,638	11,790	24,454	10,811	47,055	54,693
Mississippi	1,372	3,872	92	5,336	12,894	4,360	5,843	23,097	28,433
Missouri	3,134	5,249	42	8,425	4,793	13,688	7,260	25,741	34,166
Montana	905	5,494	22	6,421	5,236	13,745	1,508	20,489	26,910
Nebraska	1,103	3,043	12	4,158	13,365	19,196	5,656	38,217	42,375
Nevada	1,175	7,070	166	8,411	8,939	8,074	131	17,144	25,555
New Hampshire	608	1,212	3	1,823	3,914	11,725	387	16,026	17,849
New Jersey	2,257	11,279	67	13,603	40,668	102,661	4,383	147,712	161,315
New Mexico	1,390	7,441	362	9,193	14,414	17,303	818	32,535	41,728
New York	8,577	19,952	260	28,789	73,477	79,305	43,729	196,511	225,300
North Carolina	1,854	5,903	65	7,822	30,444	46,870	23,850	101,164	108,986
North Dakota	610	2,103	78	2,791	3,594	6,666	1,659	11,919	14,710
Ohio	3,165	9,883	99	13,147	62,271	77,419	24,303	163,993	177,140
Oklahoma	1,540	5,330	161	7,031	11,792	48,580	16,537	76,909	83,940
Oregon	1,401	9,884	82	11,367	27,962	24,053	10,298	62,313	73,680
Pennsylvania	5,163	13,909	145	19,217	43,867	55,357	8,407	107,631	126,848
Rhode Island	243	1,215	7	1,465	4,794	4,436	7	9,237	10,702
South Carolina	1,614	5,362	38	7,014	10,054	23,534	13,458	47,046	54,060
South Dakota	572	2,902	140	3,614	3,689	11,960	1,767	17,416	21,030
Tennessee	3,421	10,455	94	13,970	20,926	51,706	15,605	88,237	102,207
Texas	6,420	25,345	295	32,060	113,304	226,324	72,585	412,213	444,273
Utah	946	4,857	45	5,848	10,777	12,208	793	23,778	29,626
Vermont	338	524	5	867	2,563	5,463	1,157	9,183	10,050
Virginia	2,590	9,661	287	12,538	32,881	27,193	15,337	75,411	87,949
Washington	2,853	13,726	232	16,811	18,874	30,261	8,309	57,444	74,255
West Virginia	895	2,186	53	3,134	12,762	24,735	1,959	39,456	42,590
Wisconsin	1,126	5,208	28	6,362	16,217	45,239	4,870	66,326	72,688
Wyoming	394	3,172	12	3,578	5,644	11,536	2,186	19,366	22,944
Total	**108,529**	**387,062**	**5,821**	**501,412**	**1,315,086**	**1,871,946**	**484,144**	**3,671,176**	**4,172,588**

(1) Vehicles of the civilian branches of the federal government are given in this table. Vehicles of the military services are not included. Distribution by state is estimated by the Federal Highway Administration.

(2) This information, compiled chiefly from reports of state authorities, is incomplete in many cases. Some States give state owned vehicles only; others exclude certain classes, such as fire apparatus and police vehicles. For the states not reporting state, county and municipal vehicles separately from private and commercial vehicles and those reporting unsegregated totals only, classification by vehicle type has been estimated on the basis of other available data.

SOURCE: U.S. Department of Transportation, Federal Highway Administration.

Vehicles in Operation by Year

U.S. VEHICLES IN OPERATION BY YEAR (as of July 1 of each year)

Year	Cars	Trucks	Total	% Change	Truck % of Total
2008	135,882,003	114,356,659	250,238,662	0.6	45.7
2007	135,222,259	113,478,738	248,700,997	1.7	45.6
2006	135,046,706	109,595,904	244,642,610	2.6	44.8
2005	132,908,828	105,475,340	238,384,168	2.7	44.2
2004	132,469,269	99,697,867	232,167,136	2.8	42.9
2003	131,072,466	94,809,637	225,882,103	2.2	42.0
2002	129,906,797	91,120,324	221,027,121	2.0	41.2
2001	128,714,022	87,968,915	216,682,937	1.6	40.6
2000	127,720,809	85,578,504	213,299,313	1.8	40.1
1999	126,868,744	82,640,417	209,509,161	2.2	39.4
1998	125,965,709	79,076,930	205,042,639	2.0	38.6
1997	124,672,920	76,397,477	201,070,397	1.4	38.0
1996	124,612,787	73,680,672	198,293,459	2.5	37.2
1995	123,241,881	70,198,512	193,440,393	2.5	36.3
1994	121,996,580	66,717,417	188,713,997	1.3	35.4
1993	121,055,398	65,260,066	186,315,464	2.6	35.0
1992	120,346,746	61,172,404	181,519,150	--	33.7
1991	123,327,046	58,178,883	181,505,929	1.2	32.1
1990	123,276,268	56,022,934	179,299,202	1.9	31.2
1989	122,758,378	53,201,657	175,960,035	2.5	30.2
1988	121,519,074	50,221,502	171,740,576	2.7	29.2
1987	119,848,769	47,344,319	167,193,088	3.1	28.3
1986	117,268,071	44,825,523	162,093,594	3.2	27.7
1985	114,662,333	42,386,882	157,049,215	3.2	27.0
1984	112,018,640	40,142,872	152,161,512	3.4	26.4
1983	108,961,215	38,143,304	147,104,519	2.3	25.9
1982	106,867,108	36,986,537	143,853,645	1.4	25.7
1981	105,838,582	36,069,197	141,907,779	1.5	25.4
1980	104,563,781	35,267,535	139,831,316	1.9	25.2
1979	104,676,507	32,582,991	137,259,498	2.8	23.7
1978	102,956,713	30,564,701	133,521,414	4.2	22.9
1977	99,903,594	28,221,661	128,125,255	3.0	22.0
1976	97,818,221	26,560,296	124,378,517	3.6	21.4
1975	95,240,602	24,812,843	120,053,445	3.6	20.7
1974	92,607,551	23,312,245	115,919,796	4.2	20.1
1973	89,805,159	21,411,931	111,217,090	4.7	19.3
1972	86,438,957	19,772,938	106,211,895	4.5	18.6
1971	83,137,324	18,462,287	101,599,611	3.5	18.2
1970	80,448,463	17,687,505	98,135,968	3.2	18.0
1969	78,494,938	16,586,368	95,081,306	4.4	17.4
1968	75,358,034	15,684,917	91,042,951	3.5	17.2
1967	72,967,686	14,988,491	87,956,177	2.7	17.0
1966	71,263,738	14,356,591	85,620,329	4.3	16.8
1965	68,939,770	13,126,579	82,066,349	4.5	16.0
1964	66,051,415	12,444,964	78,496,379	4.1	15.9
1963	63,493,277	11,902,039	75,395,316	4.2	15.8
1962	60,919,579	11,463,381	72,382,960	3.6	15.8
1961	58,854,380	11,042,770	69,897,150	2.9	15.8
1960	57,102,676	10,802,959	67,905,635	3.5	15.9
1959	55,086,761	10,532,145	65,618,906	4.9	16.1
1958	52,492,509	10,056,567	62,549,076	2.2	16.1
1957	51,432,460	9,775,950	61,208,410	3.1	16.0
1956	49,803,977	9,544,082	59,348,059	5.0	16.1
1955	47,377,970	9,162,444	56,540,414	6.3	16.2

NOTE: 2008 estimated by *Ward's*.
SOURCE: R.L. Polk Company. Permission for further use must be obtained from the Polk Company.

U.S. Market Used Vehicle Sales and Consumer Leases

USED VEHICLE SALES (in Thousands)

Year	Franchised Dealers	Independent Dealers	Casual	Total
2008	13,190	11,742	11,599	36,531
2007	14,285	13,077	14,056	41,418
2006	14,319	13,710	14,536	42,565
2005	16,450	14,210	13,478	44,138
2004	15,953	14,751	11,841	42,545
2003	16,171	13,732	13,668	43,571
2002	16,470	13,078	13,478	43,026
2001	15,945	14,416	12,263	42,624
2000	16,178	13,559	11,883	41,620
1999	16,504	12,786	11,448	40,738
1998	15,684	13,182	11,976	40,842
1997	15,796	12,685	12,757	41,238
1996	15,713	13,247	11,871	40,831
1995	15,679	14,124	11,958	41,761
1994	15,047	14,548	10,541	40,136
1993	14,792	14,011	9,257	38,060

SOURCE: CNW Marketing Research, Inc.

AVERAGE USED VEHICLE TRANSACTION PRICES

Year	Franchised Dealers	Independent Dealers	Casual	Total
2008	$9,643	$8,358	$5,725	$7,986
2007	$10,100	$8,650	$5,810	$8,186
2006	$9,750	$8,492	$5,838	$8,009
2005	$10,516	$8,545	$4,471	$8,036
2004	$11,414	$8,490	$4,263	$8,410
2003	$12,177	$7,632	$4,002	$8,180
2002	$12,537	$7,157	$3,688	$8,130
2001	$12,238	$8,275	$4,316	$8,618
2000	$12,748	$7,613	$4,539	$8,896
1999	$12,630	$7,590	$4,505	$8,828
1998	$12,165	$7,172	$4,190	$8,341
1997	$12,350	$7,155	$4,164	$8,399
1996	$12,256	$7,076	$4,283	$8,257
1995	$11,585	$7,413	$4,316	$8,093
1994	$11,150	$7,209	$3,762	$7,781
1993	$9,871	$7,157	$3,554	$7,335

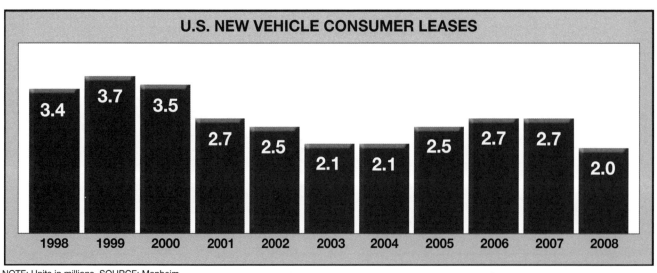

U.S. NEW VEHICLE CONSUMER LEASES

1998	1999	2000	2001	2002	2003	2004	2005	2006	2007	2008
3.4	3.7	3.5	2.7	2.5	2.1	2.1	2.5	2.7	2.7	2.0

NOTE: Units in millions. SOURCE: Manheim.

Light Vehicle Fleet Registrations

LIGHT VEHICLE FLEET REGISTRATIONS BY MODEL YEAR, 2007

Make	Commercial	Rental	Government	Total Fleet	Total Sales	Fleet % of Total Sales
Audi	3,426	1,442	15	4,883	71,321	6.8
BMW/Mini	3,888	990	50	4,928	263,438	1.9
Buick	4,217	21,422	810	26,449	134,808	19.6
Cadillac	3,770	17,477	60	21,307	122,107	17.4
Chevrolet	58,994	230,978	43,048	333,020	747,036	44.6
Chrysler	13,825	81,656	1,751	97,232	218,454	44.5
Dodge	17,859	122,125	7,981	147,965	307,316	48.1
Ford	35,415	115,640	54,331	205,386	592,523	34.7
Honda/Acura	6,485	19,838	1,617	27,940	849,322	3.3
Hyundai/Kia	3,492	98,403	90	101,985	457,052	22.3
Jaguar	323	574	4	901	15,668	5.8
Lincoln/Mercury	5,720	50,664	419	56,803	170,371	33.3
Mazda	2,456	37,043	201	39,700	206,988	19.2
Mercedes-Benz	4,548	4,968	65	9,581	165,313	5.8
Mitsubishi	413	21,970	24	22,407	88,891	25.2
Nissan/Infiniti	7,122	59,338	209	66,669	612,420	10.9
Pontiac	8,770	131,099	1,175	141,044	324,540	43.5
Porsche	369	26	2	397	21,712	1.8
Saab	1,535	265	8	1,808	27,850	6.5
Saturn	1,331	21,411	202	22,944	134,371	17.1
Scion	1,324	146	28	1,498	133,704	1.1
Subaru	2,026	11,898	30	13,954	121,880	11.4
Suzuki	361	4,546	3	4,910	58,670	8.4
Toyota/Lexus	30,157	77,035	3,871	111,063	1,340,454	8.3
Volkswagen	2,190	11,385	77	13,652	211,821	6.4
Volvo	3,960	7,561	47	11,568	72,125	16.0
Other	195	2	238	435	1,253	34.7
Total Cars	**224,171**	**1,149,902**	**116,356**	**1,490,429**	**7,471,408**	**19.9**
Audi	1,396	414	19	1,829	17,578	10.4
BMW	1,194	59	17	1,270	57,673	2.2
Buick	570	8,503	39	9,112	55,827	16.3
Cadillac	3,286	3,998	27	7,311	83,661	8.7
Chevrolet	168,616	160,608	48,136	377,360	1,497,741	25.2
Chrysler	18,193	116,329	448	134,970	328,066	41.1
Dodge	54,036	97,251	16,081	167,368	732,839	22.8
Ford	197,417	132,652	76,377	406,446	1,402,543	29.0
Freightliner	785	802	55	1,642	3,041	54.0
GMC	33,474	25,245	4,840	63,559	471,311	13.5
Honda/Acura	6,454	1,964	354	8,772	679,572	1.3
Hummer	1,298	4,620	39	5,957	59,202	10.1
Hyundai/Kia	3,446	44,787	72	48,305	295,329	16.4
Isuzu	82	10	5	97	6,823	1.4
Jeep	13,068	70,150	3,384	86,602	484,379	17.9
Land Rover	1,555	248	13	1,816	48,172	3.8
Lincoln/Mercury	4,341	9,982	76	14,399	120,006	12.0
Mazda	933	2,137	46	3,116	75,127	4.1
Mercedes-Benz	2,058	311	35	2,404	69,038	3.5
Mitsubishi	203	9,193	13	9,409	42,753	22.0
Nissan/Infiniti	4,154	44,178	278	48,610	428,271	11.4
Pontiac	537	7,627	52	8,216	37,300	22.0
Porsche	483	13	6	502	10,097	5.0
Saab	69	1	1	71	5,161	1.4
Saturn	1,749	13,191	177	15,117	110,370	13.7
Sprinter	16	—	—	16	109	14.7
Subaru	1,027	7,395	36	8,458	63,955	13.2
Suzuki	242	4,773	8	5,023	38,000	13.2
Toyota/Lexus	22,698	53,296	765	76,759	1,084,321	7.1
Volkswagen	181	3	4	188	7,250	2.6
Volvo Truck	777	519	14	1,310	32,306	4.1
Total Trucks	**544,338**	**820,259**	**151,417**	**1,516,014**	**8,347,821**	**18.2**
Total	**768,509**	**1,970,161**	**267,773**	**3,006,443**	**15,819,229**	**19.0**

NOTE: Total sales includes fleet plus retail.
SOURCE: Bobit Business Media, Automotive Fleet Fact Book 2008.

Total Vehicle Registrations by Country

VEHICLES IN OPERATION BY COUNTRY

Country	2007					2006		
	Cars	Commercial Vehicles	Total	Population (000)	Persons Per Car	Cars	Commercial Vehicles	Total
AFRICA								
Algeria	427,000	553,000	980,000	33,363	78.1	425,000	552,000	977,000
Angola	48,200	66,500	114,700	12,264	254.4	48,000	66,000	114,000
Benin	10,500	17,350	27,850	8,278	788.4	10,250	16,800	27,050
Botswana	62,500	88,000	150,500	1,913	30.6	61,000	87,000	148,000
Burkina Faso	50,750	31,500	82,250	14,797	291.6	50,500	31,100	81,600
Burundi	28,900	24,900	53,800	8,391	290.3	28,800	24,600	53,400
Cameroon	169,000	88,000	257,000	18,060	106.9	166,500	86,250	252,750
Central African Republic	1,950	1,850	3,800	4,377	2,244.6	1,900	1,800	3,700
Congo	42,000	18,000	60,000	3,802	90.5	42,500	18,500	61,000
Congo, Democratic Republic of	911,000	704,000	1,615,000	64,390	70.7	903,400	699,500	1,602,900
Egypt	2,625,800	721,000	3,346,800	80,335	30.6	2,560,700	710,000	3,270,700
Ethiopia	73,100	54,750	127,850	79,936	1,093.5	72,500	54,000	126,500
Ghana	112,000	59,500	171,500	22,931	204.7	110,200	58,000	168,200
Ivory Coast	21,500	94,500	116,000	19,747	918.5	21,400	94,000	115,400
Kenya	293,000	128,000	421,000	36,914	126.0	287,000	124,500	411,500
Liberia	12,200	37,300	49,500	3,196	262.0	12,150	37,500	49,650
Libya	413,000	385,000	798,000	6,037	14.6	401,500	379,000	780,500
Madagascar	75,900	50,000	125,900	19,449	256.2	75,100	49,000	124,100
Malawi	12,650	16,750	29,400	13,603	1,075.3	12,600	16,500	29,100
Mali	9,500	11,900	21,400	11,995	1,262.6	9,000	11,500	20,500
Mauritania	12,500	8,650	21,150	2,981	238.5	12,500	8,500	21,000
Mauritius	123,000	45,000	168,000	1,264	10.3	122,100	44,600	166,700
Morocco	1,354,000	428,500	1,782,500	33,826	25.0	1,347,000	424,600	1,771,600
Mozambique	33,250	31,000	64,250	20,906	628.8	33,000	30,750	63,750
Namibia	80,000	88,700	168,700	2,069	25.9	79,000	88,200	167,200
Niger	23,500	21,000	44,500	14,215	604.9	23,000	20,500	43,500
Nigeria	736,000	458,000	1,194,000	143,312	194.7	725,000	450,000	1,175,000
Reunion	235,700	94,600	330,300	814	3.5	233,400	93,900	327,300
Sierra Leone	20,200	9,250	29,450	6,152	304.6	20,600	9,500	30,100
South Africa	4,616,707	2,504,393	7,121,100	48,367	10.5	4,850,000	2,330,000	7,180,000
Sudan	39,500	49,500	89,000	39,379	996.9	39,000	48,900	87,900
Tanzania	23,000	51,500	74,500	39,384	1,712.3	22,650	51,000	73,650
Togo	104,500	48,000	152,500	5,702	54.6	101,250	47,100	148,350
Tunisia	635,000	312,500	947,500	10,281	16.2	625,100	308,000	933,100
Uganda	56,000	45,500	101,500	30,263	540.4	54,600	44,100	98,700
Zambia	130,200	76,000	206,200	11,477	88.1	126,500	73,100	199,600
Zimbabwe	378,500	64,000	442,500	11,443	30.2	373,000	63,500	436,500
Total Africa	**14,002,007**	**7,487,893**	**21,489,900**	**885,615**	**63.2**	**14,087,700**	**7,253,800**	**21,341,500**
AMERICA, Caribbean								
Bahamas	88,500	30,250	118,750	306	3.5	86,250	30,100	116,350

Total Vehicle Registrations by Country

VEHICLES IN OPERATION BY COUNTRY — continued

Country	2007 Cars	2007 Commercial Vehicles	2007 Total	Population (000)	Persons Per Car	2006 Cars	2006 Commercial Vehicles	2006 Total
Barbados	76,500	17,000	93,500	282	3.7	75,000	16,500	91,500
Bermuda	30,700	8,100	38,800	67	2.2	30,650	7,900	38,550
Cuba	199,500	218,000	417,500	11,394	57.1	196,650	216,500	413,150
Dominican Republic	197,500	223,000	420,500	9,366	47.4	192,000	220,000	412,000
Haiti	36,000	35,750	71,750	8,711	242.0	36,500	36,000	72,500
Jamaica	128,000	33,900	161,900	2,782	21.7	127,000	33,750	160,750
Netherlands Antilles	81,000	35,750	116,750	224	2.8	80,000	35,100	115,100
Puerto Rico	1,044,000	449,300	1,493,300	3,942	3.8	1,032,500	445,600	1,478,100
Trinidad and Tobago	311,500	40,250	351,750	1,233	4.0	308,000	39,800	347,800
Virgin Islands (US)	34,500	19,250	53,750	110	3.2	34,000	19,000	53,000
Total Caribbean	**2,227,700**	**1,110,550**	**3,338,250**	**38,417**	**17.2**	**2,198,550**	**1,100,250**	**3,298,800**
AMERICA, Central & South								
Argentina	6,003,730	2,197,059	8,200,789	40,049	6.7	5,700,000	1,524,000	7,224,000
Belize	11,900	15,100	27,000	295	24.8	11,650	14,800	26,450
Bolivia	213,500	304,000	517,500	9,426	44.1	210,250	302,100	512,350
Brazil	20,430,000	5,166,000	25,596,000	193,919	9.5	19,446,000	4,823,200	24,269,200
Chile	1,505,000	776,500	2,281,500	16,304	10.8	1,465,100	770,400	2,235,500
Colombia	985,000	603,000	1,588,000	44,380	45.1	965,000	592,000	1,557,000
Costa Rica	401,000	260,000	661,000	4,137	10.3	395,000	256,000	651,000
Ecuador	580,000	291,000	871,000	14,135	24.4	567,000	288,000	855,000
El Salvador	82,000	111,000	193,000	6,948	84.7	78,600	107,200	185,800
Guatemala	139,000	151,500	290,500	12,728	91.6	137,500	149,500	287,000
Guyana	30,000	14,200	44,200	769	25.6	29,250	13,800	43,050
Honduras	29,500	92,000	121,500	7,484	253.7	29,000	91,000	120,000
Nicaragua	70,100	109,750	179,850	5,680	81.0	69,500	108,500	178,000
Panama	276,500	179,000	455,500	3,258	11.8	273,000	177,000	450,000
Paraguay	92,000	88,750	180,750	6,669	72.5	90,000	87,000	177,000
Peru	418,000	289,000	707,000	28,809	68.9	410,000	283,000	693,000
Suriname	72,500	31,200	103,700	471	6.5	71,000	30,100	101,100
Uruguay	598,000	120,500	718,500	3,461	5.8	593,100	119,800	712,900
Venezuela	1,705,000	1,210,000	2,915,000	26,024	15.3	1,650,000	1,190,000	2,840,000
Total Central & S. America	**33,642,730**	**12,009,559**	**45,652,289**	**424,945**	**12.6**	**32,190,950**	**10,927,400**	**43,118,350**
AMERICA, North								
Canada	19,198,954	871,843	20,070,797	32,936	1.7	18,738,935	841,306	19,580,241
Mexico	16,164,550	8,222,317	24,386,867	108,701	6.7	15,566,300	7,912,200	23,478,500
United States	135,222,259	113,478,738	248,700,997	301,280	2.2	135,046,706	108,975,048	244,021,754
Total North America	**170,585,763**	**122,572,898**	**293,158,661**	**442,916**	**2.6**	**169,351,941**	**117,728,554**	**287,080,495**
ASIA, Far East								
Afghanistan	29,000	24,500	53,500	31,890	1,099.7	30,000	25,000	55,000
Bangladesh	37,750	71,500	109,250	152,034	4,027.4	37,500	71,000	108,500
Brunei	84,000	18,900	102,900	375	4.5	83,000	18,500	101,500

Total Vehicle Registrations by Country

VEHICLES IN OPERATION BY COUNTRY — continued

Country	2007					2006		
	Cars	Commercial Vehicles	Total	Population (000)	Persons Per Car	Cars	Commercial Vehicles	Total
Burma	8,200	17,750	25,950	47,374	5,777.3	8,100	17,500	25,600
Hong Kong	511,000	213,500	724,500	6,980	13.7	500,000	211,000	711,000
India	8,594,771	5,327,400	13,922,171	1,129,866	131.5	8,100,000	4,850,000	12,950,000
Indonesia	4,355,000	3,345,000	7,700,000	234,694	53.9	4,100,000	3,250,000	7,350,000
Japan	57,623,753	16,505,195	74,128,948	127,433	2.2	57,521,043	16,731,091	74,252,134
Korea, South	12,099,793	4,328,452	16,428,245	48,250	4.0	11,607,000	4,288,400	15,895,400
Malaysia	6,804,000	1,313,500	8,117,500	24,835	3.7	6,600,000	1,257,500	7,857,500
Pakistan	427,500	431,000	858,500	169,341	396.1	425,000	428,000	853,000
Peoples Republic of China	13,758,000	26,336,000	40,094,000	1,321,852	96.1	11,000,000	24,000,000	35,000,000
Philippines	798,600	2,139,000	2,937,600	94,157	117.9	793,100	2,137,700	2,930,800
Singapore	450,500	156,900	607,400	4,553	10.1	440,583	152,592	593,175
Sri Lanka	347,500	404,000	751,500	20,926	60.2	343,000	400,000	743,000
Taiwan	5,759,513	1,010,178	6,769,691	22,859	4.0	5,698,324	1,001,948	6,700,272
Thailand	3,850,000	6,210,000	10,060,000	65,068	16.9	3,700,000	5,800,000	9,500,000
Vietnam	150,300	169,500	319,800	85,262	567.3	145,000	165,000	310,000
Total Far East	**115,689,180**	**68,022,275**	**183,711,455**	**3,587,750**	**31.0**	**111,131,650**	**64,805,231**	**175,936,881**
ASIA, Middle East								
Azerbaijan	436,000	139,000	575,000	8,120	18.6	425,000	136,000	561,000
Bahrain	306,250	135,500	441,750	709	2.3	301,000	133,000	434,000
Cyprus	435,500	149,900	585,400	788	1.8	345,000	135,000	480,000
Iran	2,996,000	780,100	3,776,100	65,398	21.8	2,889,500	764,600	3,654,100
Iraq	864,000	152,500	1,016,500	27,500	31.8	857,115	150,300	1,007,415
Israel	1,779,301	409,525	2,188,826	6,990	3.9	1,652,055	374,459	2,026,514
Jordan	362,500	127,500	490,000	6,053	16.7	355,500	125,000	480,500
Kuwait	881,000	229,000	1,110,000	2,506	2.8	858,900	222,100	1,081,000
Lebanon	425,900	89,000	514,900	3,926	9.2	422,900	87,800	510,700
Oman	291,500	122,000	413,500	3,207	11.0	284,800	119,300	404,100
Qatar	178,500	92,500	271,000	815	4.6	175,200	90,000	265,200
Saudi Arabia	3,308,000	1,860,000	5,168,000	27,587	8.3	3,197,900	1,835,100	5,033,000
Syria	246,000	342,000	588,000	19,315	78.5	241,800	336,000	577,800
Turkey	6,472,156	3,181,390	9,653,546	74,768	11.6	6,140,992	2,938,500	9,079,492
United Arab Emirates	299,500	86,000	385,500	4,444	14.8	295,000	84,000	379,000
Yemen	297,200	336,500	633,700	22,231	74.8	295,100	334,800	629,900
Total Middle East	**19,579,307**	**8,232,415**	**27,811,722**	**274,354**	**14.0**	**18,737,762**	**7,865,959**	**26,603,721**
EUROPE, East								
Belarus	1,702,000	36,000	1,738,000	9,725	5.7	1,680,000	33,250	1,713,250
Bulgaria	2,820,000	366,000	3,186,000	7,323	2.6	2,660,000	353,000	3,013,000
Croatia	1,491,100	170,700	1,661,800	4,493	3.0	1,435,800	164,100	1,599,900
Czech Republic	4,280,081	573,243	4,853,324	10,229	2.4	4,108,610	562,255	4,670,865
Hungary	3,012,165	433,944	3,446,109	9,956	3.3	2,953,737	422,388	3,376,125
Poland	14,589,000	2,609,000	17,198,000	38,518	2.6	13,384,229	2,329,790	15,714,019
Romania	3,541,000	536,000	4,077,000	22,276	6.3	3,603,400	585,700	4,189,100

Total Vehicle Registrations by Country

VEHICLES IN OPERATION BY COUNTRY — continued

Country	2007 Cars	2007 Commercial Vehicles	2007 Total	Population (000)	Persons Per Car	2006 Cars	2006 Commercial Vehicles	2006 Total
Russian Federation	28,300,000	5,805,000	34,105,000	141,378	5.0	26,800,000	5,890,000	32,690,000
Serbia & Montenegro	1,491,200	164,600	1,655,800	8,132	5.5	1,526,800	135,100	1,661,900
Slovak Republic	1,433,926	206,621	1,640,547	5,448	3.8	1,333,749	181,563	1,515,312
Slovenia	1,005,000	75,300	1,080,300	2,009	2.0	950,000	69,300	1,019,300
Ukraine	6,932,300	1,241,000	8,173,300	46,300	6.7	6,433,800	1,171,600	7,605,400
Total Eastern Europe	**70,597,772**	**12,217,408**	**82,815,180**	**305,786**	**4.3**	**66,870,125**	**11,898,046**	**78,768,171**
EUROPE, West								
Austria	4,245,583	381,944	4,627,527	8,200	1.9	4,204,969	373,620	4,578,589
Belgium	5,019,720	757,380	5,777,100	10,392	2.1	4,944,500	734,300	5,678,800
Denmark	2,074,519	546,357	2,620,876	5,468	2.6	2,026,000	518,700	2,544,700
Finland	2,570,356	419,525	2,989,881	5,238	2.0	2,489,287	383,479	2,872,766
France	30,550,000	6,297,000	36,847,000	63,682	2.1	30,400,000	6,261,000	36,661,000
Germany	41,183,594	2,837,021	44,020,615	82,401	2.0	46,569,657	3,172,042	49,741,699
Greece	4,752,362	1,033,580	5,785,942	10,706	2.3	4,446,528	1,017,000	5,463,528
Iceland	197,900	30,200	228,100	302	1.5	188,000	28,000	216,000
Ireland	1,900,000	377,000	2,277,000	4,109	2.2	1,720,000	331,000	2,051,000
Italy	35,680,098	4,687,968	40,368,066	58,148	1.6	35,297,600	4,579,600	39,877,200
Latvia	822,011	131,748	953,759	2,260	2.7	735,000	135,000	870,000
Luxembourg	220,000	98,000	318,000	480	2.2	215,000	95,000	310,000
Malta	213,800	45,500	259,300	402	1.9	212,100	45,300	257,400
Netherlands	7,597,000	1,095,000	8,692,000	16,571	2.2	7,413,000	1,070,000	8,483,000
Norway	2,153,730	531,423	2,685,153	4,628	2.1	2,083,106	509,724	2,592,830
Portugal	4,379,000	1,348,100	5,727,100	10,643	2.4	4,290,000	1,335,000	5,625,000
Spain	21,760,174	5,414,322	27,174,496	40,448	1.9	20,908,700	5,146,400	26,055,100
Sweden	4,258,463	517,400	4,775,863	9,031	2.1	4,202,463	493,437	4,695,900
Switzerland	3,955,787	372,153	4,327,940	7,555	1.9	3,899,917	360,465	4,260,382
United Kingdom	31,225,329	4,164,465	35,389,794	60,776	1.9	30,920,000	4,054,500	34,974,500
Total Western Europe	**204,759,426**	**31,086,086**	**235,845,512**	**401,440**	**2.0**	**207,165,827**	**30,643,567**	**237,809,394**
PACIFIC								
Australia	11,462,000	2,757,289	14,219,289	20,750	1.8	10,850,000	2,560,000	13,410,000
Fiji	79,750	54,250	134,000	919	11.5	78,400	53,900	132,300
French Polynesia	44,000	23,200	67,200	279	6.3	43,500	23,000	66,500
Guam	138,000	53,750	191,750	174	1.3	137,200	53,000	190,200
New Caledonia	63,900	28,500	92,400	222	3.5	63,750	27,200	90,950
New Zealand	2,361,823	476,835	2,838,658	4,132	1.7	2,324,900	435,300	2,760,200
Papua New Guinea	36,600	91,000	127,600	5,806	158.6	36,000	90,000	126,000
Samoa (American)	7,175	7,350	14,525	214	29.8	7,150	7,300	14,450
Vanuatu	8,900	4,900	13,800	212	23.8	8,750	4,800	13,550
Total Pacific	**14,202,148**	**3,497,074**	**17,699,222**	**32,708**	**2.3**	**13,549,650**	**3,254,500**	**16,804,150**
WORLD TOTAL	**645,286,033**	**266,236,158**	**911,522,191**	**6,393,931**	**9.9**	**635,284,155**	**255,477,307**	**890,761,462**

SOURCE: International Road Federation, VDA, World Bank and *Ward's* estimates.

U.S. Vehicle Exports by Country of Destination and Vehicle Type

U.S. EXPORTS BY COUNTRY OF DESTINATION AND VEHICLE TYPE, 2008

	Cars		Trucks		Buses		Total	
COUNTRY	Units	Value ($000)	Units	Value ($000)	Units	Value ($000)	Units	Value ($000)
Afghanistan	1,617	66,691	257	14,949	—	—	1,874	81,640
Algeria	31	711	13	897	—	—	44	1,608
Angola	828	15,850	317	7,437	1,057	113,506	2,202	136,793
Anguilla	32	572	—	—	—	—	32	572
Antigua Barbuda	72	979	39	748	2	158	113	1,885
Argentina	2,424	56,793	57	1,555	2	49	2,483	58,397
Armenia	119	3,559	—	—	—	—	119	3,559
Aruba	271	4,988	24	599	—	—	295	5,587
Australia	16,620	532,983	4,350	205,686	23	654	20,993	739,323
Austria	1,333	35,371	—	—	—	—	1,333	35,371
Azerbaijan	54	3,336	1	6	—	—	55	3,342
Bahamas	1,682	20,945	883	10,159	7	175	2,572	31,279
Bahrain	6,220	144,571	166	5,018	7	125	6,393	149,714
Barbados	58	1,196	26	480	—	—	84	1,676
Belarus	64	1,373	—	—	—	—	64	1,373
Belgium	6,815	181,758	564	13,846	42	952	7,421	196,556
Belize	138	522	243	2,626	3	62	384	3,210
Benin	613	8,825	33	592	3	38	649	9,455
Bermuda	32	127	32	820	—	—	64	947
Bolivia	367	4,583	307	5,268	41	783	715	10,634
Bosnia-Hercegovina	16	354	—	—	—	—	16	354
British Virgin Islands	208	3,099	72	1,152	4	97	284	4,348
Brazil	3,369	89,775	57	1,637	24	607	3,450	92,019
Brunei	13	241	—	—	—	—	13	241
Bulgaria	518	11,415	11	171	—	—	529	11,586
Cambodia	187	3,861	21	674	4	130	212	4,665
Cameroon	65	1,119	21	384	2	41	88	1,544
Canada	748,749	12,400,411	247,810	7,614,518	10,273	598,015	1,006,832	20,612,944
Cayman Islands	634	12,817	127	2,533	—	—	761	15,350
Chile	13,042	203,466	4,380	155,447	50	1,097	17,472	360,010
China	23,942	588,310	873	25,240	38	1,247	24,853	614,797
Colombia	3,256	53,913	994	31,145	4	246	4,254	85,304
Congo (ROC)	107	1,582	17	226	3	45	127	1,853
Costa Rica	1,266	25,237	1,109	23,471	85	1,484	2,460	50,192
Cote d'Ivoire	209	3,461	10	146	—	—	219	3,607
Croatia	422	10,133	—	—	—	—	422	10,133
Cyprus	115	2,850	—	—	—	—	115	2,850
Czech Republic	338	9,527	6	92	—	—	344	9,619
Denmark	435	9,663	24	265	8	171	467	10,099
Djibouti	5	124	—	—	—	—	5	124
Dominica Islands	15	309	6	100	—	—	21	409
Dominican Republic	2,647	54,311	721	17,979	7	112	3,375	72,402
Ecuador	1,717	20,515	809	49,101	6	175	2,532	69,791
Egypt	959	11,042	94	2,386	3	124	1,056	13,552

U.S. Vehicle Exports by Country of Destination and Vehicle Type

U.S. EXPORTS BY COUNTRY OF DESTINATION AND VEHICLE TYPE, 2008 — continued

	Cars		Trucks		Buses		Total	
COUNTRY	Units	Value ($000)	Units	Value ($000)	Units	Value ($000)	Units	Value ($000)
El Salvador	349	3,901	438	4,509	19	270	806	8,680
Eq Guinea	19	290	2	77	—	—	21	367
Estonia	201	5,415	7	106	—	—	208	5,521
Ethiopia	5	93	—	—	—	—	5	93
Fed. States Micronesia	5	95	6	134	—	—	11	229
Finland	5,186	123,290	827	26,957	463	10,502	6,476	160,749
French Polynesia	425	8,482	37	793	4	98	466	9,373
France	5,055	133,002	226	3,496	—	—	5,281	136,498
Gabon	45	816	77	2,142	—	—	122	2,958
Gambia	42	733	25	359	31	2,344	98	3,436
Georgia	747	15,373	15	321	4	98	766	15,792
Germany	179,197	6,935,401	2,518	62,818	621	25,375	182,336	7,023,594
Ghana	712	10,086	80	1,963	1	32	793	12,081
Greece	2,649	52,366	6	400	3	97	2,658	52,863
Grenada	17	476	2	75	—	—	19	551
Guadeloupe	17	294	—	—	—	—	17	294
Guatemala	1,725	25,341	1,307	13,812	21	373	3,053	39,526
Guinea	72	1,000	11	165	4	53	87	1,218
Guyana	81	1,392	24	347	1	13	106	1,752
Haiti	121	3,426	187	13,014	—	—	308	16,440
Honduras	788	9,737	1,128	15,237	224	3,131	2,140	28,105
Hong Kong	1,085	38,207	13	268	19	949	1,117	39,424
Hungary	448	10,397	—	—	—	—	448	10,397
Iceland	720	17,308	3	110	—	—	723	17,418
India	224	7,109	91	4,893	—	—	315	12,002
Indonesia	1	—	49	2,041	—	—	50	2,041
Iraq	5,902	71,545	212	16,080	—	—	6,114	87,625
Ireland	150	4,053	2	119	1	70	153	4,242
Israel	7,342	137,386	1,256	35,031	21	553	8,619	172,970
Italy	9,854	265,618	101	3,701	18	564	9,973	269,883
Jamaica	522	8,803	319	7,730	3	56	844	16,589
Japan	12,900	352,862	2,381	74,977	16	539	15,297	428,378
Jordan	3,115	56,609	156	4,928	1	37	3,272	61,574
Kazakhstan	469	13,053	46	1,382	—	—	515	14,435
Kenya	22	452	39	1,925	1	53	62	2,430
Korea	9,122	202,047	125	2,715	1,512	46,710	10,759	251,472
Kuwait	24,507	529,966	2,593	54,288	244	7,354	27,344	591,608
Laos	6	106	2	26	—	—	8	132
Latvia	231	9,175	12	548	15	466	258	10,189
Lebanon	5,318	99,798	38	715	5	77	5,361	100,590
Liberia	57	869	48	2,024	3	91	108	2,984
Libya	812	10,755	45	2,976	—	—	857	13,731
Lithuania	398	7,399	10	628	41	1,509	449	9,536
Luxembourg	55	1,416	—	—	—	—	55	1,416

U.S. Vehicle Exports by Country of Destination and Vehicle Type

U.S. EXPORTS BY COUNTRY OF DESTINATION AND VEHICLE TYPE, 2008 — continued

	Cars		Trucks		Buses		Total	
COUNTRY	Units	Value ($000)	Units	Value ($000)	Units	Value ($000)	Units	Value ($000)
Macao	1	35	—	—	—	—	1	35
Malawi	15	319	52	1,045	—	—	67	1,364
Malaysia	12	232	—	—	—	—	12	232
Mali	17	342	2	78	4	77	23	497
Malta & Gozo	2	25	—	—	1	38	3	63
Marshall Islands	7	15	7	90	2	152	16	257
Mexico	191,534	2,991,452	40,026	760,340	1,592	33,896	233,152	3,785,688
Moldova	9	259	—	—	—	—	9	259
Monaco	2	91	—	—	—	—	2	91
Mongolia	122	3,633	4	142	—	—	126	3,775
Montserrat	4	32	4	130	—	—	8	162
Morocco	283	5,804	142	5,931	—	—	425	11,735
Mozambique	6	109	819	15,112	—	—	825	15,221
Namibia	122	2,615	286	3,952	10	218	418	6,785
Netherlands	4,868	126,799	320	7,205	65	1,657	5,253	135,661
Netherlands Antilles	635	11,635	83	1,623	3	104	721	13,362
New Zealand	1,108	36,227	516	17,087	3	164	1,627	53,478
Nicaragua	260	3,632	194	2,903	9	144	463	6,679
Niger	2	28	54	734	2	31	58	793
Nigeria	6,424	118,119	7,652	149,735	182	4,343	14,258	272,197
Norway	989	25,046	61	1,475	9	348	1,059	26,869
Oman	12,929	316,871	496	15,319	1	38	13,426	332,228
Pakistan	119	1,319	11	226	—	—	130	1,545
Palau	5	345	—	—	—	—	5	345
Panama	2,406	59,156	1,464	28,776	22	461	3,892	88,393
Paraguay	1,156	21,718	192	2,158	4	131	1,352	24,007
Peru	1,675	37,740	717	30,091	12	319	2,404	68,150
Philippines	958	24,658	88	1,345	2	98	1,048	26,101
Poland	2,278	45,158	570	3,024	13	290	2,861	48,472
Portugal	886	24,321	5	47	—	—	891	24,368
Qatar	10,428	261,399	1,083	24,866	42	1,159	11,553	287,424
Romania	486	14,603	—	—	1	85	487	14,688
Russia	24,224	610,207	7,566	211,197	18	444	31,808	821,848
Samoa	4	48	—	—	1	16	5	64
Saudi Arabia	83,629	2,217,286	4,519	105,738	162	3,504	88,310	2,326,528
Senegal	215	4,161	4	47	3	102	222	4,310
Sierra Leone	37	438	55	1,006	1	13	93	1,457
Singapore	362	11,403	44	2,447	7	168	413	14,018
Slovak Republic	306	9,233	15	143	—	—	321	9,376
Slovenia	95	2,744	—	—	1	29	96	2,773
South Africa	7,460	222,555	2,906	178,712	16	303	10,382	401,570
Spain	4,096	116,866	20	650	5	124	4,121	117,640
St. Kitts-Nevis	65	1,351	1	10	—	—	66	1,361
St. Lucia Islands	9	210	11	255	—	—	20	465
St. Vincent & Grenadines	13	317	13	128	—	—	26	445

U.S. Vehicle Exports by Country of Destination and Vehicle Type

U.S. EXPORTS BY COUNTRY OF DESTINATION AND VEHICLE TYPE, 2008 — continued

COUNTRY	Cars Units	Cars Value ($000)	Trucks Units	Trucks Value ($000)	Buses Units	Buses Value ($000)	Total Units	Total Value ($000)
Suriname	84	1,635	6	92	—	—	90	1,727
Sweden	2,283	56,241	50	1,421	—	—	2,333	57,662
Switzerland	1,107	28,821	7	171	20	578	1,134	29,570
Syria	1	28	—	—	—	—	1	28
Taiwan	390	9,341	41	1,087	21	777	452	11,205
Tajikistan	2	95	—	—	—	—	2	95
Tanzania	17	232	21	1,073	3	80	41	1,385
Thailand	228	5,349	6	131	3	62	237	5,542
Togo	331	4,431	41	832	3	59	375	5,322
Trinidad & Tobago	88	2,098	58	3,702	—	—	146	5,800
Tunisia	46	1,123	8	163	—	—	54	1,286
Turkey	1,769	49,383	5	353	7	90	1,781	49,826
Turks & Caicos Islands	419	8,429	31	2,435	3	51	453	10,915
Uganda	1	11	2	199	—	—	3	210
Ukraine	4,535	98,545	93	1,650	—	—	4,628	100,195
United Arab Emirates	59,539	1,569,393	3,112	95,542	322	22,337	62,973	1,687,272
United Kingdom	22,359	860,656	172	4,616	11	374	22,542	865,646
Uruguay	126	3,529	13	196	—	—	139	3,725
Uzbekistan	13	548	3	20	—	—	16	568
Venezuela	7,392	78,187	6,094	158,929	9	263	13,495	237,379
Vietnam	3,179	90,586	1,435	38,582	113	3,578	4,727	132,746
Yemen	604	10,378	2	63	—	—	606	10,441
Zambia	4	106	7	158	—	—	11	264
Zimbabwe	—	—	2	31	—	—	2	31
Other	954	19,800	159	7,617	86	6,811	1,199	34,228
Total	**1,588,076**	**34,008,711**	**360,308**	**10,454,013**	**17,788**	**905,023**	**1,966,172**	**45,367,747**

NOTE: Data for 2008 include new cars only and are not directly comparable to prior years.
SOURCE: Compiled from official statistics of the U.S. Department of Commerce.

U.S. EXPORTS OF CARS BY COUNTRY OF DESTINATION

Year	Canada	France	Germany	Japan	Kuwait	Mexico	Saudi Arabia	Taiwan	Other Countries	Total Exports
2008	748,749	5,055	179,197	12,900	24,507	191,534	83,629	390	342,115	1,588,076
2007	643,559	11,788	171,461	17,078	22,822	250,362	98,646	1,069	722,359	1,939,144
2006	620,234	5,572	145,238	17,823	25,057	264,937	96,975	1,262	495,542	1,672,640
2005	623,840	3,124	120,135	25,689	37,406	275,845	125,675	5,483	459,528	1,676,725
2004	581,139	3,389	129,664	26,929	24,814	247,218	77,876	3,568	327,218	1,421,815
2003	605,246	2,107	130,867	25,608	20,887	209,163	48,027	2,978	232,964	1,277,847
2002	687,440	1,486	97,110	25,455	16,126	247,197	54,725	3,045	193,678	1,326,262
2001	612,070	5,815	77,054	27,265	6,957	227,131	31,271	4,720	187,946	1,180,229
2000	611,696	3,834	55,812	40,441	4,307	191,885	23,138	10,932	188,050	1,130,095
1999	583,999	2,782	42,415	36,602	1,650	117,018	5,076	8,054	107,814	905,410
1998	566,481	2,675	44,611	43,580	2,519	70,130	11,956	9,604	147,080	898,636
1997	626,629	2,514	57,426	71,789	2,565	62,911	10,146	24,697	216,626	1,075,303
1996	502,652	3,802	59,462	109,917	7,708	46,562	18,253	35,141	190,137	973,634
1995	492,107	2,538	26,690	130,524	6,661	18,649	12,523	61,002	238,673	989,367
1994	559,513	6,083	39,568	100,400	9,246	36,569	18,587	72,491	176,801	1,019,258

NOTE: Data include used vehicles prior to 2008.
SOURCE: Compiled from official statistics of the U.S. Department of Commerce.

U.S. Vehicle Imports by Country of Origin and Vehicle Type

U.S. IMPORTS BY COUNTRY OF ORIGIN AND VEHICLE TYPE, 2008

Country of Origin	Cars Units	Cars Value ($000)	Trucks Units	Trucks Value ($000)	Buses Units	Buses Value ($000)	Total Units	Total Value ($000)
Australia	34,079	863,540	313	521	—	—	34,392	864,061
Austria	19,768	726,663	—	—	29	103	19,797	726,766
Belgium	39,706	696,377	6	398	393	141,103	40,105	837,878
Brazil	52	939	48	1,043	13	1,166	113	3,148
Canada	1,598,115	31,226,339	135,173	4,843,083	1,525	417,634	1,734,813	36,487,056
Finland	5,362	234,450	25	3,383	—	—	5,387	237,833
France	39,497	125,459	9	3,849	—	—	39,506	129,308
Germany	679,624	20,055,852	3,042	84,913	1,023	69,363	683,689	20,210,128
Hungary	5,061	155,273	—	—	1	135	5,062	155,408
Italy	5,473	814,577	64	3,002	16	84	5,553	817,663
Japan	3,119,746	42,060,189	10,381	261,081	41	33,073	3,130,168	42,354,343
Korea, South	800,447	7,850,049	128	2,130	1	80	800,576	7,852,259
Mexico	912,841	13,841,772	307,048	8,206,461	94	5,025	1,219,983	22,053,258
Netherlands	109	3,853	16	3,228	—	—	125	7,081
Slovak Republic	20,363	728,512	—	—	—	—	20,363	728,512
South Africa	62,878	1,823,266	—	—	—	—	62,878	1,823,266
Spain	12	262	—	—	12	6,539	24	6,801
Sweden	59,172	1,477,063	24	1,327	1	13	59,197	1,478,403
Switzerland	—	—	11	5,768	1	20	12	5,788
Taiwan	40	58	4	19	—	—	44	77
United Kingdom	111,880	3,933,482	91	5,099	65	36,005	112,036	3,974,586
Other	22,344	395,258	2,637	24,535	76	14,563	25,057	434,356
Total	**7,536,569**	**127,013,233**	**459,020**	**13,449,840**	**3,291**	**724,906**	**7,998,880**	**141,187,979**

SOURCE: Compiled from official statistics of the U.S. Department of Commerce.

U.S. IMPORTS OF NEW ASSEMBLED CARS BY COUNTRY OF ORIGIN

Year	Canada	Germany	Japan	South Korea	Mexico	Sweden	United Kingdom	Other	Total Imports
2008	1,598,115	679,624	3,119,746	800,447	912,841	59,172	111,880	254,744	7,536,569
2007	1,907,775	753,898	3,504,443	891,237	875,417	91,788	112,399	302,423	8,439,380
2006	1,927,382	695,364	3,693,385	888,256	945,726	80,380	147,403	254,459	8,632,355
2005	1,955,072	544,971	1,628,313	730,431	692,659	92,617	184,138	144,056	5,972,257
2004	2,004,890	545,634	1,538,805	860,057	650,400	97,992	185,059	190,114	6,072,951
2003	1,751,958	560,381	1,575,599	690,885	677,771	119,833	205,937	174,990	5,757,354
2002	1,815,323	571,164	1,827,434	623,810	838,829	89,347	156,258	157,992	6,080,157
2001	1,809,236	492,177	1,616,950	631,945	853,264	89,412	81,261	178,380	5,752,625
2000	2,076,181	489,086	1,661,906	560,728	927,574	85,713	79,639	125,007	6,005,834
1999	2,125,876	456,246	1,560,857	369,264	637,486	82,808	67,689	99,590	5,399,816
1998	1,817,836	372,632	1,317,702	207,165	586,973	84,404	49,037	65,690	4,501,439
1997	1,722,199	298,032	1,383,519	222,535	539,384	79,725	43,726	68,100	4,357,220
1995	1,678,276	206,892	1,387,193	216,618	463,305	82,634	42,176	36,823	4,113,917
1990	1,220,221	245,286	1,867,794	201,475	215,986	93,084	27,271	73,485	3,944,602
1985	1,144,805	473,110	2,527,467	—	13,647	142,640	24,474	71,536	4,397,679
1980	594,770	338,711	1,991,502	—	—	61,496	32,517	97,451	3,116,448
1975	733,766	370,012	695,573	—	—	51,993	67,106	156,203	2,074,653
1970	692,783	674,945	381,338	—	—	57,844	76,257	130,253	2,013,420
1965	33,378	376,950	25,538	—	—	26,010	66,565	35,232	563,673

NOTE: Figures include imports into Puerto Rico and do not include automobiles assembled in U.S. foreign trade zones.
SOURCE: Compiled from official statistics of the U.S. Department of Commerce.

World Trade in Vehicles

EXPORTS AND IMPORTS OF VEHICLES FOR SELECTED COUNTRIES, 2008

Country	Exports			Imports		
	Cars	Commercial Vehicles	Total	Cars	Commercial Vehicles	Total
Argentina	221,259	129,833	351,092	22,770	17,300	40,070
Austria	124,665	25,055	149,720	341,559	44,029	385,588
Belgium	610,784	42,085	652,869	535,947	77,951	613,898
Brazil	422,679	145,903	568,582	229,011	155,175	384,186
Czech Republic	616,529	3,739	620,268	59,404	43,320	102,724
Finland	—	—	—	139,647	21,329	160,976
France	3,736,921	585,270	4,322,191	967,613	197,484	1,165,097
Germany	4,131,660	369,147	4,500,807	1,234,240	126,967	1,361,207
Italy	279,670	281,283	560,953	1,468,242	108,786	1,577,028
Japan	5,915,429	811,662	6,727,091	206,278	12,953	219,231
Korea, South	1,693,325	990,640	2,683,965	61,648	17,825	79,473
Mexico	1,106,040	592,107	1,698,147	314,258	303,420	617,678
Portugal	130,902	38,840	169,742	NA	NA	NA
Romania	153,595	2,503	156,098	189,050	43,505	232,555
Spain	1,655,154	525,698	2,180,852	860,173	144,198	1,004,371
Sweden	384,487	174,377	558,864	NA	NA	NA
Switzerland	—	—	—	288,525	30,218	318,743
Turkey	525,301	384,969	910,270	206,793	99,294	306,087
United Kingdom	1,130,899	125,512	1,256,411	1,840,901	272,000	2,112,901
United States	1,588,076	378,096	1,966,172	7,536,569	462,311	7,998,880
Total	**24,427,375**	**5,606,719**	**30,034,094**	**16,502,628**	**2,178,065**	**18,680,693**

NA - Not available.
SOURCE: Compiled by Ward's Automotive Group from various sources.

WORLD VEHICLE EXPORTS

Year	World Total[1]	Vehicle Exports by Country of Origin (In Thousands)								
		Belgium	Canada	France	Germany	Italy	Japan	Sweden	United Kingdom	United States
2008	30,034.1	652.9	NA	4,322.2	4,500.8	561.0	6,727.1	558.9	1,256.4	1,966.2
2007	31,496.6	758.3	NA	4,696.7	4,664.3	650.5	6,550.2	750.8	1,317.0	2,395.6
2006	27,821.9	848.2	NA	3,126.0	4,182.7	596.0	5,966.7	643.9	1,242.2	2,054.7
2005	27,533.7	868.8	NA	4,319.4	4,080.6	497.6	5,053.1	628.4	1,316.5	2,064.2
2004	26,962.8	870.8	NA	4,268.9	3,924.1	595.7	4,957.7	648.4	1,307.9	1,793.6
2003	24,999.7	871.9	NA	4,045.6	3,935.9	703.6	4,756.3	565.3	1,246.7	1,613.9
2002	26,765.7	1,014.6	2,373.0	3,916.7	3,875.1	733.7	4,698.2	546.3	1,161.0	1,658.5
2001	25,577.3	1,140.8	2,023.3	3,734.7	3,915.8	813.7	4,166.2	575.4	991.8	1,462.3
2000	25,886.6	993.7	2,323.0	3,619.0	3,722.8	911.6	4,454.9	453.5	1,127.9	1,298.2
1999	24,241.3	983.0	2,331.8	3,255.5	3,675.8	797.8	4,408.9	221.0	1,213.5	1,219.2
1998	24,145.6	1,026.3	2,220.5	3,122.8	3,510.9	812.4	4,528.9	425.9	1,123.6	1,247.8
1997	23,620.8	1,050.8	2,220.5	2,822.5	3,035.6	739.3	4,553.2	416.6	1,065.3	1,591.0
1996	21,691.1	1,192.7	2,134.8	2,272.0	2,841.8	799.2	3,711.7	194.5	1,073.3	1,289.6
1995	20,142.7	1,218.8	1,908.6	2,261.2	2,639.5	806.5	3,790.8	206.3	837.0	1,243.6
1994	19,795.6	1,215.7	1,852.0	2,428.5	2,410.3	669.6	4,460.3	192.8	718.2	1,293.2
1993	19,095.9	1,097.8	2,023.8	2,264.0	2,176.1	504.0	5,017.8	194.4	633.0	1,045.3
1992	20,250.5	1,130.6	1,765.4	2,295.8	2,729.9	697.6	5,667.7	210.8	708.4	1,012.5
1991	19,598.6	1,127.8	1,639.1	2,420.6	2,346.7	806.2	5,753.4	203.4	702.0	962.9
Percent of World Vehicle Exports										
2008	100.0	2.2	NA	14.4	15.0	1.9	22.4	1.9	4.2	6.5
2007	100.0	2.4	NA	14.9	14.8	2.1	20.8	2.4	4.2	7.6
2006	100.0	3.0	NA	11.2	15.0	2.1	21.4	2.3	4.5	7.4
2005	100.0	3.2	NA	15.7	14.8	1.8	18.4	2.3	4.8	7.5
2004	100.0	3.2	NA	15.8	14.6	2.2	18.4	2.4	4.9	6.7
2003	100.0	3.5	NA	16.2	15.7	2.8	19.0	2.3	5.0	6.5
2002	100.0	3.8	8.9	14.6	14.5	2.7	17.6	2.0	4.3	6.2
2001	100.0	4.5	7.9	14.6	15.3	3.2	16.3	2.2	3.9	5.7
2000	100.0	3.8	9.0	14.0	14.4	3.5	17.2	1.8	4.4	5.0
1999	100.0	4.1	9.6	13.4	15.2	3.3	18.2	1.0	5.0	5.4
1998	100.0	4.3	9.2	12.9	14.5	3.4	18.8	1.8	4.7	5.2
1997	100.0	4.4	9.4	11.9	12.9	3.1	19.3	1.8	4.5	6.7
1996	100.0	5.5	9.8	10.5	13.1	3.7	17.1	0.9	4.9	5.9
1995	100.0	6.1	9.5	11.2	13.1	4.0	18.8	1.0	4.2	6.2
1994	100.0	6.1	9.4	12.3	12.2	3.4	22.5	1.0	3.6	6.5
1993	100.0	5.7	10.6	11.9	11.4	2.6	26.3	1.0	3.3	5.5
1992	100.0	5.6	8.7	11.3	13.5	3.4	28.0	1.0	3.5	5.0
1991	100.0	5.8	8.4	12.4	12.0	4.1	29.4	1.0	3.6	4.9

(1) World total includes countries with vehicle exports not shown separately. NA - Not available.
SOURCE: Compiled by Ward's Data Group from various sources.

Material Usage by the Automotive Industry

AUTOMOTIVE CONSUMPTION OF MATERIALS BY TYPE

Material	U.S. Total Consumption	Automotive Consumption	Automotive Percentage	Material	U.S. Total Consumption	Automotive Consumption	Automotive Percentage
ALUMINUM (Thousands of Pounds)				**PLASTIC (Thousands of Pounds)**			
2008	18,595,000	4,473,000	24.1	2008	NA	NA	NA
2007	21,415,000	5,923,000	27.7	2007	115,879,000	4,638,160	4.0
2006	23,151,000	6,397,000	27.6	2006	113,015,000	4,882,248	4.3
2005	23,113,000	6,529,000	28.2	2005	110,606,000	5,017,000	4.5
2004	22,904,000	6,585,000	28.8	2004	113,940,000	5,190,000	4.6
COPPER AND COPPER ALLOY (Thousands of Pounds)				**RUBBER (Tire & Tire Products in Metric Tons)**			
2008	5,892,000	637,000	10.8	2008	1,656,000	1,540,000	93.0
2007	6,617,000	737,000	11.1	2007	1,716,620	1,596,456	93.0
2006	7,279,000	778,000	10.7	2006	1,751,656	1,629,040	93.0
2005	7,786,000	794,400	10.2	2005	1,860,000	1,729,800	93.0
2004	7,755,900	835,700	10.8	2004	1,943,000	1,806,990	93.0
GRAY IRON (Tons)				**RUBBER (Non-Tire Products in Metric Tons)**			
2008	4,158,000	793,000	19.1	2008	1,024,200	409,600	40.0
2007	4,440,000	915,000	20.6	2007	1,061,423	424,569	40.0
2006	4,650,000	1,065,000	22.9	2006	1,094,250	437,700	40.0
2005	4,700,000	1,010,000	21.5	2005	1,162,000	464,800	40.0
2004	4,850,000	1,085,000	22.4	2004	1,215,000	486,000	40.0
DUCTILE IRON (Tons)				**ALLOY STEEL (Tons)**			
2008	3,994,000	839,000	21.0	2008	5,403,008	694,867	12.9
2007	4,440,000	1,005,000	22.6	2007	5,159,400	670,722	13.0
2006	4,500,000	1,015,000	22.6	2006	5,501,615	698,705	12.7
2005	4,400,000	1,136,000	25.8	2005	5,182,650	647,831	12.5
2004	4,271,000	1,077,000	25.2	2004	5,032,638	634,112	12.6
MALLEABLE IRON (Tons)				**STAINLESS STEEL (Tons)**			
2008	NA	NA	NA	2008	1,876,668	401,320	21.4
2007	NA	NA	NA	2007	2,275,823	455,164	20.0
2006	NA	NA	NA	2006	2,524,434	499,838	19.8
2005	105,000	56,000	53.3	2005	2,361,300	448,647	19.0
2004	120,000	63,000	52.5	2004	2,521,850	484,195	19.2
TOTAL IRON (Tons)				**TOTAL STEEL (Tons)**			
2008	8,152,000	1,632,000	20.0	2008	101,964,789	12,851,000	12.6
2007	8,880,000	1,920,000	21.6	2007	110,169,806	13,631,755	12.4
2006	9,150,000	2,080,000	22.7	2006	109,501,703	15,528,000	14.2
2005	9,205,000	2,202,000	23.9	2005	104,970,522	14,477,000	13.8
2004	9,291,000	2,240,000	24.1	2004	111,385,462	13,857,470	12.4
LEAD (Metric Tons)				**ZINC (Tons)**			
2008	1,600,000	1,178,200	73.6	2008	955,000	205,300	21.5
2007	1,590,000	1,162,800	73.1	2007	1,110,000	244,200	22.0
2006	1,510,000	1,132,500	75.0	2006	1,130,000	248,600	22.0
2005	1,510,000	1,126,400	74.6	2005	939,000	206,580	22.0
2004	1,520,000	1,135,200	74.7	2004	1,160,000	261,000	22.5

NA - Not available.
NOTE: For most materials listed, automotive consumption includes materials used for cars, trucks, buses and replacement parts.
SOURCE: Ward's Automotive Group from various sources.

Material Usage, Vehicles Retired From Use and Vehicle Recycling

AVERAGE MATERIALS CONTENT OF NORTH AMERICAN LIGHT VEHICLES

Material	2007 Pounds	2007 Percent	2006 Pounds	2006 Percent	2000 Pounds	2000 Percent	1995 Pounds	1995 Percent
Regular Steel	1,644	40.3	1,622	40.1	1,655	42.4	1,630	44.1
High and Medium Strength Steel	518	12.7	500	12.4	408	10.5	324	8.8
Stainless Steel	75	1.8	73	1.8	62	1.6	51	1.4
Other Steels	34	0.8	35	0.9	26	0.7	46	1.2
Iron Castings	322	7.9	331	8.2	432	11.1	466	12.6
Aluminum	313	7.7	323	8.0	268	6.9	231	6.3
Magnesium Castings	10	0.2	10	0.2	8	0.2	4	0.1
Copper and Brass	53	1.3	61	1.5	52	1.3	50	1.4
Lead	42	1.0	39	1.0	36	0.9	33	0.9
Zinc Castings	9	0.2	10	0.2	13	0.3	19	0.5
Powder Metal	43	1.1	42	1.0	36	0.9	29	0.8
Other Metals	5	0.1	5	0.1	4	0.1	4	0.1
Plastics and Plastic Composites	331	8.1	338	8.4	286	7.3	240	6.5
Rubber	189	4.6	174	4.3	166	4.3	149	4.0
Coatings	29	0.7	29	0.7	25	0.6	23	0.6
Textiles	46	1.1	48	1.2	44	1.1	42	1.1
Fluids and Lubricants	215	5.3	211	5.2	207	5.3	192	5.2
Glass	106	2.6	105	2.6	103	2.6	97	2.6
Other Materials	92	2.3	88	2.2	71	1.9	64	1.7
Total	**4,076**	**100.0**	**4,044**	**100.0**	**3,902**	**100.0**	**3,694**	**100.0**

SOURCE: American Chemistry Council. Data reflects Light Vehicles built in North America.

VEHICLES RETIRED FROM USE
(in Thousands)

Year Ending June 30	Cars	Trucks & Buses	Total
2008	6,896	7,149	14,045
2007	7,008	5,699	12,707
2006	6,750	5,258	12,008
2005	6,478	3,511	9,989
2004	5,524	6,379	11,903
2003	6,864	5,226	12,090
2002	7,310	5,986	13,296
2001	7,650	6,472	14,122
2000	8,085	6,214	14,299
1999	7,216	4,447	11,663
1998	6,819	4,846	11,665
1997	8,244	4,265	12,509
1996	7,527	3,284	10,811
1995	7,414	2,918	10,332
1994	7,824	4,545	12,369
1993	7,366	1,048	8,414
1992	11,194	1,587	12,781
1991	8,565	2,284	10,849
1989	8,981	2,189	11,170
1987	8,103	2,364	10,467
1985	7,729	2,100	9,829
1983	6,243	1,491	7,734
1981	7,542	1,519	9,061
1979	9,312	1,916	11,228
1977	8,234	1,668	9,902
1975	5,669	908	6,577
1973	7,987	1,208	9,195
1971	6,021	1,044	7,065
1969	6,348	966	7,314
1967	6,984	947	7,931

NOTE: Car and truck splits are estimated. Figures represent vehicles which are not re-registered.
SOURCE: The Polk Company. Permission for further use must be obtained from The Polk Company.

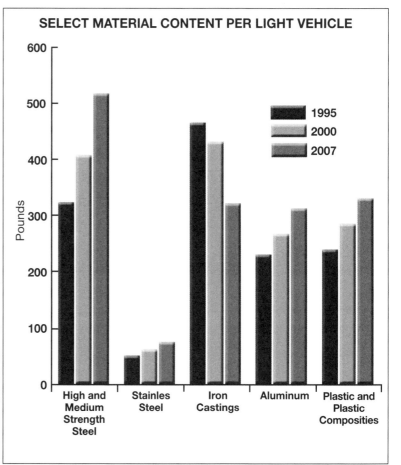

SELECT MATERIAL CONTENT PER LIGHT VEHICLE

LICENSED DRIVERS

Licensed Drivers by Age Group, Gender and State

LICENSED DRIVERS BY STATE, 2007

State	Male (000)	Female (000)	Total (000)
Alabama	1,807	1,885	3,692
Alaska	263	232	495
Arizona	2,080	2,074	4,154
Arkansas	1,012	1,034	2,046
California	11,999	11,468	23,467
Colorado	1,792	1,710	3,502
Connecticut	1,413	1,435	2,848
Delaware	304	320	624
Dist. of Columbia	195	201	396
Florida	6,964	7,175	14,139
Georgia	2,952	3,182	6,134
Hawaii	451	412	863
Idaho	518	510	1,028
Illinois	4,044	4,146	8,190
Indiana	2,124	2,185	4,309
Iowa	1,028	1,065	2,093
Kansas	1,003	1,015	2,018
Kentucky	1,452	1,482	2,934
Louisiana	1,473	1,561	3,034
Maine	501	508	1,009
Maryland	1,810	1,928	3,738
Massachusetts	2,338	2,362	4,700
Michigan	3,477	3,582	7,059
Minnesota	1,591	1,559	3,150
Mississippi	921	1,006	1,927
Missouri	2,050	2,112	4,162
Montana	374	362	736
Nebraska	668	663	1,331
Nevada	864	798	1,662
New Hampshire	515	511	1,026
New Jersey	2,849	2,934	5,783
New Mexico	677	689	1,366
New York	5,907	5,462	11,369
North Carolina	3,165	3,219	6,384
North Dakota	238	233	471
Ohio	3,864	4,111	7,975
Oklahoma	1,045	1,238	2,283
Oregon	1,432	1,396	2,828
Pennsylvania	4,281	4,320	8,601
Rhode Island	368	376	744
South Carolina	1,501	1,626	3,127
South Dakota	294	294	588
Tennessee	2,149	2,277	4,426
Texas	7,598	7,586	15,184
Utah	832	820	1,652
Vermont	268	267	535
Virginia	2,561	2,698	5,259
Washington	2,526	2,353	4,879
West Virginia	676	682	1,358
Wisconsin	2,046	2,020	4,066
Wyoming	205	193	398
Total	**102,465**	**103,277**	**205,742**

SOURCE: U.S. Department of Transportation, Federal Highway Administration.

DRIVERS BY AGE GROUP AND GENDER, 2007

Age (in Years)	Male (000)	Female (000)	Total (000)
Under 16	127	124	251
16	682	670	1,352
17	1,150	1,108	2,258
18	1,480	1,394	2,874
19	1,638	1,547	3,185
20	1,682	1,624	3,306
21	1,712	1,677	3,389
22	1,740	1,715	3,455
23	1,743	1,726	3,469
24	1,792	1,778	3,570
25-29	9,073	9,077	18,150
30-34	8,852	8,767	17,619
35-39	9,763	9,635	19,398
40-44	10,117	10,042	20,159
45-49	10,583	10,642	21,225
50-54	9,870	9,994	19,864
55-59	8,581	8,724	17,305
60-64	6,891	6,976	13,867
65-69	4,982	5,095	10,077
70-74	3,734	3,877	7,611
75-79	2,933	3,188	6,121
80-84	2,000	2,306	4,306
85 and over	1,340	1,590	2,930
Total	**102,465**	**103,277**	**205,742**

SOURCE: U.S. Department of Transportation, Federal Highway Administration.

DRIVERS BY GENDER

Year	Male (000)	Percent Male	Female (000)	Percent Female	Total (000)
2007	102,465	49.80	103,277	50.20	205,742
2006	101,116	49.86	101,694	50.14	202,810
2005	100,252	49.99	100,297	50.01	200,549
2004	99,571	50.06	99,318	49.94	198,889
2003	98,228	50.07	97,937	49.93	196,165
2002	97,461	50.16	96,834	49.84	194,295
2001	95,792	50.08	95,483	49.92	191,275
2000	95,796	50.30	94,829	49.70	190,625
1999	94,166	50.31	93,004	49.69	187,170
1998	93,105	50.33	91,875	49.67	184,980
1997	91,905	50.30	90,804	49.70	182,709
1996	90,519	50.42	89,021	49.58	179,540
1995	89,214	50.51	87,414	49.49	176,628
1994	89,194	50.85	86,209	49.15	175,403
1993	87,993	50.82	85,156	49.18	173,149
1992	88,387	51.05	84,738	48.95	173,125
1991	86,665	51.28	82,330	48.72	168,995
1990	85,792	51.37	81,223	48.63	167,015
1989	85,378	51.57	80,177	48.43	165,555
1988	85,230	51.91	78,967	48.09	164,197
1987	84,084	51.91	77,891	48.09	161,975
1986	82,494	52.02	76,100	47.98	158,594
1985	81,592	52.01	75,276	47.99	156,868
1984	80,977	52.10	74,447	47.90	155,424
1983	80,894	52.40	73,495	47.60	154,389
1982	78,553	52.29	71,681	47.71	150,234
1981	77,888	52.96	69,187	47.04	147,075
1980	77,187	53.12	68,108	46.88	145,295
1979	76,531	53.41	66,753	46.59	143,284
1978	75,594	53.67	65,249	46.33	140,843

SOURCE: U.S. Department of Transportation, Federal Highway Administration.

Demographics of New Vehicle Buyers and Initial Vehicle Quality

DEMOGRAPHICS OF NEW VEHICLE BUYERS AND INITIAL VEHICLE QUALITY, 2009 MODEL YEAR

Characteristic	New Passenger Car Buyers				New Light Trucks Buyers				New CUV Buyers			
	Domestic[1]	European[2]	Asian[2]	Total	Domestic[1]	European[2]	Asian[2]	Total	Domestic[1]	European[2]	Asian[2]	Total
Gender												
Male	56.3%	57.5%	50.2%	52.8%	76.7%	53.2%	62.4%	70.6%	51.7%	55.1%	44.5%	48.1%
Female	38.9	37.9	45.0	42.4	18.4	40.6	33.2	24.7	44.5	38.7	51.1	47.6
No Answer	4.8	4.6	4.8	4.8	4.9	6.2	4.4	4.7	3.8	6.2	4.4	4.3
Total	100.0	100.0	100.0	100.0	100.0	100.0	100.0	100.0	100.0	100.0	100.0	100.0
Age of Principal Purchaser (In Years)												
Under 25	3.0%	3.1%	4.5%	3.9%	1.4%	0.5%	1.4%	1.4%	1.0%	1.1%	1.2%	1.1%
25-29	4.1	6.0	7.2	6.2	2.8	3.9	3.4	3.1	4.0	3.1	4.5	4.2
30-34	3.5	6.3	5.9	5.3	4.2	10.6	7.6	5.7	5.6	8.3	6.8	6.5
35-39	4.2	8.4	5.2	5.4	5.9	13.5	11.7	8.3	6.9	12.0	6.9	7.3
40-44	6.0	9.2	6.8	6.9	7.8	17.5	11.4	9.5	7.2	13.1	7.2	7.7
45-49	9.4	11.3	9.9	9.9	10.2	14.1	11.8	10.9	9.6	14.8	10.3	10.4
50-54	11.8	13.9	11.7	12.1	11.8	10.3	10.6	11.3	11.7	13.4	13.0	12.5
55-59	13.1	13.3	12.7	12.9	13.0	7.9	11.2	12.2	13.1	11.4	14.3	13.5
60-64	13.4	12.1	12.5	12.7	14.9	8.7	11.8	13.6	14.7	10.2	14.9	14.5
65 and over	31.5	16.4	23.6	24.7	28.0	13.0	19.1	24.0	26.2	12.6	20.9	22.3
Total	100.0	100.0	100.0	100.0	100.0	100.0	100.0	100.0	100.0	100.0	100.0	100.0
Highest Education Level												
8th Grade or Less	0.7%	0.1%	0.3%	0.4%	1.0%	0.1%	0.5%	0.8%	0.5%	0.1%	0.1%	0.2%
Some High School	2.0	0.6	1.1	1.3	2.6	0.3	1.3	2.0	1.2	0.6	0.8	0.9
High School Graduate	20.2	6.5	12.1	13.3	23.0	6.1	11.2	18.0	16.5	5.7	10.7	12.5
Technical/Trade School	8.9	4.2	6.0	6.5	11.2	5.3	6.9	9.4	8.4	3.3	5.8	6.5
Some College	24.9	17.8	21.1	21.6	25.1	18.3	22.1	23.7	23.6	14.2	19.2	20.5
College Graduate	20.7	28.8	26.6	25.4	19.8	31.7	25.7	22.4	23.7	33.1	26.3	25.9
Post Graduate	5.9	7.6	7.0	6.8	4.6	6.8	6.4	5.3	6.6	7.1	7.7	7.3
Advanced Degree	16.7	34.4	25.8	24.7	12.7	31.4	25.9	18.4	19.5	35.9	29.4	26.2
Total	100.0	100.0	100.0	100.0	100.0	100.0	100.0	100.0	100.0	100.0	100.0	100.0
Census Region												
Northeast	19.9%	23.6%	23.9%	22.9%	17.6%	23.8%	21.9%	19.4%	16.8%	27.2%	28.8%	24.2%
Midwest	41.0	16.2	17.0	22.9	39.0	23.8	17.1	30.2	46.1	16.9	21.0	30.1
South	28.6	33.0	36.8	34.2	32.2	30.0	39.3	34.9	26.1	29.8	30.4	28.7
West	10.5	27.2	22.3	20.0	11.2	22.4	21.7	15.5	11.0	26.1	19.8	17.0
Total	100.0	100.0	100.0	100.0	100.0	100.0	100.0	100.0	100.0	100.0	100.0	100.0
Median Household Income	$75,916	$130,214	$82,255	$85,927	$89,576	$178,468	$99,447	$94,782	$88,302	$187,958	$99,983	$98,553
Initial Quality (Problems per 100 Passenger Cars)												
Study Results	103	113	100	103	113	134	116	115	128	119	109	117

NOTE: Study conducted among personal use buyers of '09 model year vehicles.
(1) Domestic figures include captive import buyers.
(2) Import figures include buyers of North American assembled vehicles.
SOURCE: J.D. Power and Associates, 2009 Initial Quality Study.

Car Operating Costs

CAR OPERATING COSTS

| Model Year | Variable Cost in Cents Per Mile | | | | Cost Per 10,000 Miles | | | |
	Gas & Oil	Maintenance	Tires	Total	Variable Cost	Fixed Cost	Total Cost	Total Cost Per Mile
2009	10.09	4.56	0.77	15.42	$1,542	$5,526	$7,068	70.68¢
2008	11.67	4.57	0.72	16.96	1,696	5,399	7,095	70.95
2007	8.90	4.90	0.70	14.50	1,450	4,765	6,215	62.15
2006	9.50	4.90	0.70	15.10	1,510	4,686	6,196	61.96
2005	8.20	5.30	0.60	14.10	1,410	5,412	6,822	68.22
2004	6.50	5.40	0.70	12.60	1,260	5,633	6,893	68.93
2003	7.20	4.10	1.80	13.10	1,310	4,884	6,194	61.94
2002	5.90	4.10	1.80	11.80	1,180	4,874	6,054	60.54
2001	7.90	3.90	1.80	13.60	1,360	4,621	5,981	59.81
2000	6.90	3.60	1.70	12.20	1,220	4,724	5,944	59.44
1999	5.60	3.30	1.70	10.60	1,060	4,660	5,720	57.20
1998	6.20	3.10	1.40	10.70	1,070	4,528	5,598	55.98
1997	6.60	2.80	1.40	10.80	1,080	4,348	5,428	54.28
1996	5.60	2.80	1.20	9.60	960	4,193	5,153	51.53
1995	5.80	2.60	1.20	9.60	960	4,005	4,965	49.65
1994	5.60	2.50	1.00	9.10	910	3,836	4,746	47.46
1993	5.90	2.40	0.90	9.20	920	3,722	4,642	46.42
1992	5.90	2.20	0.90	9.00	900	3,784	4,684	46.84
1991	6.60	2.20	0.90	9.70	970	3,566	4,536	45.36
1990	5.40	2.10	0.90	8.40	840	3,256	4,096	40.96
1989	5.30	1.90	0.80	8.00	800	2,920	3,720	37.20
1987	4.40	1.50	0.80	6.70	670	2,328	2,998	29.98
1985	5.57	1.20	0.65	7.42	742	2,061	2,803	28.03
1983	6.13	0.98	0.69	7.80	780	2,084	2,864	28.64
1981	6.27	1.18	0.72	8.17	817	2,375	3,192	31.92

ANNUAL FIXED COST OF OPERATING A CAR

| Model Year | Insurance | | | License, Registration & Taxes | Depreciation | Finance Charge | Total | Average Fixed Cost Per Day |
	Fire & Theft[2]	Collision[3]	Property Damage & Liability[4]					
2009[1]	NA	$976	NA	$567	$3,461	$779	$5,783	$15.84
2008[1]	NA	943	NA	554	3,321	758	5,576	15.28
2007[1]	NA	985	NA	538	3,392	733	5,648	15.47
2006[1]	NA	926	NA	535	3,392	716	5,569	15.26
2005[1]	NA	1,288	NA	389	3,879	739	6,295	17.25
2004[1]	NA	1,603	NA	415	3,782	741	6,541	17.92
2003	203	401	498	205	3,738	744	5,789	15.86
2002	173	357	484	201	3,721	828	5,764	15.79
2001	167	345	479	208	3,548	866	5,613	15.38
2000	163	326	481	223	3,492	849	5,534	15.16
1999	162	324	484	226	3,436	828	5,460	14.96
1998	134	287	479	226	3,364	813	5,303	14.53
1997	120	326	401	216	3,272	768	5,103	13.98
1996	144	275	426	215	3,170	718	4,948	13.56
1995	121	252	410	203	3,073	686	4,745	13.00
1994	123	246	400	194	2,940	648	4,551	12.47
1993	116	243	385	178	2,830	670	4,422	12.12
1992	128	286	373	174	2,717	796	4,474	12.26
1991	108	247	353	168	2,504	266	3,646	9.99
1990	110	245	318	165	2,357	680	3,875	10.62
1989	102	234	309	144	2,018	588	3,395	9.30
1987	87	196	252	128	1,494	526	2,683	7.35
1985	75	177	213	110	1,262	534	2,371	6.50
1983	67	181	222	97	1,298	529	2,394	6.56
1981	76	180	254	88	1,287	490	2,375	6.51

NOTE: Methodology changed beginning in 2004; data is not comparable to prior years. Beginning in 1985 ownership costs are based on a six year/60,000 mile retention cycle rather than four year/60,000 miles.
NA - Not available.
(1) Individual component costs of insurance are no longer available, therefore insurance costs for 2004 forward reflect the total amount of a full coverage policy.
(2) $100 deductible 1981-1992; $250 deductible 1993-2003, $100 deductible 2004-2009.
(3) $250 deductible 1981-1992; $500 deductible 1993-2009.
(4) Coverage: 1967 to 2009-$100,000/$300,000
SOURCE: American Automobile Association.

Light Truck Operating Costs

LIGHT TRUCK OPERATING COSTS

| Model Year | Variable Cost in Cents Per Mile | | | | Cost Per 10,000 Miles | | | |
	Gas & Oil	Maintenance	Tires	Total	Variable Cost	Fixed Cost	Total Cost	Total Cost Per Mile
2009	14.39	4.94	0.95	20.28	$2,028	$6,942	$8,970	89.70¢
2008	17.05	5.47	0.93	23.45	2,345	6,750	9,095	90.95
2007	12.60	5.50	0.90	19.00	1,900	6,247	8,147	81.47
2006	13.70	5.60	0.80	20.10	2,010	5,890	7,900	79.00
2005	10.80	5.30	0.90	17.00	1,700	6,074	7,774	77.74
2004	8.40	4.30	1.00	13.70	1,370	5,903	7,273	72.73
2003	7.90	4.10	1.50	13.50	1,350	5,527	6,877	68.77
2002	5.80	4.10	1.70	11.60	1,160	4,332	5,492	54.92
2001	8.05	4.00	1.60	13.65	1,365	5,197	6,562	65.62
2000	7.55	3.90	1.55	13.00	1,300	4,379	5,679	56.79
1999	6.15	3.60	1.35	11.10	1,110	5,312	6,422	64.22

ANNUAL FIXED COST OF OPERATING A LIGHT TRUCK

| Model Year | Insurance | | | License, Registration & Taxes | Depreciation | Finance Charge | Total | Average Fixed Cost Per Day |
	Fire & Theft[2]	Collision[3]	Property Damage & Liability[4]					
2009[1]	NA	$948	NA	$727	$4,519	$1,023	$7,217	$19.77
2008[1]	NA	888	NA	715	4,327	1,000	6,930	18.99
2007[1]	NA	950	NA	695	4,531	971	7,147	19.58
2006[1]	NA	918	NA	683	4,254	935	6,790	18.60
2005[1]	NA	1,398	NA	435	4,300	891	7,024	19.24
2004[1]	NA	1,491	NA	454	4,043	865	6,853	18.78
2003	159	402	389	289	4,286	867	6,392	17.51
2002	204	451	389	261	3,220	662	5,187	14.21
2001	182	423	389	285	3,720	980	5,979	16.38
2000	202	491	481	355	2,940	638	5,107	13.99
1999	205	455	484	401	3,558	924	6,027	16.51

NOTE: Methodology changed beginning in 2004; data is not comparable to prior years.

NA - Not available

(1) Individual component costs of insurance are no longer available, therefore insurance costs for 2004 forward reflect the total amount of a full coverage policy.

(2) $100 deductible in 1992; $250 deductible 1993-2003, $100 deductible 2004-2009.

(3) $250 deductible in 1992; $500 deductible 1993-2009.

(4) Coverage: 1992 to 2009-$100,000/$300,000

SOURCE: American Automobile Association.

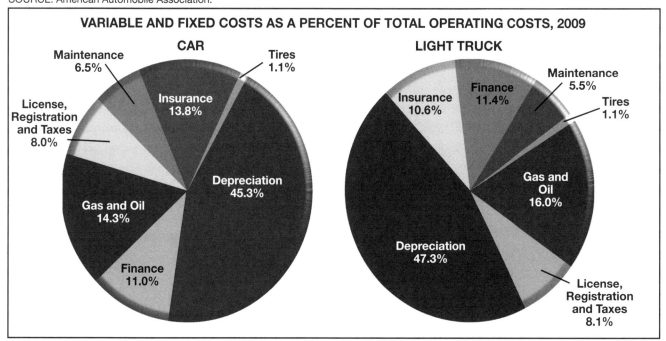

VARIABLE AND FIXED COSTS AS A PERCENT OF TOTAL OPERATING COSTS, 2009

CAR

- Maintenance 6.5%
- Tires 1.1%
- Insurance 13.8%
- License, Registration and Taxes 8.0%
- Depreciation 45.3%
- Gas and Oil 14.3%
- Finance 11.0%

LIGHT TRUCK

- Finance 11.4%
- Maintenance 5.5%
- Insurance 10.6%
- Tires 1.1%
- Gas and Oil 16.0%
- Depreciation 47.3%
- License, Registration and Taxes 8.1%

Automobile Financing

NEW AND USED CAR FINANCING WITH FINANCE COMPANIES

Year	Average Interest Rate	Average Maturity (Months)	Average Amount Financed	Average Monthly Payment
NEW CARS				
2008	5.5	63.4	$26,178	$476.73
2007	4.9	62.0	28,287	517.35
2006	5.0	63.0	26,620	481.30
2005	6.0	60.0	24,133	466.56
2004	4.9	60.7	24,888	463.76
2003	3.4	61.4	26,295	467.19
2002	4.3	56.8	24,747	482.31
2001	5.7	55.1	22,822	471.73
2000	6.6	54.9	20,923	442.58
1999	6.7	52.7	19,880	436.49
1998	6.3	52.1	19,083	419.60
1997	7.1	54.1	18,077	391.45
1996	9.8	51.6	16,987	404.75
1994	9.8	54.0	15,375	353.25
1992	9.8	54.0	13,607	313.01
USED CARS				
2008	8.7	59.8	$16,664	$344.41
2007	9.2	60.7	17,095	353.29
2006	9.6	59.4	16,671	353.70
2005	8.8	58.6	16,228	341.68
2004	8.8	57.9	15,136	321.77
2003	9.7	57.7	14,613	317.90
2002	10.7	57.6	14,532	323.70
2001	12.2	57.5	14,416	332.33
2000	13.6	57.0	14,058	336.16
1999	12.6	55.9	13,642	324.15
1998	12.6	53.5	12,691	311.51
1997	13.3	51.0	12,281	316.54
1996	13.5	51.4	12,182	313.39
1994	13.5	50.2	10,709	280.37
1992	13.7	47.9	9,211	250.70

SOURCE: Board of Governors of The Federal Reserve.

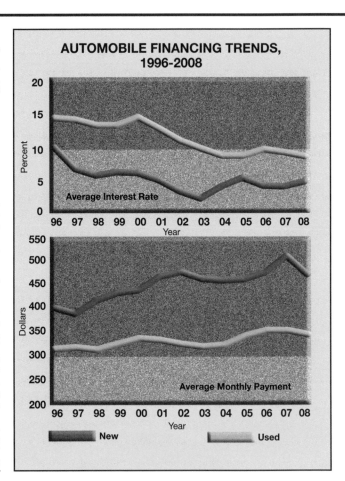

AUTOMOBILE FINANCING TRENDS, 1996-2008

CONSUMER CREDIT OUTSTANDING BY HOLDER (in Billions of Dollars)

Year	Commercial Banks	Finance Companies	Credit Unions	Savings Institutions	Nonfinancial Business	Other	Total
2008	878.5	575.8	235.0	86.3	55.6	726.1	2,557.3
2007	804.1	584.1	235.7	90.8	55.2	782.0	2,551.9
2006	741.2	534.4	234.5	95.6	56.8	755.8	2,418.3
2005	707.0	516.5	228.6	109.1	58.8	693.9	2,313.9
2004	704.3	492.3	215.4	91.3	58.5	670.4	2,232.2
2003	669.4	393.0	205.9	77.9	58.5	711.4	2,116.1
2002	602.6	237.8	195.7	68.7	77.5	766.7	1,949.0
2001	571.8	238.1	189.6	71.1	88.8	719.2	1,878.6
2000	554.0	220.5	184.4	64.6	90.0	625.6	1,739.1
1999	499.8	201.5	167.9	61.5	78.7	448.6	1,458.0
1998	508.9	183.3	155.4	51.6	74.9	372.4	1,346.5
1997	511.2	161.1	147.8	46.8	70.2	281.9	1,219.0
1996	506.0	154.3	137.2	42.7	73.4	237.5	1,151.1
1995	475.3	142.1	125.6	38.9	80.1	172.4	1,034.4

SOURCE: Board of Governors of the Federal Reserve.

Expenditures for Transportation

AVERAGE EXPENDITURE PER NEW CAR

Year	Average Expenditure Per New Car[1]			Estimated Average New Car Price for a 1967 "Comparable Car"		Annual Median Family Earnings[4]	Weeks of Median Family Earnings to Equal Cost of "Comparable Car"		
	Domestic*	Import	Average	With Added Safety & Emissions Equipment[2]	Without Added Safety & Emissions Equipment[3]		Average New Car Expenditure[5]	With Added Safety & Emissions Equipment[6]	Without Added Safety & Emissions Equipment[7]
2008	$20,490	$28,174	$23,051	$13,429	$8,859	$78,483	15.3	8.9	5.9
2007	20,434	29,735	23,336	13,465	8,795	75,610	16.0	9.2	6.1
2006	20,342	29,625	23,140	13,461	8,811	71,196	16.9	9.8	6.4
2005	19,833	29,172	22,497	13,404	8,799	66,977	17.5	10.4	6.8
2004	18,910	28,409	21,637	12,950	8,784	63,485	17.7	10.6	7.2
2003	18,536	28,139	21,169	12,965	8,838	60,135	18.3	11.2	7.6
2001	18,755	27,539	20,945	13,402	9,116	56,628	19.2	12.3	8.4
1999	18,339	28,695	20,381	13,236	9,157	50,784	20.9	13.6	9.4
1997	17,907	27,722	19,531	13,267	9,297	45,326	22.4	15.2	10.7
1995	16,864	23,202	17,959	12,989	9,115	40,572	23.0	16.5	11.7
1993	15,976	20,261	16,871	12,153	8,631	36,764	23.9	16.7	12.2
1991	15,192	16,327	15,475	11,321	8,224	34,775	23.1	16.7	12.3
1989	13,936	15,510	14,371	10,282	7,825	32,448	23.0	16.5	12.5
1987	12,922	14,470	13,386	9,775	7,518	29,744	23.4	17.1	13.1
1985	11,589	12,853	11,838	9,014	6,958	27,144	22.7	17.3	13.3
1983	10,516	10,868	10,606	8,415	6,544	24,580	22.4	17.8	13.8
1981	8,912	8,896	8,910	7,726	6,115	22,388	20.7	17.9	14.2
1979	6,889	6,704	6,847	6,198	5,337	19,661	18.1	16.4	14.1
1977	5,985	5,072	5,814	5,292	4,593	16,009	18.9	17.2	14.9
1975	5,084	4,384	4,950	4,689	4,103	13,719	18.8	17.8	15.6
1967	3,313	2,276	3,216	3,196	3,185	7,933	21.1	20.9	20.9

NOTE: *Includes transplants.
(1) U.S. Departments of Commerce, Bureau of Economic Analysis (BEA) , "Average Transaction Price Per New Car." Includes purchases by business, government, and consumers.
(2) 1967 "Average Transaction Price" plus the value of added safety and emissions equipment as determined by the U.S. Bureau of Labor Statistics (BLS), all inflated to current dollars using the BLS, "New Car Consumer Price Index-All Urban Consumers." For example, 1969 is equal to the 1968 value plus the BLS stated value of added safety and emissions equipment for the 1969 model year multiplied by 1968-1969 monthly changes in the New Car Consumer Price Index. The cost to improve fuel economy, which prior to 1980 was included with "Other Quality Adjustments", has since been included by the BLS with the cost of emissions improvements.
(3) 1967 "Average Transaction Price" inflated to current dollars.
(4) BLS, "Median Family Earnings."
(5) "Average Expenditure," as reported by the BEA, divided by "Annual Median Family Earnings", multiplied by 52 weeks. This index is not a good reflection of car prices because it includes upgrading-the purchase of more expensive types of vehicles with more options-and downgrading.
(6) "Estimated Average New Car Price of Comparable Cars With New Safety and Emissions Equipment Added", divided by "Annual Median Family Earnings," multiplied by 52 weeks. This index is a good reflection of price as seen by car purchasers who would not otherwise buy safety/emissions equipment.
(7) "Estimated Average New Car Price of Comparable Cars Without New Safety and Emissions Equipment" divided by "Annual Median Family Earnings," multiplied by 52 weeks. This index is a good reflection of price as seen by purchasers who place full value on new safety/emissions equipment.

INDICES OF CONSUMER COSTS

Year	Consumer Price Index - All Urban Consumers (1982-84 = 100)							
	All Items	Housing	Medical Care	Public Transportation	Gasoline	New Cars	New Trucks	Used Cars & Trucks
2008	215.3	216.3	364.1	250.5	277.5	135.4	137.1	134.0
2007	207.3	209.6	351.0	230.0	238.0	135.9	140.7	135.7
2006	201.6	203.2	336.2	226.6	219.9	136.4	141.5	140.0
2005	195.3	195.7	323.2	217.3	194.7	135.2	144.4	139.4
2004	188.9	189.5	310.1	209.1	159.7	133.9	147.2	133.3
2003	184.0	184.8	297.1	209.3	135.1	134.7	146.4	142.9
2002	179.9	180.3	285.6	207.4	116.0	137.3	148.6	152.0
2001	177.1	176.4	272.8	210.6	124.0	138.9	152.0	158.7
2000	172.2	169.6	260.8	209.6	128.6	139.6	152.2	155.8
1999	166.6	163.9	250.6	197.7	100.1	139.6	153.1	152.0
1998	163.0	160.4	242.1	190.3	91.6	140.7	152.1	150.6
1997	160.5	156.8	234.6	186.7	105.8	141.7	151.4	151.1
1996	156.9	152.8	228.2	181.9	105.9	141.5	149.5	157.1
1995	152.4	148.5	220.5	175.9	99.8	139.0	145.9	156.5
1994	148.2	144.8	211.0	172.0	98.2	136.0	141.7	141.7
1993	144.5	141.2	201.4	167.0	97.7	131.5	135.7	133.9

NA: Not Available.
SOURCE: U.S. Department of Labor, Bureau of Labor Statistics.

Personal Consumption Expenditures for Transportation

PERSONAL CONSUMPTION EXPENDITURES FOR TRANSPORTATION (in Millions of Dollars)

	2008	2007	2006	2005	2004	2003	2002	2001
User-Operated Transportation								
New Autos	90,771	102,046	106,478	103,121	97,652	97,175	101,703	103,239
Net Purchases of Used Autos	51,425	56,471	57,856	57,190	54,299	54,848	60,355	59,652
Other Motor Vehicles*	174,625	219,087	209,042	225,093	230,528	227,648	216,911	195,889
Tires, Tubes, Accessories and Parts	62,774	62,838	60,619	57,742	54,364	52,038	50,295	49,105
Repair, Greasing, Washing, Parking, Storage, Rental and Leasing	235,711	224,184	212,711	198,567	189,488	286,818	185,952	189,066
Gasoline and Oil	383,451	340,574	313,788	283,593	231,440	192,701	164,525	171,642
Bridge, Tunnel, Ferry and Road Tolls	7,981	7,351	6,965	6,531	5,992	5,510	5,270	5,122
Insurance Premiums, Less Claims Paid	61,812	59,409	57,161	57,803	53,690	49,233	45,842	44,599
Total User-Operated Transportation	**1,068,550**	**1,071,960**	**1,024,620**	**989,640**	**917,453**	**965,971**	**830,853**	**818,314**
Purchased Local Transportation								
Transit Systems	13,348	11,875	11,443	10,679	10,166	9,519	9,000	9,242
Taxicabs	4,822	4,533	4,297	3,947	3,648	3,500	3,336	3,228
Total Purchased Local Transportation	**18,170**	**16,408**	**15,740**	**14,626**	**13,814**	**13,019**	**12,336**	**13,278**
Purchased Intercity Transportation								
Railway Excluding Commutation	784	715	639	578	568	563	573	559
Bus	35,899	2,010	2,170	5,175	2,254	2,322	2,353	2,366
Airline	35,899	36,675	35,918	34,370	33,256	31,216	28,319	31,377
Other	10,380	10,256	9,937	9,650	9,136	8,627	7,786	7,281
Total Purchased Intercity Transportation	**82,962**	**49,656**	**48,664**	**49,773**	**45,214**	**42,728**	**39,031**	**41,583**
Total Transportation Expenditures	**1,169,682**	**1,138,024**	**1,089,024**	**1,054,039**	**976,481**	**1,021,718**	**882,220**	**873,175**
Total Personal Consumption Expenditures	**10,058,506**	**9,710,167**	**9,207,208**	**8,694,112**	**8,195,862**	**7,703,630**	**7,350,721**	**7,055,038**

*New and used trucks, recreation vehicles, etc.
SOURCE: U.S. Department of Commerce, Bureau of Economic Analysis.

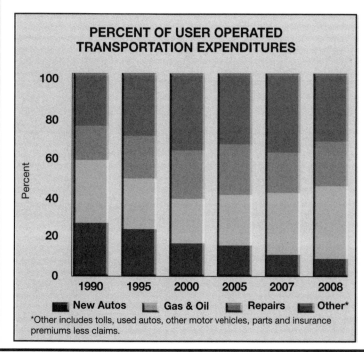

PERCENT OF USER OPERATED TRANSPORTATION EXPENDITURES

Legend: New Autos, Gas & Oil, Repairs, Other*

*Other includes tolls, used autos, other motor vehicles, parts and insurance premiums less claims.

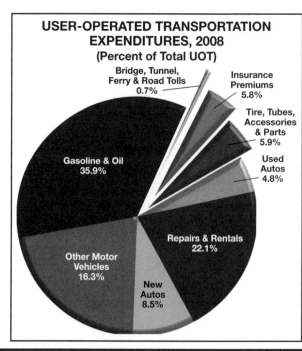

USER-OPERATED TRANSPORTATION EXPENDITURES, 2008
(Percent of Total UOT)

- Bridge, Tunnel, Ferry & Road Tolls 0.7%
- Insurance Premiums 5.8%
- Tire, Tubes, Accessories & Parts 5.9%
- Used Autos 4.8%
- Gasoline & Oil 35.9%
- Repairs & Rentals 22.1%
- Other Motor Vehicles 16.3%
- New Autos 8.5%

U.S. Vehicle Thefts by State, Area and Year

U.S. VEHICLE THEFTS BY STATE

State	2007	2006	Percent Change	State	2007	2006	Percent Change
Alabama	14,230	14,840	-4.11	Montana	1,755	1,748	0.40
Alaska	2,418	2,529	-4.39	Nebraska	5,201	5,038	3.24
Arizona	48,389	54,849	-11.78	Nevada	22,331	26,961	-17.17
Arkansas	7,010	7,463	-6.07	New Hampshire	1,299	1,422	-8.65
California	219,392	242,693	-9.60	New Jersey	21,953	24,724	-11.21
Colorado	16,792	20,795	-19.25	New Mexico	8,939	9,225	-3.10
Connecticut	9,167	10,390	-11.77	New York	28,030	32,134	-12.77
Delaware	2,316	2,816	-17.76	North Carolina	27,966	30,126	-7.17
Dist. of Columbia	7,600	7,321	3.81	North Dakota	914	1,012	-9.68
Florida	73,656	76,437	-3.64	Ohio	33,779	37,425	-9.74
Georgia	42,594	43,163	-1.32	Oklahoma	13,459	13,358	0.76
Hawaii	6,715	7,763	-13.50	Oregon	14,549	14,460	0.62
Idaho	2,226	2,429	-8.36	Pennsylvania	26,461	29,540	-10.42
Illinois	33,887	37,641	-9.97	Rhode Island	3,226	3,582	-9.94
Indiana	19,557	21,866	-10.56	South Carolina	17,026	16,402	3.80
Iowa	4,885	5,006	-2.42	South Dakota	735	718	2.37
Kansas	8,564	8,703	-1.60	Tennessee	21,658	22,593	-4.14
Kentucky	8,675	9,243	-6.15	Texas	93,899	95,429	-1.60
Louisiana	15,180	15,640	-2.94	Utah	8,812	8,299	6.18
Maine	1,259	1,340	-6.04	Vermont	641	586	9.39
Maryland	28,393	30,522	-6.98	Virginia	14,054	14,814	-5.13
Massachusetts	14,992	17,961	-16.53	Washington	37,622	45,899	-18.03
Michigan	42,151	50,017	-15.73	West Virginia	3,492	3,921	-10.94
Minnesota	12,526	13,379	-6.38	Wisconsin	13,433	14,031	-4.26
Mississippi	7,381	8,347	-11.57	Wyoming	796	776	2.58
Missouri	23,784	25,433	-6.48	**Total**	**1,095,769**	**1,192,809**	**-8.14**

SOURCE: Federal Bureau of Investigation.

U.S. VEHICLE THEFTS

Year	Thefts*	Vehicle Registrations	Ratio of Vehicles Stolen/Registered	Year	Thefts*	Vehicle Registrations	Ratio of Vehicles Stolen/Registered
2007	1,095,769	248,700,997	1 in 227	1994	1,539,287	188,713,997	1 in 123
2006	1,192,809	244,642,610	1 in 205	1993	1,563,060	186,315,464	1 in 119
2005	1,235,226	238,384,168	1 in 193				
2004	1,237,114	232,167,136	1 in 188				
2003	1,260,471	225,882,103	1 in 179				
2002	1,246,096	221,027,121	1 in 177				
2001	1,226,457	216,682,937	1 in 177				
2000	1,177,304	213,299,313	1 in 181				
1999	1,148,305	209,509,161	1 in 182				
1998	1,317,324	205,042,639	1 in 156				
1997	1,353,707	201,070,397	1 in 149				
1996	1,394,238	198,293,459	1 in 142				
1995	1,472,441	193,440,393	1 in 131				

* Includes cars, motorcycles, trucks and buses

U.S. TOP TEN VEHICLE THEFT AREAS

	2007	2006
1	Detroit, Michigan	Detroit, Michigan
2	Las Vegas, Nevada	Las Vegas, Nevada
3	Modesto, California	Oakland, California
4	San Francisco, California	Seattle, Washington
5	Phoenix, Arizona	Phoenix, Arizona
6	San Diego, California	Stockton, California
7	Salinas, California	Visalia, California
8	Seattle, Washington	San Francisco, California
9	Stockton, California	Yakima, Washington
10	Fresno, California	Modesto, California

SOURCE: Federal Bureau of Investigation

Vehicle Miles of Travel and Fuel Consumption

VEHICLE MILES OF TRAVEL AND FUEL CONSUMPTION

	Cars	Light Trucks	Light Vehicle Total	Medium Duty Trucks	Heavy Duty Trucks	Buses	Motorcycles	Total Vehicles
Vehicle Miles of Travel (in Millions)								
2007	1,670,994	1,111,277	2,782,271	81,954	145,008	6,976	13,612	3,029,821
2006	1,682,671	1,089,013	2,771,684	80,331	142,706	6,994	12,401	3,014,116
2005	1,708,421	1,041,051	2,749,472	79,174	144,028	6,980	10,454	2,990,108
2004	1,699,890	1,027,164	2,727,054	78,441	142,370	6,801	10,122	2,964,788
2003	1,672,079	984,094	2,656,173	77,757	140,160	6,783	9,577	2,890,450
2002	1,658,474	966,034	2,624,508	75,866	138,737	6,845	9,552	2,855,508
2001	1,628,332	943,207	2,571,539	72,448	136,584	7,077	9,639	2,797,287
2000	1,600,287	923,059	2,523,346	70,500	135,020	7,590	10,469	2,746,925
1999	1,569,100	901,022	2,470,122	70,304	132,384	7,662	10,584	2,691,056
1998	1,549,577	868,275	2,417,852	68,021	128,359	7,007	10,283	2,631,522
1996	1,469,854	816,540	2,286,394	64,072	118,899	6,563	9,920	2,485,848
1994	1,416,329	764,634	2,180,963	61,284	108,932	6,409	(1)	2,357,588
1990	1,417,823	574,571	1,992,394	51,901	94,341	5,726	(1)	2,144,362
Average Annual Miles Traveled Per Vehicle								
2007	12,293	12,040	11,720	12,040	65,290	8,360	1,907	11,910
2006	12,427	11,857	12,197	13,038	70,986	8,509	1,855	12,408
2005	12,510	10,920	11,856	12,274	69,020	8,649	1,679	12,082
2004	12,460	11,184	11,946	12,732	70,819	8,552	1,755	12,200
2003	12,325	11,287	11,919	13,295	73,445	8,734	1,783	12,208
2002	12,202	11,364	11,879	13,426	60,939	8,998	1,909	12,171
2001	11,831	11,204	11,593	12,702	63,404	9,442	1,966	11,887
2000	11,976	11,672	11,863	11,897	64,399	10,173	2,409	12,164
1998	11,754	12,173	11,901	11,861	64,265	9,793	2,651	12,211
1996	11,330	11,811	11,497	12,167	68,075	9,446	2,562	11,813
1994	10,759	12,156	11,205	12,491	64,783	9,560	(1)	11,683
1990	10,277	11,902	10,693	11,567	55,206	9,133	(1)	11,107
Fuel Consumed (Millions of Gallons)								
2007	74,355	61,816	136,171	10,036	28,515	1,144	242	176,108
2006	74,983	60,662	135,645	9,843	28,075	1,147	221	174,931
2005	77,418	58,869	136,287	9,501	27,689	1,120	189	174,786
2004	75,402	63,417	138,819	8,959	24,191	1,360	202	173,531
2003	75,455	60,758	136,213	8,880	23,815	969	192	170,069
2002	75,471	55,220	130,691	10,321	26,480	1,000	191	168,683
2001	73,559	53,522	127,081	9,667	25,512	1,026	193	163,479
2000	73,065	52,939	126,004	9,563	25,666	1,112	209	162,554
1998	71,695	50,462	122,157	6,817	25,157	1,040	206	155,379
1996	69,221	47,354	116,575	9,408	20,193	990	198	147,365
1994	68,079	44,112	112,191	9,032	18,653	964	(1)	140,839
1990	69,759	35,611	105,370	8,357	16,133	895	(1)	130,755
Average Annual Fuel Consumption Per Vehicle (Gallons)								
2007	547	609	574	1,474	12,839	1,371	34	692
2006	554	660	597	1,598	13,965	1,396	33	720
2005	567	617	588	1,486	13,269	1,388	30	706
2004	553	690	608	1,454	12,033	1,710	35	714
2003	556	697	611	1,518	12,479	1,248	36	718
2002	555	650	592	1,826	11,631	1,314	38	719
2001	534	636	573	1,695	11,843	1,369	39	695
2000	547	669	592	1,614	12,241	1,490	48	720
1998	544	707	601	1,189	12,596	1,454	53	721
1996	534	685	586	1,787	11,561	1,425	51	700
1994	517	701	580	1,841	11,093	1,438	(1)	698
1990	506	738	569	1,862	9,441	1,428	(1)	677

NA - Not available. (1) Cars include motorcycles through 1994.
SOURCE: U.S. Department of Transportation, Federal Highway Administration

Annual Vehicle Miles of Travel

VEHICLE MILES OF TRAVEL, 2007 (in Millions)

	Rural Interstate	Total Rural	Urban Interstate	Total Urban	Total
Alabama	5,933	29,793	7,577	31,617	61,410
Alaska	852	2,577	699	2,576	5,153
Arizona	7,344	19,586	6,082	43,377	62,963
Arkansas	4,692	20,082	3,879	13,089	33,171
California	18,879	60,771	70,332	267,541	328,312
Colorado	4,596	15,650	7,334	33,063	48,713
Connecticut	710	3,994	9,699	28,059	32,053
Delaware	—	2,809	1,289	6,674	9,483
Dist. of Columbia	—	—	409	3,609	3,609
Florida	10,169	38,044	25,882	168,077	206,121
Georgia	10,277	41,396	20,095	71,145	112,541
Hawaii	111	2,487	1,903	7,858	10,345
Idaho	2,260	9,519	1,323	6,263	15,782
Illinois	9,319	28,166	21,691	79,317	107,483
Indiana	7,244	34,657	9,705	36,821	71,478
Iowa	4,848	18,852	2,581	12,401	31,253
Kansas	3,247	14,297	3,727	15,751	30,048
Kentucky	6,806	27,673	6,287	20,390	48,063
Louisiana	5,464	19,500	7,396	25,876	45,376
Maine	2,289	10,848	847	4,187	15,035
Maryland	3,564	14,589	13,451	41,914	56,503
Massachusetts	1,271	4,223	15,092	50,848	55,071
Michigan	5,649	32,075	16,418	72,539	104,614
Minnesota	4,756	27,154	7,998	30,079	57,233
Mississippi	4,223	26,702	3,488	16,635	43,337
Missouri	6,209	28,002	12,365	41,149	69,151
Montana	2,535	8,634	370	2,673	11,307
Nebraska	2,777	11,265	1,400	8,174	19,439
Nevada	2,024	5,527	3,617	16,619	22,146
New Hampshire	1,267	5,919	1,597	7,540	13,459
New Jersey	1,590	6,907	14,356	69,245	76,152
New Mexico	4,619	15,558	2,658	11,292	26,850
New York	6,333	33,766	20,664	102,971	136,737
North Carolina	6,487	38,471	14,528	65,127	103,598
North Dakota	1,447	5,627	384	2,217	7,844
Ohio	9,377	36,625	23,306	74,006	110,631
Oklahoma	5,031	22,928	4,663	24,644	47,572
Oregon	4,381	15,247	4,575	19,503	34,750
Pennsylvania	10,825	39,034	14,974	69,665	108,699
Rhode Island	427	924	1,969	7,712	8,636
South Carolina	7,694	25,339	6,176	25,770	51,109
South Dakota	1,958	6,416	606	2,589	9,005
Tennessee	9,094	29,101	11,442	42,078	71,179
Texas	18,398	85,966	37,132	157,477	243,443
Utah	3,360	8,084	6,133	18,748	26,832
Vermont	1,266	5,731	375	1,963	7,694
Virginia	9,076	30,894	15,263	51,183	82,077
Washington	4,622	16,725	10,940	40,214	56,939
West Virginia	3,202	12,158	2,835	8,406	20,564
Wisconsin	5,395	28,195	5,348	31,298	59,493
Wyoming	2,541	6,816	455	2,550	9,366
U.S. Total	**256,438**	**1,035,303**	**483,315**	**1,994,519**	**3,029,822**

NOTE: Includes travel by motorcycle.
SOURCE: U.S. Department of Transportation, Federal Highway Administration.

TOTAL VEHICLE MILES TRAVELED (in Billions)

Year	Rural	Urban	Total	% Change
2007	1,035	1,995	3,030	0.5
2006	1,037	1,977	3,014	0.8
2005	1,038	1,952	2,990	0.9
2004	1,070	1,892	2,962	2.5
2003	1,085	1,806	2,891	1.2
2002	1,128	1,728	2,856	2.7
2001	1,105	1,676	2,781	1.1
2000	1,085	1,665	2,750	2.2
1999	1,063	1,628	2,691	2.5
1998	1,033	1,592	2,625	3.7
1997	985	1,547	2,532	2.0
1996	960	1,522	2,482	2.5
1995	933	1,489	2,422	2.7
1994	909	1,449	2,358	2.7
1993	887	1,410	2,297	2.2
1992	884	1,363	2,247	3.4
1991	884	1,289	2,173	1.2
1990	870	1,277	2,147	1.9
1989	849	1,258	2,107	4.0
1988	818	1,208	2,026	5.5
1987	780	1,141	1,921	4.7
1986	748	1,087	1,835	3.4
1985	730	1,044	1,774	3.1
1984	718	1,002	1,720	4.1
1983	701	952	1,653	3.6
1982	689	906	1,595	2.7
1981	686	867	1,553	1.7
1980	672	855	1,527	-0.2
1979	676	854	1,530	-0.9
1978	682	862	1,544	5.2
1977	651	816	1,467	4.6
1976	625	777	1,402	5.6
1975	602	726	1,328	3.8
1974	585	695	1,280	-2.5
1973	606	707	1,313	4.2
1972	590	670	1,260	6.9
1971	573	606	1,179	6.3
1970	539	570	1,109	4.5
1969	524	537	1,061	4.4
1968	506	510	1,016	5.4
1967	481	483	964	4.1
1966	476	450	926	4.3
1965	464	424	888	5.0
1964	441	405	846	5.1
1963	420	385	805	5.0
1962	399	368	767	3.9
1961	398	340	738	2.6
1960	387	332	719	2.6
1959	377	324	701	5.4
1958	358	307	665	2.8
1957	350	297	647	2.5
1956	344	287	631	4.1
1955	331	275	606	7.8
1954	314	248	562	3.3
1953	308	236	544	6.0
1952	289	224	513	4.5
1951	268	223	491	7.2
1950	240	218	458	8.0
1949	219	205	424	6.5
1948	199	199	398	7.3

SOURCE: U.S. Department of Transportation, Federal Highway Administration.

Selected Travel Data by State

TRAVEL DATA BY STATE, 2007

State	Resident Population in Thousands	Population Per Vehicle	Annual Miles Traveled Per Vehicle	Annual Miles Traveled Per Licensed Driver	Public Road and Street Mileage Rural	Public Road and Street Mileage Urban	Public Road and Street Mileage Total	State Gasoline Tax Rate
Alabama	4,627	0.99	13,128	16,634	75,299	22,024	97,323	18.0
Alaska	681	1.00	7,576	10,405	12,081	2,357	14,438	8.0
Arizona	6,353	1.45	14,401	15,158	37,675	22,918	60,593	18.0
Arkansas	2,831	1.41	16,501	16,212	87,592	11,966	99,558	21.5
California	36,378	1.07	9,675	13,990	83,445	87,709	171,154	18.0
Colorado	4,843	0.92	9,297	13,907	68,934	19,229	88,163	22.0
Connecticut	3,490	1.15	10,518	11,252	6,187	15,108	21,295	25.0
Delaware	862	1.01	11,140	15,186	3,279	2,963	6,242	23.0
District of Columbia	588	2.70	16,592	9,109	--	1,505	1,505	20.0
Florida	18,200	1.10	12,512	14,578	40,256	81,270	121,526	15.3
Georgia	9,523	1.12	13,221	18,346	81,096	37,683	118,779	7.5
Hawaii	1,277	1.29	10,417	11,989	2,041	2,300	4,341	17.0
Idaho	1,496	1.17	12,311	15,360	42,810	5,606	48,416	25.0
Illinois	12,826	1.31	11,016	13,124	98,205	40,952	139,157	19.0
Indiana	6,336	1.24	13,964	16,589	73,320	22,149	95,469	18.0
Iowa	2,983	0.89	9,301	14,928	102,905	11,288	114,193	21.0
Kansas	2,777	1.14	12,370	14,888	127,612	12,659	140,271	24.0
Kentucky	4,236	1.19	13,552	16,385	66,108	12,479	78,587	21.0
Louisiana	4,373	1.11	11,556	14,956	44,731	16,277	61,008	20.0
Maine	1,315	1.22	13,923	14,889	19,805	2,987	22,792	27.6
Maryland	5,619	1.25	12,527	15,116	14,024	17,276	31,300	23.5
Massachusetts	6,468	1.21	10,262	11,719	7,967	28,041	36,008	21.0
Michigan	10,050	1.19	12,393	14,820	85,837	35,756	121,593	19.0
Minnesota	5,182	1.09	12,034	18,174	119,310	18,383	137,693	20.0
Mississippi	2,921	1.45	21,584	22,490	63,843	10,779	74,622	18.4
Missouri	5,878	1.20	14,064	16,615	106,412	22,710	129,122	17.0
Montana	957	1.01	11,921	15,368	70,220	2,983	73,203	27.8
Nebraska	1,769	1.02	11,178	14,608	87,176	6,222	93,398	27.0
Nevada	2,554	1.79	15,548	13,328	26,794	7,078	33,872	24.0
New Hampshire	1,312	1.11	11,359	13,111	11,017	4,822	15,839	19.6
New Jersey	8,653	1.39	12,190	13,170	7,297	31,455	38,752	10.5
New Mexico	1,964	1.23	16,788	19,667	60,351	7,988	68,339	18.9
New York	19,429	1.69	11,896	12,027	65,874	47,866	113,740	24.7
North Carolina	9,042	1.43	16,399	16,229	71,306	33,106	104,412	30.0
North Dakota	638	0.90	11,040	16,663	84,945	1,897	86,842	23.0
Ohio	11,478	1.06	10,198	13,871	80,478	44,682	125,160	28.0
Oklahoma	3,608	1.12	14,753	20,836	97,289	15,633	112,922	17.0
Oregon	3,736	1.21	11,252	12,291	46,975	12,783	59,758	24.0
Pennsylvania	12,420	1.25	10,938	12,638	76,451	45,130	121,581	31.2
Rhode Island	1,053	1.32	10,840	11,611	1,270	5,240	6,510	30.0
South Carolina	4,405	1.25	14,515	16,345	49,826	16,422	66,248	16.0
South Dakota	796	0.92	10,412	15,300	80,866	2,878	83,744	22.0
Tennessee	6,149	1.15	13,330	16,082	69,345	21,713	91,058	20.0
Texas	23,843	1.32	13,471	16,033	221,661	84,194	305,855	20.0
Utah	2,669	1.15	11,565	16,244	32,672	11,549	44,221	24.5
Vermont	621	1.10	13,618	14,395	12,979	1,421	14,400	20.0
Virginia	7,699	1.16	12,410	15,605	50,350	22,312	72,662	17.5
Washington	6,450	1.12	9,889	11,669	60,880	22,551	83,431	36.0
West Virginia	1,810	1.28	14,549	15,137	32,995	5,279	38,274	31.5
Wisconsin	5,599	1.12	11,856	14,631	92,557	22,148	114,705	30.9
Wyoming	523	0.80	14,363	23,516	25,410	2,642	28,052	14.0
Total	**301,290**	**1.20**	**12,061**	**14,726**	**2,987,758**	**1,044,368**	**4,032,126**	**19.3**

SOURCE: U.S. Department of Commerce, Bureau of the Census, and U.S. Department of Transportation.

State Highway Agency
Capital Outlay and Maintenance

STATE HIGHWAY AGENCY CAPITAL OUTLAY AND MAINTENANCE (in Thousands of Dollars)

	Capital Outlay		Maintenance		Total		'07 vs. '06 Percent Change
	2007	2006	2007	2006	2007	2006	
Alabama	1,110,432	1,087,402	178,679	159,233	1,289,111	1,246,635	3.4
Alaska	369,286	343,155	62,492	40,153	431,778	383,308	12.6
Arizona	836,037	1,003,424	103,342	94,730	939,379	1,098,154	-14.5
Arkansas	596,014	623,516	234,360	148,829	830,374	772,345	7.5
California	5,064,561	3,826,989	365,577	364,299	5,430,138	4,191,288	29.6
Colorado	640,569	563,760	149,639	227,213	790,208	790,973	-0.1
Connecticut	498,891	527,013	141,462	130,158	640,353	657,171	-2.6
Delaware	276,511	391,715	66,236	73,705	342,747	465,420	-26.4
District of Columbia	215,228	207,600	20,360	39,819	235,588	247,419	-4.8
Florida	5,330,414	4,737,573	755,980	953,406	6,086,394	5,690,979	6.9
Georgia	2,145,198	1,711,890	151,825	164,881	2,297,023	1,876,771	22.4
Hawaii	185,718	154,993	21,676	17,834	207,394	172,827	20.0
Idaho	430,812	369,780	79,888	53,572	510,700	423,352	20.6
Illinois	3,140,057	2,959,877	372,302	335,313	3,512,359	3,295,190	6.6
Indiana	1,362,634	813,924	56,687	388,410	1,419,321	1,202,334	18.0
Iowa	566,937	531,763	78,507	81,539	645,444	613,302	5.2
Kansas	812,656	906,178	130,775	138,373	943,431	1,044,551	-9.7
Kentucky	1,486,302	1,077,890	299,003	280,901	1,785,305	1,358,791	31.4
Louisiana	1,369,067	1,249,852	224,774	226,820	1,593,841	1,476,672	7.9
Maine	277,672	327,081	108,366	117,000	386,038	444,081	-13.1
Maryland	1,273,780	1,171,434	122,271	102,198	1,396,051	1,273,632	9.6
Massachusetts	978,593	1,073,516	57,034	67,247	1,035,627	1,140,763	-9.2
Michigan	2,450,820	2,397,215	201,246	216,794	2,652,066	2,614,009	1.5
Minnesota	806,633	866,704	279,950	299,530	1,086,583	1,166,234	-6.8
Mississippi	1,220,937	933,102	76,800	68,439	1,297,737	1,001,541	29.6
Missouri	1,469,208	1,342,114	353,613	351,724	1,822,821	1,693,838	7.6
Montana	315,063	332,548	59,241	73,414	374,304	405,962	-7.8
Nebraska	623,529	414,480	310,738	76,300	934,267	490,780	90.4
Nevada	649,736	579,372	91,317	87,943	741,053	667,315	11.0
New Hampshire	252,192	269,047	128,597	2,966	380,789	272,013	40.0
New Jersey	1,905,421	1,740,220	175,072	129,216	2,080,493	1,869,436	11.3
New Mexico	382,692	382,692	96,518	96,518	479,210	479,210	0.0
New York	3,188,416	2,967,829	696,406	623,940	3,884,822	3,591,769	8.2
North Carolina	1,743,043	1,846,784	775,086	637,870	2,518,129	2,484,654	1.3
North Dakota	317,052	363,269	12,318	22,257	329,370	385,526	-14.6
Ohio	2,077,489	1,967,657	168,467	172,005	2,245,956	2,139,662	5.0
Oklahoma	688,299	709,730	158,025	157,413	846,324	867,143	-2.4
Oregon	821,088	679,213	238,556	222,137	1,059,644	901,350	17.6
Pennsylvania	2,553,171	2,272,207	1,235,501	1,023,552	3,788,672	3,295,759	15.0
Rhode Island	266,352	253,158	60,966	68,244	327,318	321,402	1.8
South Carolina	602,211	794,309	378,219	369,264	980,430	1,163,573	-15.7
South Dakota	262,908	353,107	32,502	31,109	295,410	384,216	-23.1
Tennessee	984,710	951,575	252,033	236,346	1,236,743	1,187,921	4.1
Texas	9,645,909	5,822,909	1,311,537	1,749,878	10,957,446	7,572,787	44.7
Utah	745,153	563,568	90,588	76,640	835,741	640,208	30.5
Vermont	184,514	152,917	50,392	48,788	234,906	201,705	16.5
Virginia	1,077,432	965,835	819,790	888,784	1,897,222	1,854,619	2.3
Washington	1,464,654	1,250,710	266,375	287,587	1,731,029	1,538,297	12.5
West Virginia	644,353	700,175	171,223	167,542	815,576	867,717	-6.0
Wisconsin	1,183,003	1,227,052	62,531	86,422	1,245,534	1,313,474	-5.2
Wyoming	273,247	230,982	87,551	80,034	360,798	311,016	16.0
Total	**67,766,604**	**58,990,805**	**12,422,393**	**12,558,289**	**80,188,997**	**71,549,094**	**12.1**

SOURCE: U.S. Department of Transportation, Federal Highway Administration.

Vehicle and Equipment Manufacturing Employment by State

VEHICLE AND EQUIPMENT MANUFACTURING EMPLOYMENT BY STATE, 2006

State	Vehicle Manufacturing	Vehicle Body & Trailer	Engine & Engine Parts	Electrical Components	Transmission, Brake & Suspension Parts	Other Vehicle Parts Manufacturing
Alabama	12,113	4,614	882	2,228	4,139	7,400
Alaska	—	12	—	—	—	—
Arizona	30	1,255	125	35	455	1,500
Arkansas	1,600	2,293	1,658	325	740	2,895
California	6,877	10,995	3,774	2,948	2,675	13,151
Colorado	120	945	125	40	48	825
Connecticut	—	50	275	625	852	782
Delaware	1,400	10	8	—	155	310
District of Columbia	—	—	—	—	—	—
Florida	275	4,532	808	885	597	1,934
Georgia	5,959	4,590	1,357	826	2,166	4,573
Hawaii	—	12	—	8	11	22
Idaho	60	1,450	8	12	15	50
Illinois	6,264	3,200	1,617	6,429	5,328	9,809
Indiana	14,180	39,561	8,813	12,095	28,383	17,846
Iowa	47	8,506	1,080	1,036	1,477	2,663
Kansas	2,000	2,608	222	1,030	207	1,468
Kentucky	18,025	2,045	1,247	2,638	8,946	13,814
Louisiana	7,200	300	25	650	110	694
Maine	—	150	11	45	340	50
Maryland	10	650	37	700	368	277
Massachusetts	43	526	275	625	65	160
Michigan	39,946	2,402	18,910	5,922	28,965	40,428
Minnesota	2,326	2,903	125	432	525	716
Mississippi	3,750	838	50	2,559	851	2,785
Missouri	1,720	2,354	650	650	4,944	6,165
Montana	—	316	45	12	8	55
Nebraska	8	1,970	625	150	1,091	1,660
Nevada	—	72	175	200	70	160
New Hampshire	10	135	8	650	47	710
New Jersey	40	432	344	165	198	324
New Mexico	32	300	9	60	9	55
New York	740	1,195	5,709	3,814	4,432	5,806
North Carolina	4,999	4,156	1,695	1,371	7,271	7,911
North Dakota	500	471	10	700	—	85
Ohio	26,844	4,936	8,459	9,668	24,176	23,871
Oklahoma	11,587	3,635	411	561	1,910	959
Oregon	2,750	5,467	45	437	380	2,322
Pennsylvania	1,100	8,135	340	4,222	4,729	1,920
Rhode Island	—	150	7	9	—	175
South Carolina	7,000	1,100	2,562	725	4,974	4,194
South Dakota	145	1,671	150	7	85	454
Tennessee	12,772	2,281	4,766	3,695	8,208	18,384
Texas	6,500	9,187	1,495	3,016	845	6,320
Utah	40	1,090	60	10	278	3,745
Vermont	—	45	10	685	—	10
Virginia	3,175	1,997	1,833	655	2,493	2,092
Washington	1,400	1,518	340	725	68	1,525
West Virginia	—	315	625	325	45	—
Wisconsin	6,250	5,763	4,124	2,642	1,369	5,925
Wyoming	10	350	50	50	9	35
Total	**211,162**	**155,649**	**76,649**	**77,631**	**156,928**	**219,342**

NOTE: In some cases, an average was taken based on the Bureau of the Census employment range.
Omission of data for individual states is due to either the absences of such business from the state or the necessity of withholding the data to avoid discosure of individual firms data.
SOURCE: U.S. Department of Commerce, Bureau of the Census.

Vehicle and Equipment Manufacturing Employment by State

VEHICLE AND EQUIPMENT MANUFACTURING EMPLOYMENT BY STATE, 2006 — continued

State	Vehicle Metal Stamping	Tire Manufacturing	Storage Batteries	Total Vehicle & Equipment Manufacturing	Total State Manufacturing Employment	Vehicle and Equipment % of Total State Manufacturing Employment
Alabama	3,178	6,200	20	40,774	291,239	14.0
Alaska	—	10	—	22	10,221	0.2
Arizona	150	150	265	3,965	179,122	2.2
Arkansas	10	1,250	270	11,041	200,622	5.5
California	1,653	1,304	1,005	44,382	1,449,769	3.1
Colorado	30	125	319	2,577	134,598	1.9
Connecticut	462	35	120	3,201	182,138	1.8
Delaware	—	10	110	2,003	33,155	6.0
District of Columbia	—	—	—	—	1,718	—
Florida	647	498	110	10,286	372,151	2.8
Georgia	1,252	2,896	1,050	24,669	430,697	5.7
Hawaii	—	8	—	61	15,211	0.4
Idaho	—	10	—	1,605	64,212	2.5
Illinois	5,360	3,653	265	41,925	666,711	6.3
Indiana	11,003	2,087	270	134,238	557,359	24.1
Iowa	1,250	2,537	571	19,167	227,492	8.4
Kansas	—	1,500	1,005	10,040	176,444	5.7
Kentucky	4,820	300	525	52,360	256,670	20.4
Louisiana	—	200	105	9,284	141,459	6.6
Maine	—	300	—	896	59,322	1.5
Maryland	325	25	100	2,492	131,108	1.9
Massachusetts	276	20	8	1,998	275,180	0.7
Michigan	41,482	243	110	178,408	614,888	29.0
Minnesota	1,500	150	35	8,712	336,776	2.6
Mississippi	350	1,800	—	12,983	172,656	7.5
Missouri	641	554	1,000	18,678	305,447	6.1
Montana	—	35	—	471	19,878	2.4
Nebraska	125	145	—	5,774	105,419	5.5
Nevada	—	10	8	695	46,747	1.5
New Hampshire	45	35	—	1,640	76,358	2.1
New Jersey	50	236	510	2,299	297,021	0.8
New Mexico	10	10	—	485	35,250	1.4
New York	1,659	1,464	265	25,084	551,471	4.5
North Carolina	271	7,030	1,100	35,804	535,689	6.7
North Dakota	—	10	—	1,776	25,584	6.9
Ohio	24,268	3,138	1,055	126,415	787,946	16.0
Oklahoma	144	5,826	—	25,033	142,148	17.6
Oregon	175	300	300	12,176	188,896	6.4
Pennsylvania	1,174	1,857	6,100	29,577	663,812	4.5
Rhode Island	—	—	10	351	54,061	0.6
South Carolina	2,049	4,713	—	27,317	263,605	10.4
South Dakota	10	10	—	2,532	42,215	6.0
Tennessee	2,981	6,026	275	59,388	393,385	15.1
Texas	600	1,862	300	30,125	846,465	3.6
Utah	45	30	—	5,298	118,492	4.5
Vermont	300	10	10	1,070	36,964	2.9
Virginia	10	3,461	10	15,726	289,176	5.4
Washington	50	35	45	5,706	257,611	2.2
West Virginia	600	30	—	1,940	63,382	3.1
Wisconsin	1,539	62	325	27,999	492,822	5.7
Wyoming	—	10	—	514	10,474	4.9
Total	**110,578**	**62,478**	**18,213**	**1,088,630**	**13,631,236**	**8.0**

NOTE: In some cases, an average was taken based on the Bureau of the Census employment range.
Omission of data for individual states is due to either the absences of such business from the state or the necessity of withholding the data to avoid discosure of individual firms data.
SOURCE: U.S. Department of Commerce, Bureau of the Census.

U.S. Vehicle and Related Industries Employment

U.S. EMPLOYMENT IN VEHICLE AND RELATED INDUSTRIES, 2006

Industry	Companies	Employees	Payrolls $ (000)
Motor Vehicle and Equipment Manufacturing			
Light vehicle manufacturing	275	179,040	12,736,623
Heavy truck manufacturing	95	32,122	1,542,456
Motor vehicle body & trailers	2,157	155,649	5,589,965
Motor vehicle engine and engine parts	992	76,649	4,050,387
Motor vehicle electrical & electrical equipment	799	77,631	3,452,326
Motor vehicle suspension, brake and powertrains	1,033	156,928	8,063,171
Motor vehicle seating and Interior trim	421	52,842	2,140,871
Other motor vehicle parts manufacturing	1,530	166,500	6,549,110
Motor vehicle metal stamping	781	110,578	5,386,895
Tires and Inner Tubes	663	62,478	3,062,626
Storage Batteries	125	18,213	829,193
Subtotal	**8,871**	**1,088,630**	**53,403,623**
Motor Freight Transportation and Related Services			
Trucking and courier services (1)	134,053	2,103,696	78,919,152
Road transportation support activities	1,756	21,039	609,166
Arrangement of transportation of freight & cargo	17,434	198,326	9,451,962
Misc. services incidental to transportation	1,637	31,227	1,264,945
Subtotal	**154,880**	**2,354,288**	**90,245,225**
Petroleum Refining and Wholesale Distribution			
Petroleum Refining	352	62,636	5,925,159
Asphalt paving mixtures and blocks	1,431	14,471	794,289
Lubricating oils and greases	350	10,542	612,342
Petroleum bulk stations and terminals	4,342	67,487	3,556,879
Petroleum and petroleum products wholesalers, except bulk stations and terminals	2,833	35,266	2,258,384
Subtotal	**9,308**	**190,402**	**13,147,053**
Passenger Transportation			
Local and suburban transportation	4,208	110,333	3,031,649
Taxi & Limousine service	7,013	69,226	1,542,694
Intercity and rural bus transportation	475	16,465	464,663
Bus charter service	1,207	27,929	647,760
School and Employee bus transportation	4,321	194,765	3,392,839
Arrangement of passenger transportation	23,268	253,539	10,749,023
Passenger car rental	6,683	120,313	3,679,498
Passenger car leasing	667	8,791	414,248
Truck, utility trailer and RV rental	6,274	55,364	2,162,232
Automobile parking	12,321	111,841	1,944,535
Recreational vehicle parks and campsites	7,190	38,308	1,048,569
Subtotal	**73,627**	**1,006,874**	**29,077,710**
Automotive Sales and Servicing			
Retail automotive dealers-New	25,964	1,158,275	51,322,647
Retail automotive dealers-Used	26,208	128,513	4,191,625
Auto parts, accessories and tire stores	59,439	493,354	13,521,633
Gasoline service stations (2)	116,855	913,467	15,025,898
Recreational vehicle dealers	3,054	43,508	1,662,495
Wholesale trade in motor vehicles	24,521	367,505	15,988,666
Automotive repair and maintenance	164,334	888,301	24,645,141
Motor Vehicle Towing	7,789	50,792	1,524,066
Subtotal	**428,164**	**4,043,715**	**127,882,171**
Total of Motor Vehicle and Related Industries	**674,850**	**8,683,909**	**313,755,782**
U.S. Total	**7,601,160**	**119,917,165**	**4,792,429,911**
Motor Vehicle Percent of U.S. Total	**8.9%**	**7.2%**	**6.5%**

(1) Except by air or by the U.S. Postal Service. (2) Includes truck stops and stations with and without convenience stores.
SOURCE: U.S. Department of Commerce, Bureau of the Census.

New Car Dealerships

FRANCHISED NEW CAR DEALERSHIPS BY STATE, 2008

State	Dealer-ships[1]	Sales (Millions)	Paid Employees	Payrolls (Millions)	State	Dealer-ships[1]	Sales (Millions)	Paid Employees	Payrolls (Millions)
Alabama	343	8,288	15,422	709	Montana	129	2,138	4,923	169
Alaska	35	1,258	2,587	123	Nebraska	207	3,472	6,986	296
Arizona	253	13,896	25,775	1,376	Nevada	116	5,008	9,042	565
Arkansas	257	5,039	9,049	368	New Hampshire	163	3,662	6,652	346
California	1,492	62,032	108,059	6,591	New Jersey	548	21,999	33,330	1,900
Colorado	280	9,661	17,172	905	New Mexico	137	3,544	7,434	330
Connecticut	302	7,462	13,722	786	New York	1,058	31,842	54,226	2,680
Delaware	62	1,685	3,343	186	North Carolina	656	16,410	30,182	1,504
Dist. of Columbia	1	70	32	2	North Dakota	95	1,671	3,845	137
Florida	923	35,876	58,852	3,501	Ohio	901	20,131	39,141	1,798
Georgia	576	16,374	29,483	1,574	Oklahoma	285	15,964	18,500	815
Hawaii	64	2,092	4,062	234	Oregon	264	6,084	12,314	629
Idaho	121	2,390	4,989	237	Pennsylvania	1,097	24,521	50,072	2,182
Illinois	903	22,771	40,664	2,138	Rhode Island	60	1,705	3,096	157
Indiana	503	10,640	19,864	942	South Carolina	318	7,429	14,118	671
Iowa	358	5,844	12,744	508	South Dakota	114	1,626	3,462	144
Kansas	256	5,134	10,275	449	Tennessee	410	11,318	21,364	1,070
Kentucky	291	5,946	12,786	542	Texas	1,312	53,782	94,351	4,703
Louisiana	332	8,863	18,190	771	Utah	152	4,866	9,675	426
Maine	142	2,532	5,320	231	Vermont	91	1,345	2,769	121
Maryland	342	10,628	21,023	1,149	Virginia	537	14,723	29,893	1,491
Massachusetts	459	12,872	22,958	1,220	Washington	371	11,039	22,101	1,138
Michigan	745	21,488	34,434	1,841	West Virginia	170	2,985	6,457	231
Minnesota	412	9,974	18,686	866	Wisconsin	574	9,458	19,672	849
Mississippi	232	4,301	8,691	376	Wyoming	70	1,268	2,825	107
Missouri	480	10,892	20,584	995	**Total**	**19,999**	**575,997**	**1,045,198**	**53,079**

(1) The number of establishments are NADA estimates as of Jan. 1, 2009.
SOURCE: National Automobile Dealers Assn.

DEALER SERVICE AND PARTS SALES

Year	$ Billions	% Change
2008	81.84	-1.8
2007	83.35	3.5
2006	80.45	-5.5
2005	85.16	-0.4
2004	85.48	0.2
2003	85.35	2.7
2002	83.11	3.8
2001	80.10	8.5
2000	73.83	9.1
1999	67.66	6.5
1998	63.56	1.7

SOURCE: National Automobile Dealers Assn.

DEALER SERVICE AND PARTS SALES BY TYPE
(Billions of Dollars)

Service Labor Sales	2008	% Chg. '08 vs. '07	2007
Customer Mechanical	$18.10	4.9	$17.25
Customer Body	4.26	-32.7	6.33
Warranty	5.58	-5.3	5.89
Sublet	2.52	-0.8	2.54
Internal	5.40	5.1	5.14
Other	0.45	—	0.45
Total Service Labor	**36.31**	**-3.4**	**37.60**

Parts Sales	2008	% Chg. '08 vs. '07	2007
Customer Mechanical	12.96	-1.1	13.10
Customer Body	3.07	-3.5	3.18
Wholesale	13.67	7.5	12.72
Counter	2.34	-7.5	2.53
Warranty	7.03	-8.6	7.69
Internal	3.67	-11.4	4.14
Other	2.79	16.3	2.40
Total Parts	**45.53**	**-0.5**	**45.76**

SOURCE: National Automobile Dealers Association.

SHARE OF TOTAL DEALERSHIP SALES DOLLARS BY DEPARTMENT, 2008

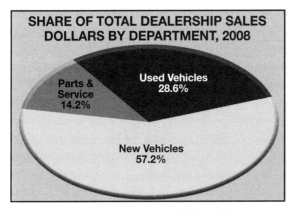

- Used Vehicles 28.6%
- Parts & Service 14.2%
- New Vehicles 57.2%

PROFILE OF FRANCHISED DEALER SERVICE AND PARTS OPERATIONS, 2008

	Average Dealership	All Dealers
Total service and parts sales	$4,092,205	$81.84 Billion
Total gross profit as percent of service and parts sales	45.9%	—
Total net profit as percent of service and parts sales	8.4%	—
Total number of repair orders written	13,191	264 Million
Total service and parts sales per customer repair order	$219	—
Total service and parts sales per warranty repair order	$242	—
Number of technicians	12	246,648
Number of service bays (excluding body)	18	357,779
Total parts inventory	$317,646	$6.60
Average customer mechanical labor rate	$88	—

SOURCE: National Automobile Dealers Assn.

Personal Income of Vehicle and Equipment Manufacturing Employees by State

PERSONAL INCOME OF VEHICLE AND EQUIPMENT MANUFACTURING EMPLOYEES

| State | Personal Income (in Millions of Dollars) | | | | 2007 Vehicle & Equipment Percent of Total Manufacturing | 2006 Vehicle & Equipment Percent of Total Manufacturing |
| | Vehicle and Equipment Manufacturing Employees | | All Manufacturing Employees | | | |
	2007	2006	2007	2006		
Alabama	2,525	2,619	18,251	18,222	13.8%	14.4%
Alaska	—	—	827	800	—	—
Arizona	—	—	14,441	14,746	—	—
Arkansas	471	—	9,394	9,455	5.0%	—
California	2,477	2,619	133,810	131,718	1.9%	2.0%
Colorado	—	124	11,654	11,593	—	1.1%
Connecticut	—	—	19,337	18,989	—	—
Delaware	—	—	3,114	2,806	—	—
District of Columbia	—	—	182	192	—	—
Florida	833	843	26,412	26,474	3.2%	3.2%
Georgia	—	1,562	27,490	27,707	—	5.6%
Hawaii	—	2	1,003	978	—	—
Idaho	—	—	4,361	4,175	—	—
Illinois	2,997	2,915	53,124	51,759	5.6%	5.6%
Indiana	9,558	9,835	39,948	40,376	23.9%	24.4%
Iowa	—	—	14,442	14,120	—	—
Kansas	—	—	13,461	13,250	—	—
Kentucky	4,056	4,104	16,620	16,666	24.4%	24.6%
Louisiana	—	—	12,010	11,333	—	—
Maine	29	31	3,807	3,829	0.7%	0.8%
Maryland	—	—	11,145	10,668	—	—
Massachusetts	—	—	27,541	26,242	—	—
Michigan	21,206	22,141	54,118	54,833	39.2%	40.4%
Minnesota	533	438	24,601	23,858	2.2%	1.8%
Mississippi	—	—	8,562	8,582	—	—
Missouri	2,473	2,643	19,825	19,893	12.5%	13.3%
Montana	22	21	1,288	1,209	1.7%	1.7%
Nebraska	—	—	5,478	5,390	—	—
Nevada	—	—	3,420	3,259	—	—
New Hampshire	30	38	6,235	6,028	0.5%	0.6%
New Jersey	—	—	32,530	31,523	—	—
New Mexico	—	—	2,658	2,468	—	—
New York	2,103	2,318	46,202	44,918	4.6%	5.2%
North Carolina	1,777	1,897	35,101	34,597	5.1%	5.5%
North Dakota	—	—	1,535	1,490	—	—
Ohio	9,778	10,700	55,366	55,876	17.7%	19.2%
Oklahoma	524	645	14,552	12,943	3.6%	5.0%
Oregon	584	624	14,440	14,050	4.0%	4.4%
Pennsylvania	1,254	1,364	48,706	47,948	2.6%	2.8%
Rhode Island	12	—	3,362	3,327	0.4%	—
South Carolina	—	—	15,735	15,542	—	—
South Dakota	—	—	2,244	2,154	—	—
Tennessee	—	4,064	25,444	25,739	—	15.8%
Texas	2,744	2,690	92,757	87,250	3.0%	3.1%
Utah	—	—	7,986	7,555	—	—
Vermont	—	—	2,449	2,392	—	—
Virginia	—	—	17,995	17,977	—	—
Washington	—	—	24,327	23,935	—	—
West Virginia	—	190	3,925	4,005	—	4.7%
Wisconsin	—	—	32,264	32,017	—	—
Wyoming	—	—	737	707	—	—
Total	**81,907**	**86,198**	**1,066,218**	**1,047,560**	**7.7%**	**8.2%**

NOTE: Personal Income is measured as the sum of wage and salary disbursements, other labor income, proprietors' income, rental income, personal dividend income and personal interest income.
Omission of data for individual state is due to either the absences of such business from the state or the necessity of withholding the data to avoid disclosure of individual firm's data. Total includes states not listed individually.
SOURCE: U.S. Department of Commerce, Bureau of Economic Analysis.

Automotive Employment and Compensation

HOURLY COMPENSATION OF AUTOMOTIVE PRODUCTION EMPLOYMENT IN SELECTED COUNTRIES

Country	National Currency	2006 Exchange Rate Per U.S. Dollar	Hourly Compensation						2006 Percent of U.S. Earnings
			National Currency			U.S. Currency			
			2006	2005	2004	2006	2005	2004	
France	Euro	0.796	23.41	22.77	22.02	29.41	28.34	27.39	83.7
Germany	Euro	0.796	36.56	36.26	35.83	45.93	45.14	44.56	130.8
Ireland	Euro	0.796	17.62	16.73	15.95	22.14	20.83	19.84	63.0
Italy	Euro	0.796	20.84	20.22	19.84	26.18	25.17	24.68	74.5
Japan	Yen	116.300	NA	2,986.00	2,962.00	NA	27.12	27.39	NA
Korea	Won	954.300	18,167.00	17,005.00	16,801.00	19.04	16.61	14.76	54.2
Mexico	Peso	10.910	40.73	39.48	37.98	3.73	3.62	3.36	10.6
Spain	Euro	0.796	19.24	18.14	17.23	24.18	22.58	21.43	68.8
Taiwan	Dollar	32.510	NA	249.00	249.60	NA	7.75	7.48	NA
United Kingdom	Pound	0.542	NA	16.07	16.12	NA	29.27	29.55	NA
United States	Dollar	1.000	35.12	35.62	34.09	35.12	35.57	34.09	100.0

NA: Not available.
SOURCE: U.S. Department of Labor, Bureau of Labor Statistics.

U.S. VEHICLE AND EQUIPMENT MANUFACTURING EMPLOYMENT

Year	All Employees (000)	Production Workers		
		Number (000)	Percent of Total Employees	Average Hourly Earnings
2008	885.4	701.1	79.2%	$22.19
2007	996.8	805.7	80.8%	21.98
2006	1,070.4	873.3	81.6%	22.13
2005	1,098.2	894.9	81.5%	22.27
2004	1,112.8	902.9	81.1%	21.71
2003	1,125.3	906.3	80.5%	21.68
2002	1,151.2	931.0	80.9%	21.09
2001	1,212.8	986.7	81.4%	19.62
2000	1,313.6	1,073.0	81.7%	19.07
1999	1,312.6	1,075.7	82.0%	18.45
1998	1,271.5	1,050.3	82.6%	18.19
1997	1,253.9	1,062.5	84.7%	18.35
1996	1,240.3	1,052.3	84.8%	18.07
1995	1,241.5	1,048.9	84.5%	17.63
1994	1,168.5	978.4	83.7%	17.28
1993	1,077.8	896.4	83.2%	15.13
1992	1,047.1	867.9	82.9%	14.09

NOTE: The basis for industry classification has changed from the Standard Industrial Classification System (SIC) to the North American Industry Classification System (NAICS).
SOURCE: U.S. Department of Labor, Bureau of Labor Statistics.

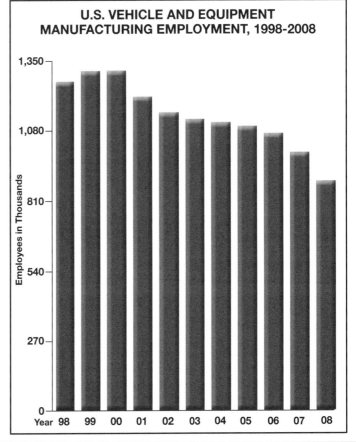

U.S. VEHICLE AND EQUIPMENT MANUFACTURING EMPLOYMENT, 1998-2008

Industrial Production and Capacity Utilization

INDUSTRIAL PRODUCTION INDEX FOR VEHICLE AND PARTS MANUFACTURERS

	Industrial Production Index			
	Total		Vehicle and Parts	
Year	Index	Percent Change	Index	Percent Change
2008	109.2	-3.1	83.4	-14.4
2007	112.7	1.3	97.4	-2.8
2006	111.2	2.5	100.2	-3.6
2005	108.5	4.0	103.9	0.2
2004	104.3	3.0	103.7	0.2
2003	101.3	1.3	103.5	3.5
2002	100.0	-0.1	100.0	9.4
2001	100.1	-4.1	91.4	-8.5
2000	104.4	4.5	99.9	-0.6
1999	99.9	5.0	100.5	10.9
1998	95.1	6.6	90.6	5.2
1997	89.2	8.5	86.1	7.8

NOTE: "Industrial Production" is an index benchmarked to 2002=100.
SOURCE: Board of Governors of the Federal Reserve System.

CAPACITY UTILIZATION FOR VEHICLE AND PARTS MANUFACTURING

Year	All Manufac- turing	Percent Change	Vehicle & Parts Mfg.	Percent Change
2008	75.1	-4.9	60.9	-14.2
2007	79.0	-0.5	71.0	-2.1
2006	79.4	1.0	72.5	-5.8
2005	78.6	3.1	77.0	0.3
2004	76.2	3.4	76.8	-2.0
2003	73.7	1.4	78.4	0.1
2002	72.7	-1.5	78.3	7.7
2001	73.8	-7.9	72.7	-11.3
2000	80.1	-0.7	82.0	-2.6
1999	80.7	-1.3	84.2	4.7
1998	81.8	-1.7	80.4	-3.8
1997	83.2	1.2	83.6	1.8

NOTE: "Capacity Utilization" is a percent of capacity.
SOURCE: Board of Governors of the Federal Reserve System.

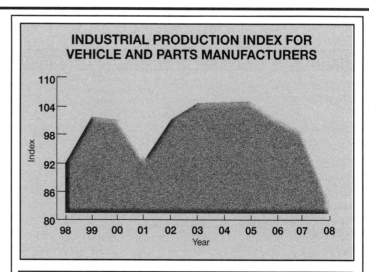

INDUSTRIAL PRODUCTION INDEX FOR VEHICLE AND PARTS MANUFACTURERS

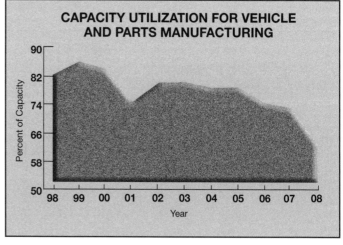

CAPACITY UTILIZATION FOR VEHICLE AND PARTS MANUFACTURING

CAR AND TRUCK OUTPUT (in Billions of U.S. Dollars)

Year	Car Output	Car Percent of GDP	Truck Output	Truck Percent of GDP	Total Vehicle Output	Percent of GDP	Gross Domestic Product (GDP)
2008	138.6	1.0	183.4	1.3	322.0	2.3	14,280.7
2007	150.6	1.1	251.6	1.8	402.2	2.9	13,807.5
2006	154.1	1.2	255.8	1.9	409.9	3.1	13,178.4
2005	146.5	1.2	267.2	2.2	413.7	3.3	12,421.9
2004	129.8	1.1	264.4	2.3	394.2	3.4	11,685.9
2003	130.1	1.2	248.5	2.3	378.6	3.5	10,971.2
2002	148.0	1.4	233.7	2.2	381.7	3.6	10,469.6
2001	141.4	1.4	203.1	2.0	344.5	3.4	10,128.0
2000	151.1	1.2	213.9	2.4	365.0	3.6	9,817.0
1999	150.4	1.4	221.5	2.4	371.9	3.7	9,268.4
1998	146.9	1.4	191.8	2.1	338.7	3.6	8,747.0
1997	144.6	1.5	175.1	2.0	319.7	3.5	8,304.3

SOURCE: U.S. Department of Commerce, Bureau of Economic Analysis.

Corporate Profits and Research and Development Spending

SELECTED AUTOMAKERS' REVENUES/NET INCOME (in Millions of U.S. Dollars)

Year	DaimlerChrysler[1] Revenues	Net Income	Ford Revenues	Net Income	General Motors Revenues	Net Income	Toyota Revenues	Net Income	Volkswagen Revenues	Net Income
2008	NA	NA	146,277	-14,672	148,979	-30,860	262,394	17,146	160,440	6,609
2007	NA	NA	172,455	-2,723	178,199	-38,732	202,864	13,927	160,389	6,071
2006	200,138	4,261	160,065	-12,613	171,179	-1,978	179,083	11,681	138,463	3,631
2005	177,402	3,371	176,835	1,440	158,623	-10,417	172,749	10,907	111,344	1,327
2004	192,319	3,338	172,255	3,487	195,351	2,701	163,637	10,995	120,405	969
2003	171,870	564	166,040	495	185,837	2,899	128,965	6,247	109,786	1,408
2002	156,838	4,947	162,256	-9,800	186,763	1,736	107,443	4,177	82,958	2,478
2001	136,072	-589	162,412	-5,453	177,260	601	106,030	5,447	78,446	4,806
2000	152,446	7,411	170,064	3,467	184,632	4,452	119,656	4,540	78,314	3,791
1999	151,035	5,785	160,658	7,237	176,558	6,002	100,990	3,747	75,525	2,534
1998	154,615	5,656	143,350	22,071	155,445	2,956	88,473	3,442	80,395	1,343
1997	61,147	2,805	153,627	6,920	178,174	6,698	99,730	3,143	63,664	765
1996	61,397	3,529	146,991	4,446	164,013	4,963	101,177	2,426	64,491	437
1995	53,195	2,025	137,137	4,139	160,254	6,881	89,715	1,458	61,168	233
1994	52,235	3,713	128,439	5,308	154,951	4,901	91,317	1,227	50,930	95
1993	43,596	-2,551	108,521	2,529	138,676	2,466	95,063	1,643	44,774	-1,134
1992	36,897	723	100,132	-7,385	132,429	-23,498	80,128	1,875	53,977	93
1991	29,370	-795	88,286	-2,258	123,056	-4,453	71,731	3,140	48,826	713
1990	30,620	68	97,650	860	124,705	-1,986	59,962	2,878	45,429	725
1989	35,186	359	96,146	3,835	126,932	4,224	61,440	2,652	37,606	597
1988	34,421	1,050	92,446	5,300	123,642	4,856	—	—	—	—
1987	28,353	1,290	79,893	4,625	114,870	3,551	—	—	—	—
1986	24,569	1,389	69,695	3,285	115,610	2,945	—	—	—	—
1985	22,738	1,610	57,616	2,515	106,656	3,999	—	—	—	—
1984	19,717	2,373	56,323	2,907	93,145	4,517	—	—	—	—
1982	10,040	170	37,067	-658	60,026	963	—	—	—	—
1980	9,225	-1,710	37,086	-1,543	57,729	-763	—	—	—	—
1978	13,618	-205	42,784	1,589	63,221	3,508	—	—	—	—
1976	15,537	423	28,840	983	47,181	2,903	—	—	—	—
1974	10,860	-52	23,621	361	31,550	950	—	—	—	—
1972	9,641	221	20,194	870	30,435	2,163	—	—	—	—
1970	7,000	-8	14,980	516	18,752	609	—	—	—	—

(1) Data for DaimlerChrysler for 1998-2006. In August 2007 Daimler AG sold 80.1% of Chrysler to private equity firm Cerberus Capital Management LP, which is not publicly traded and therefore not required to release financial information.
SOURCE: Compiled by Ward's Automotive Group from company annual reports.

RESEARCH & DEVELOPMENT EXPENDITURES FOR SELECTED MANUFACTURERS
(in Millions of U.S. Dollars)

Year	Daimler-Chrysler[1]	Ford	General Motors	Toyota	Volkswagen	Year	Daimler-Chrysler[1]	Ford	General Motors	Toyota	Volkswagen
2008	NA	7,300	NA	9,571	7,191	1996	1,602	6,821	8,900	—	—
2007	NA	7,500	8,100	7,554	7,251	1995	1,420	6,624	8,200	—	—
2006	7,038	7,200	6,600	6,912	6,057	1994	1,303	5,811	6,900	—	—
2005	6,691	8,000	6,700	7,031	4,827	1993	1,230	5,618	6,030	—	—
2004	7,660	7,400	6,500	6,455	5,637	1992	1,053	4,332	5,917	—	—
2003	7,018	7,300	6,200	5,561	5,215	1991	955	3,728	5,887	—	—
2002	6,455	7,500	6,000	4,423	4,118	1990	908	3,558	5,342	—	—
2001	5,281	7,300	6,100	3,864	3,476	1989	958	3,167	5,248	—	—
2000	5,347	6,800	6,600	4,196	3,855	1988	866	2,930	4,754	—	—
1999	7,628	6,000	6,800	4,771	3,806	1987	773	2,514	4,361	—	—
1998	7,853	5,300	7,900	3,367	3,343	1986	732	2,305	4,158	—	—
1997	1,714	6,327	8,200	3,723	2,555	1985	609	2,018	3,625	—	—

(1) Data for DaimlerChrysler for 1998-2006. In August 2007 Daimler AG sold 80.1% of Chrysler to private equity firm Cerberus Capital Management LP, which is not publicly traded and therefore not required to release financial information.
NOTE: Figures are dollars in millions.
SOURCE: Compiled by Ward's Automotive Group from company annual reports.

Use Tax Revenues by State

STATE USE TAX REVENUES, 2008 (in Thousands of Dollars)

State	Total State Tax Revenue	State Tax on Vehicle Fuel	State License Tax on Vehicles	State License Tax on Vehicle Operators	Total Vehicle Fuel and License Taxes	Percent Vehicle of Total Taxes
Alabama	9,070,530	545,726	212,687	17,762	776,175	8.6
Alaska	8,424,714	41,985	53,453	NA	95,438	1.1
Arizona	13,452,101	731,345	218,763	27,082	977,190	7.3
Arkansas	7,530,504	471,214	140,112	14,816	626,142	8.3
California	117,361,976	3,421,457	2,704,632	235,185	6,361,274	5.4
Colorado	9,624,636	637,193	219,590	13,587	870,370	9.0
Connecticut	13,367,631	450,095	201,364	39,202	690,661	5.2
Delaware	2,930,955	117,746	46,413	2,814	166,973	5.7
Florida	35,849,998	2,289,166	1,153,139	161,590	3,603,895	10.1
Georgia	18,183,117	1,011,202	296,648	64,896	1,372,746	7.5
Hawaii	5,147,480	93,991	111,262	404	205,657	4.0
Idaho	3,651,917	239,881	124,369	7,293	371,543	10.2
Illinois	31,564,804	1,438,315	1,486,308	66,742	2,991,365	9.5
Indiana	14,916,295	856,301	190,165	226,096	1,272,562	8.5
Iowa	6,892,026	442,183	404,006	15,000	861,189	12.5
Kansas	7,159,748	431,755	172,111	17,270	621,136	8.7
Kentucky	10,056,293	617,826	212,037	19,945	849,808	8.5
Louisiana	11,003,870	604,377	87,189	11,455	703,021	6.4
Maine	3,681,614	229,849	85,762	11,824	327,435	8.9
Maryland	16,605,830	808,964	442,018	29,373	1,280,355	7.7
Massachusetts	21,836,357	672,654	287,738	92,881	1,053,273	4.8
Michigan	25,043,233	994,937	892,817	51,928	1,939,682	7.7
Minnesota	18,320,891	648,565	511,513	50,168	1,210,246	6.6
Mississippi	6,618,349	442,119	123,203	34,385	599,707	9.1
Missouri	10,965,171	736,303	269,443	15,558	1,021,304	9.3
Montana	2,457,929	205,819	143,972	7,916	357,707	14.6
Nebraska	4,175,471	294,149	90,845	8,735	393,729	9.4
Nevada	6,115,584	311,953	169,896	16,133	497,982	8.1
New Hampshire	2,251,179	137,206	93,679	13,226	244,111	10.8
New Jersey	30,616,510	563,266	432,164	37,579	1,033,009	3.4
New Mexico	5,674,530	250,418	179,367	4,780	434,565	7.7
New York	65,400,355	527,840	860,519	145,084	1,533,443	2.3
North Carolina	22,781,199	1,582,400	609,158	134,196	2,325,754	10.2
North Dakota	2,312,056	143,389	88,453	4,087	235,929	10.2
Ohio	27,153,786	1,864,305	809,784	79,622	2,753,711	10.1
Oklahoma	8,484,227	384,814	631,732	14,589	1,031,135	12.2
Oregon	7,250,033	413,521	484,291	31,906	929,718	12.8
Pennsylvania	32,123,740	2,102,168	814,486	61,881	2,978,535	9.3
Rhode Island	2,761,356	126,718	52,248	660	179,626	6.5
South Carolina	8,455,463	534,252	142,120	44,717	721,089	8.5
South Dakota	1,321,368	129,619	47,285	2,513	179,417	13.6
Tennessee	11,538,430	872,892	270,176	43,827	1,186,895	10.3
Texas	44,675,953	3,103,170	1,518,188	115,935	4,737,293	10.6
Utah	5,944,879	377,261	107,158	22,257	506,676	8.5
Vermont	2,544,163	91,535	79,077	5,040	175,652	6.9
Virginia	18,408,276	920,063	355,683	45,425	1,321,171	7.2
Washington	17,944,925	1,169,900	487,422	61,978	1,719,300	9.6
West Virginia	4,879,151	404,221	86,754	947	491,922	10.1
Wisconsin	15,088,662	1,001,339	406,806	36,391	1,444,536	9.6
Wyoming	2,168,016	75,013	55,722	2,215	132,950	6.1
Total	**781,787,281**	**36,562,380**	**19,663,727**	**2,168,895**	**58,395,002**	**7.5**

SOURCE: U.S. Department of Commerce, Bureau of the Census.

New Car Corporate Average Fuel Economy

NEW CAR U.S. CORPORATE AVERAGE FUEL ECONOMY PERFORMANCE BY MANUFACTURER (Miles Per Gallon)

Manufacturer	Preliminary '08 mpg	Final Sales Basis '07 mpg	'06 mpg	'05 mpg	'03 mpg	'01 mpg	'99 mpg	'97 mpg	'95 mpg	'85 mpg	'74 mpg
DOMESTIC FLEET											
Chrysler	29.5	—	—	—	—	—	—	27.6	28.4	27.8	13.9
DaimlerChrysler[1][2]	—	28.5	26.0	28.8	29.7	27.9	27.2	—	—	—	—
Ford[1]	29.8	29.0	28.2	28.6	27.9	27.7	27.6	27.2	27.7	26.6	14.2
General Motors[1]	29.6	30.0	30.3	29.2	28.9	28.3	27.7	28.2	27.4	25.8	12.1
Honda	35.3	33.5	33.8	33.2	34.4	32.7	33.5	28.5	—	—	—
Mitsubishi	—	—	—	27.6	—	—	—	—	—	—	—
Nissan	33.7	33.4	31.1	30.4	28.9	27.9	29.9	—	—	—	—
Toyota	33.9	31.3	34.6	34.4	28.1	34.2	28.3	28.8	28.5	—	—
IMPORT FLEET											
Alfa Romeo	—	—	—	—	—	—	—	—	—	27.7	—
AMC-Renault	—	—	—	—	—	—	—	—	—	28.6	—
BMW	27.4	27.7	27.2	27.2	26.8	25.0	25.4	25.7	25.3	26.4	19.5
Daimler	26.4	—	—	—	—	—	—	—	—	—	—
DaimlerChrysler[2]	—	24.7	24.7	25.9	26.3	26.5	26.5	25.7	28.6	36.2	—
Ford	30.6	30.0	29.8	28.4	28.2	27.9	30.1	31.3	34.0	25.2	—
Fuji (Subaru)	28.5	28.5	28.3	27.9	27.6	27.8	27.7	28.3	28.9	32.6	25.7
General Motors	31.4	32.3	29.0	30.5	28.3	26.5	25.5	32.1	36.7	47.9	—
Honda	33.2	39.3	34.5	33.1	31.9	29.3	29.4	32.4	32.7	34.5	31.1
Hyundai	33.8	32.4	30.1	30.3	30.4	31.3	30.8	31.4	31.2	-	—
Isuzu	—	—	—	—	—	—	—	—	—	34.2	—
Kia	33.4	33.4	32.8	29.5	30.4	30.5	30.9	31.0	—	—	—
Mercedes-Benz	—	—	—	—	—	—	—	25.2	24.7	23.6	15.3
MG-Triumph-Jaguar	—	—	—	—	—	—	—	—	—	19.3	21.3
Mitsubishi	27.5	28.7	29.5	30.2	—	29.4	30.0	30.0	29.9	31.9	—
Nissan	29.4	29.6	24.3	24.8	27.4	28.7	29.9	29.9	29.5	30.1	24.0
Peugeot	—	—	—	—	—	—	—	—	—	25.2	19.0
Saab	—	—	—	—	—	—	—	—	—	26.4	19.8
Suzuki	31.4	30.3	30.1	29.6	33.0	35.1	35.5	35.2	40.8	58.7	—
Toyota	38.5	38.3	35.0	36.6	32.4	30.6	29.9	30.1	30.4	33.5	22.5
Volvo	—	—	—	—	—	—	26.2	25.8	26.0	27.2	19.4
Volkswagen	28.8	28.8	30.1	29.1	29.8	28.5	28.2	29.0	29.0	30.5	25.9

NOTE: Data are for model years.
(1) Domestic fleet excludes captive imports after '79.
(2) DaimlerChrysler includes Mercedes-Benz and the Chrysler Group from '99-'07.
SOURCE: U.S. Department of Transportation.

NEW CAR U.S. CORPORATE AVERAGE FUEL ECONOMY (Sales Weighted Combined City/Highway Miles Per Gallon)

Model Year	Federal Standard	Domestic Fleet	Import Fleet	Total Fleet
2008 (prelim.)	27.5	31.0	31.7	31.4
2007	27.5	30.6	32.2	31.2
2006	27.5	30.4	29.7	30.2
2005	27.5	30.5	29.9	30.3
2004	27.5	29.9	28.7	29.5
2003	27.5	29.1	29.9	29.5
2002	27.5	29.1	28.8	29.0
2001	27.5	28.7	29.0	28.8
2000	27.5	28.7	28.3	28.5
1999	27.5	28.0	29.0	28.3
1998	27.5	28.6	29.2	28.8
1997	27.5	27.8	30.1	28.7
1996	27.5	28.1	29.6	28.5
1994	27.5	27.5	29.7	28.3
1992	27.5	27.0	29.2	27.9
1990	27.5	26.9	29.9	28.0
1988	26.0	27.4	31.5	28.8
1986	26.0	26.6	31.6	28.2
1984	27.0	25.6	32.0	26.9
1982	24.0	25.0	31.1	26.6
1980	20.0	22.6	29.6	24.3
1978	18.0	18.7	27.3	19.9
1976	—	16.6	25.4	17.5

NOTE: After 1979, domestic fleet excludes captive imports.
SOURCE: U.S. Department of Transportation.

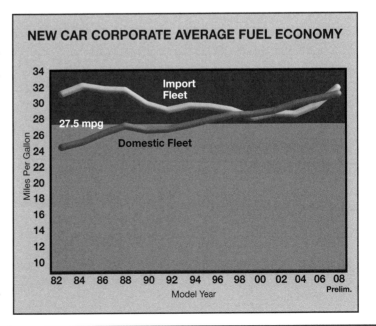

NEW CAR CORPORATE AVERAGE FUEL ECONOMY

New Light Truck Corporate Average Fuel Economy

NEW LIGHT TRUCK[1] U.S. CORPORATE AVERAGE FUEL ECONOMY
(Sales Weighted Combined City/Highway Miles Per Gallon)

Model Year	Federal Standard	Other[3]	Captive Import[4]	Total Fleet
2008	22.5	—	—	23.6
2007	22.2	—	—	23.1
2006	21.6	—	—	22.5
2005	21.0	—	—	22.1
2004	20.7	—	—	21.5
2003	20.7	—	—	21.8
2002	20.7	—	—	21.4
2001	20.7	—	—	20.9
2000	20.7	—	—	21.3
1999	20.7	—	—	20.9
1998	20.7	20.8	—	21.1
1997	20.7	20.4	—	20.6

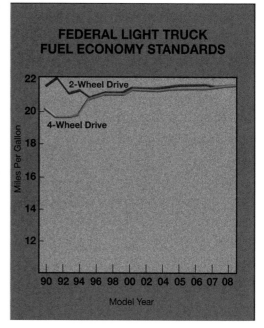

FEDERAL LIGHT TRUCK FUEL ECONOMY STANDARDS

	2-Wheel Drive			4-Wheel Drive		
	Federal Standard	Sales Weighted Average Domestic*	Import	Federal Standard	Sales Weighted Average Domestic*	Import
1991**	20.7	20.9[2]	23.0[2]	19.1	20.9[2]	23.0[2]
1990**	20.5	20.3[2]	23.0[2]	19.0	20.3[2]	23.0[2]
1989**	21.5	20.4[2]	23.5[2]	19.0	20.4[2]	23.5[2]
1988**	21.0	20.6[2]	24.6[2]	19.5	20.6[2]	24.6
1987**	21.0	20.4	27.5	19.5	19.4	25.3
1985**	19.7	19.9	27.4	18.9	19.6	24.7[2]
1983**	19.5	19.6[2]	27.1[2]	17.5	19.6[2]	27.1

* Captive imports are excluded.
** Manufacturers may elect to meet a single combined corporate fleet average of 19 mpg in 1983, 20 mpg in 1984, 19.5 mpg in 1985, 20 mpg in 1986, 20.5 mpg in 1987-89, 20 in 1990, and 20.2 in 1991.
(1) Light truck defined as 0-6,000 lbs. In 1979 and 0-8,500 lbs. in subsequent years.
(2) Combined 2-wheel and 4-wheel drive fleet average.
(3) Not a captive import light truck; 2 and 4 wheel drive combined.
(4) A light truck which is not domestically manufactured but imported by a manufacturer whose principal place of business is the United States; 2 and 4 wheel drive combined.
SOURCE: U.S. Department of Transportation.

NEW LIGHT TRUCK U.S. CORPORATE AVERAGE FUEL ECONOMY PERFORMANCE BY MANUFACTURER (Miles Per Gallon)

Manufacturer	Preliminary '08 mpg	Final Sales Basis '07 mpg	'05 mpg	'03 mpg	'01 mpg	'99 mpg	'97 mpg	'95 mpg
BMW	22.9	23.4	21.3	20.0	19.2	—	—	—
Chrysler	23.6	—	—	—	—	—	20.2	20.1
DaimlerChrysler[1][2]	—	22.9	21.4	22.2	20.7	20.8	—	—
Ford[1]	23.6	22.3	21.6	21.3	20.5	20.4	20.0	20.8
General Motors[1]	22.8	22.4	21.8	21.3	20.5	20.3	20.5	20.1
Honda	25.5	25.1	24.9	24.7	24.9	26.1	26.9	—
Hyundai	25.5	25.5	24.7	24.4	25.2	—	—	—
Isuzu	—	—	—	22.3	21.1	21.5	19.6	20.3
Kia	24.2	24.2	21.4	19.7	22.9	24.4	23.7	24.4
Mazda	—	—	—	—	—	20.4	20.5	20.9
Mitsubishi	25.9	24.7	23.6	—	—	22.3	22.3	20.2
Nissan	24.0	22.9	21.6	21.9	20.7	21.2	22.3	22.4
Porsche	19.7	—	18.5	—	—	—	—	—
Rover	—	—	—	—	—	17.0	17.2	16.3
Suzuki	23.8	23.8	22.8	21.9	22.0	23.8	27.4	28.1
Toyota	23.7	23.7	23.1	21.9	22.1	22.9	22.6	21.2
Volkswagen	20.1	19.5	20.1	21.3	20.5	19.1	18.5	19.6

NOTE: Data are for vehicles with gross vehicle weight of 8,500 lbs. or less by model years.
(1) Captive imports are excluded.
(2) DaimlerChrysler includes Mercedes-Benz and the Chrysler Group beginning in '99.
SOURCE: U.S. Department of Transportation.

Gas Guzzler Tax Receipts, Automotive Fuel Prices and New Car Quality Improvements

NEW CAR GAS GUZZLER TAX

Miles Per Gallon*	1991-09	1986-90	1985	1984	1983	1982	1981	1980
Under 12.5	$7,700	$3,850	$2,650	$2,150	$1,550	$1,200	$650	$550
12.5-13.0	6,400	3,200	2,650	1,750	1,550	950	650	550
13.0-13.5	6,400	3,200	2,200	1,750	1,250	950	550	300
13.5-14.0	5,400	2,700	2,200	1,450	1,250	750	550	300
14.0-14.5	5,400	2,700	1,800	1,450	1,000	750	450	200
14.5-15.0	4,500	2,250	1,800	1,150	1,000	600	450	200
15.0-15.5	4,500	2,250	1,500	1,150	800	600	350	0
15.5-16.0	3,700	1,850	1,500	950	800	450	350	0
16.0-16.5	3,700	1,850	1,200	950	650	450	200	0
16.5-17.0	3,000	1,500	1,200	750	650	350	200	0
17.0-17.5	3,000	1,500	1,000	750	500	350	0	0
17.5-18.0	2,600	1,300	1,000	600	500	200	0	0
18.0-18.5	2,600	1,300	800	600	350	0	0	0
18.5-19.0	2,100	1,050	800	450	350	0	0	0
19.0-19.5	2,100	1,050	600	450	0	0	0	0
19.5-20.0	1,700	850	600	0	0	0	0	0
20.0-20.5	1,700	850	500	0	0	0	0	0
20.5-21.0	1,300	650	500	0	0	0	0	0
21.0-21.5	1,300	650	0	0	0	0	0	0
21.5-22.0	1,000	500	0	0	0	0	0	0
22.0-22.5	1,000	500	0	0	0	0	0	0
22.5 & Over	0	0	0	0	0	0	0	0

NOTE: New car purchaser pays tax if car's combined city/highway fuel economy rating is lower than standard. * Combined city/highway rating.
SOURCE: Internal Revenue Service.

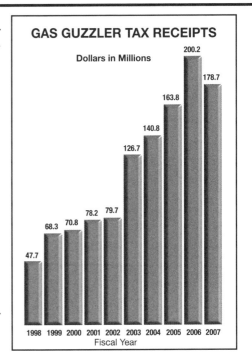

GAS GUZZLER TAX RECEIPTS
Dollars in Millions

Fiscal Year	Value
1998	47.7
1999	68.3
2000	70.8
2001	78.2
2002	79.7
2003	126.7
2004	140.8
2005	163.8
2006	200.2
2007	178.7

U.S. CITY AVERAGE RETAIL PRICES FOR AUTOMOTIVE FUEL
(Cents Per Gallon, Including Taxes)

Year	Unleaded Regular	Unleaded Premium	All Types[1]	Diesel
2008	326.6	351.9	331.7	391.5
2007	280.1	303.3	284.9	296.4
2006	258.9	280.5	263.5	281.4
2005	229.5	249.1	233.8	252.0
2004	188.0	206.8	192.3	192.1
2003	159.1	177.7	163.8	164.5
2002	135.8	155.6	144.1	142.6
2001	146.1	165.7	153.1	153.4
2000	138.2	169.3	156.3	151.1
1999	116.5	135.7	122.1	112.0
1998	105.9	125.0	111.5	104.5
1997	120.0	138.1	124.5	120.0
1996	123.1	141.3	128.8	123.6
1995	114.7	133.6	120.5	110.9
1994	111.2	130.5	117.4	112.0
1993	110.8	130.2	117.3	114.8
1992	112.7	131.6	119.0	114.5
1991(2)	114.0	132.1	119.6	124.3
1990	116.4	134.9	121.7	134.3
1989	102.1	119.7	106.0	110.0
1988	94.6	110.7	96.3	104.6
1985	120.2	134.0	119.6	129.5
1980	124.5	NA	122.1	112.4

NOTE: Prices are based on city averages. NA - Not available. (1) Includes types of motor gasoline not shown separately. (2) Price calculations changed from "Full Service" to "Self Service."

AVERAGE RETAIL PRICE INCREASES FOR NEW CAR QUALITY IMPROVEMENTS

Model Year	Safety	Emissions[1]	Other[2]	Total
	Adjusted to 2008 Dollars			
2009	NA	NA	NA	185.18
2008	82.39	0.00	87.78	170.17
2007	56.36	—	93.99	150.35
2006	—	26.59	2.43	29.03
2005	193.40	117.56	—	310.96
2004	37.58	22.04	24.27	83.89
2003	—	—	25.17	25.17
2002	—	—	67.35	67.35
2001	24.53	65.95	116.84	207.31
2000	14.80	—	—	14.80
1999	—	74.31	395.97	470.27
1998	—	50.18	171.94	222.12
1997	8.70	19.84	148.74	177.28
1996	15.82	84.61	84.28	184.71
1995	116.74	52.12	—	168.86
1994	183.26	39.29	139.48	362.03
1993	—	—	91.74	91.74
1992	36.55	—	237.40	273.95
1991	232.40	—	—	232.40
1990	199.08	—	43.07	242.15
1989	26.30	—	181.45	207.75
1988	75.77	—	208.65	284.42
1987	—	—	55.68	55.68
1986	33.57	—	194.75	228.32
1985	—	25.61	167.66	193.27
1984	-15.92	77.57	83.35	144.99
1983	—	87.62	85.92	173.54
1982	—	117.72	57.89	175.60
1981	6.20	674.33	86.57	767.10
1980	20.36	180.80	168.76	369.91

(1) Includes changes to improve fuel economy and emissions control.
(2) Includes improved warranties, corrosion protection and changes in standard equipment.
SOURCE: U.S. Department of Labor, Bureau of Labor Statistics.

Federal Exhaust Emission Standards for Cars and Light Trucks

FEDERAL EXHAUST EMISSION STANDARDS FOR CONVENTIONALLY FUELED CARS AND LIGHT TRUCKS (Grams Per Mile)

EPA Tier 1 Emission Standards for Passenger Cars and Light-Duty Trucks, FTP 75, (grams/mile)

Category	50,000 miles/5 years						100,000 miles/10 years[1]					
	THC	NMHC	CO	NOx diesel	NOx gasoline	PM	THC	NMHC	CO	NOx diesel	NOx gasoline	PM
LDV (Passenger cars)	0.41	0.25	3.4	1	0.4	0.08	—	0.31	4.2	1.25	0.6	0.1
LDT1 (LLDT, LVW <3,750 lbs)	—	0.25	3.4	1	0.4	0.08	0.8	0.31	4.2	1.25	0.6	0.1
LDT2 (LLDT, LVW >3,750 lbs)	—	0.32	4.4	—	0.7	0.08	0.8	0.4	5.5	0.97	0.97	0.1
LDT3 (HLDT, ALVW <5,750 lbs)	—	0.32	4.4	—	0.7	—	0.8	0.46	6.4	0.98	0.98	0.1
LDT4 (HLDT, ALVW >5,750 lbs)	—	0.39	5	—	1.1	—	0.8	0.56	7.3	1.53	1.53	0.12

1 - Useful life 120,000 miles/11 years for all HLDT standards and for THC standards for LDT
Abbreviations:
 LVW - loaded vehicle weight (curb weight + 300 lbs)
 ALVW - adjusted LVW (the numerical average of the curb weight and the GVWR)
 LLDT - light light-duty truck (below 6,000 lbs GVWR)
 HLDT - heavy light-duty truck (above 6,000 lbs GVWR)

EPA Tier 2 Emission Standards, FTP 75, (grams/mile)

Bin#	50,000 miles					120,000 miles				
	NMOG	CO	NOx	PM	HCHO	NMOG	CO	NOx*	PM	HCHO
Temporary Bins										
MDPVc						0.28	7.3	0.9	0.12	0.032
10a,b,d,f	0.125 (0.160)	3.4 (4.4)	0.4	—	0.015 (0.018)	0.156 (0.230)	4.2 (6.4)	0.6	0.08	0.018 (0.027)
9a,b,e	0.075 (0.140)	3.4	0.2	—	0.015	0.090 (0.180)	4.2	0.3	0.06	0.018
Permanent Bins					—					
8b	0.100 (0.125)	3.4	0.14	—	0.015	0.125 (0.156)	4.2	0.2	0.02	0.018
7	0.075	3.4	0.11	—	0.015	0.09	4.2	0.15	0.02	0.018
6	0.075	3.4	0.08	—	0.015	0.09	4.2	0.1	0.01	0.018
5	0.075	3.4	0.05	—	0.015	0.09	4.2	0.07	0.01	0.018
4	—	—	—	—	—	0.07	2.1	0.04	0.01	0.011
3	—	—	—	—	—	0.055	2.1	0.03	0.01	0.011
2	—	—	—	—	—	0.01	2.1	0.02	0.01	0.004
1	—	—	—	—	—	—	—	—	—	—

* - average manufacturer fleet NOx standard is 0.07 g/mi
NOTE: Tier 2 standards will be phased in between 2004 and 2009. For new passenger cars and light LDT's, Tier 2 standards were phased in beginning in 2004 and completed in 2007. For heavy LDT's and MDPV's, the Tier 2 standards will be phased in beginning in 2008, with full compliance in 2009.
a - Bin deleted at end of 2006 model year (2008 for HLDTs)
b - The higher temporary NMOG, CO and HCHO values apply only to HLDTs and expire after 2008
c - An additional temporary bin restricted to MDPVs, expires after model year 2008
d - Optional temporary NMOG standard of 0.195 g/mi (50,000) and 0.280 g/mi (120,000) applies for qualifying LDT4s and MDPVs only
e - Optional temporary NMOG standard of 0.100 g/mi (50,000) and 0.130 g/mi (120,000) applies for qualifying LDT2s only
f - 50,000 mile standard optional for diesels certified to bin 10

Federal Motor Vehicle Safety Standards

FEDERAL MOTOR VEHICLE SAFETY STANDARDS (FMVSS)

FMVSS NUMBER	Car	MPV	Truck	Bus	Equip.
100 SERIES Crash Avoidance					
101 Controls, Location & Identification	•	•	•	•	
102 Transmission Shift Lever Sequence	•	•	•	•	
103 Windshield Defrosting & Defogging	•	•	•	•	
104 Windshield Wiping & Washing System	•	•	•	•	
106 Brake Hoses	•	•	•	•	•
108 Lights & Reflectors	•	•	•	•	•*
110 Tire Selection & Rims for Passenger Cars	•*	•*	•*		
111 Rearview Mirrors	•	•	•	•	
113 Hood Latch System	•	•	•	•	
114 Theft Protection	•*	•*	•*		
115 Vehicle Identification Number (Location)	•	•	•	•	
116 Hydraulic Brake Fluids	•	•	•	•	•
117 Retreaded Tires	•				
118 Power-Operated Window Systems	•	•	•		
119 New Tires for Trucks, Buses, etc		•	•	•	•
120 Tire Selection & Rims for Trucks, Buses, etc.		•	•	•	•
121 Air Brake Systems			•	•	•
124 Accelerator Control Systems	•	•	•	•	
125 Warning Devices					•*
129 Non-Pneumatic Tires	•				
131 School Bus Pedestrian Safety Devices				•*	
135 Light Vehicle Brake Systems	•	•*	•*	•*	
139 New Tires for Light Vehicles	•				
200 SERIES Crashworthiness					
201 Occupant Protection in Interior Impacts	•	•*	•*	•*	
202 Head Restraints	•	•*	•*	•*	
203 Steering Wheel Impact Protection	•	•*	•*	•*	
204 Steering System Rearward Displacement	•	•*	•*	•*	
205 Glazing Materials	•	•	•	•	•
206 Door Locks & Hinges	•	•	•		
207 Anchorage of Seats	•	•	•	•	
208 Occupant Restraints	•*	•*	•*	•*	
209 Seat Belt Assemblies	•	•	•	•	
210 Seat Belt Anchorages	•	•	•	•	
212 Windshield Mounting	•	•*	•*	•*	
213 Child Restraint Systems	•	•	•	•	
214 Side Door Strength	•	•*	•*	•*	
216 Roof Crush Resistance	•*	•*	•*	•*	

FMVSS/CFR NUMBER	Car	MPV	Truck	Bus	Equip.
217 Bus Window Strength & Emergency Release				•	
219 Windshield Zone Intrusion	•	•*		•*	•*
220 School Bus Rollover Protection				•*	
221 School Bus Body Joint Strength				•*	
222 School Bus Seats				•*	
223 Rear Impact Guards					•
224 Rear Impact Protection					•*
225 Child Restraint Anchorage System	•	•	•*		
300 SERIES Post Crash Protection					
301 Fuel System Integrity	•	•*	•*	•*	
302 Flammability of Interior Materials	•	•	•	•	
303 Fuel System Integrity-CNG	•	•*	•*	•*	
304 CNG Fuel Container Integrity	•	•	•	•	
400 SERIES					
401 Interior Trunk Release	•*				
49 CFR PART NO. - Code of Federal Regulation (CFR) Parts					
— Importation of Motor Vehicles & Equipment	•	•	•	•	•
541 Theft Prevention	•	•	•	•	•
565 Vehicle Identification Number (Content)	•	•	•	•	•
566 Manufacturers Identification	•	•	•	•	•
567 Certification	•	•	•	•	•
568 Vehicles Manufactured in 2 or More Stages	•	•	•	•	•
569 Regrooved Tires	•	•	•	•	•
572 Anthropomorphic Dummy (Test Equipment)	•	•	•	•	•
573 Defect Reports	•	•	•	•	•
574 Tire Identification & Record Keeping	•	•	•	•	•
575 Consumer Information					
Truck-Camper Loading			•		
Uniform Tire Quality Grading	•				
Vehicle Rollover		•*			
577 Defect Notification	•	•	•	•	•
579 Defect & Non-Compliance Responsibility	•	•	•	•	•
580 Odometer Disclosure Requirements	•	•	•		
581 Bumper Damage Limits	•				
582 Insurance Cost Information	•	•	•		
583 Automobile Parts Content Labeling	•	•	•	•	•
595 Retrofit On-Off Switches for Air Bags					•

*Application or requirements vary for specific vehicle types or Gross Vehicle Weight Ratings (GVWR).
CAR: Vehicle with motive power, except a multipurpose passenger vehicle, motorcycle or trailer designed for carrying 10 persons or less.
MULTIPURPOSE PASSENGER VEHICLE: Vehicle with motive power, except a trailer, designed to carry 10 persons or less which is constructed either on a truck chassis or with special features for occasional off-road operation.
TRUCK: Vehicle with motive power, except a trailer, designed primarily for the transportation of property or special purpose equipment.
BUS: Vehicle with motive power, except a trailer, designed for carrying more than 10 persons.
EQUIPMENT: Individual vehicle components or systems whether installed on a new vehicle or provided as a replacement.
SOURCE: National Highway Traffic Safety Administration.

Vehicle Deaths by Type of Accident and Death Rates

VEHICLE DEATHS BY TYPE OF ACCIDENT AND DEATH RATES

Year	Total Vehicle Deaths	Pedes-trians	Other Vehicles	Rail-road Trains	Pedal cycles	Animal drawn Veh. or Animal	Fixed Objects	Deaths from Non-collision Accidents	Per 10,000 Vehicles	Per 100,000,000 Vehicle Miles	Per 100,000 Popu-lation
2007	43,100	5,900	17,200	200	1,000	100	13,500	5,200	1.69	1.44	14.3
2006	44,700	6,100	18,500	200	1,100	100	13,400	5,300	1.77	1.49	14.9
2005	45,800	6,200	19,200	300	1,000	100	13,700	5,300	1.86	1.54	15.5
2004	45,300	5,900	20,600	200	900	100	13,300	5,200	1.92	1.58	15.7
2003	44,757	5,600	19,900	300	700	100	13,000	5,200	1.87	1.56	15.4
2002	44,100	5,700	18,700	300	700	100	13,400	5,200	1.88	1.54	15.3
2001	43,788	6,100	18,800	324	800	100	12,800	4,900	1.86	1.57	15.4
2000	43,354	5,900	19,100	321	800	100	12,300	4,800	1.92	1.58	15.8
1999	42,401	6,100	18,600	314	800	100	11,800	4,700	1.98	1.57	15.5
1998	43,501	5,900	19,700	309	700	100	12,200	4,600	1.94	1.59	16.1
1997	43,458	5,900	19,900	371	800	100	12,000	4,400	2.05	1.70	16.2
1996	43,649	6,100	19,600	373	800	100	12,100	4,600	2.07	1.76	16.5
1995	43,363	6,400	19,000	514	800	100	12,100	4,400	2.11	1.79	16.5
1994	42,524	6,300	18,900	549	800	100	11,500	4,400	2.11	1.80	16.3
1993	41,893	6,400	18,300	553	800	100	11,500	4,200	2.12	1.82	16.3
1992	40,982	6,300	17,600	521	700	100	11,700	4,100	2.11	1.83	16.1
1991	43,536	6,600	18,200	541	800	100	12,600	4,700	2.26	2.00	17.3
1990	46,814	7,300	19,900	623	900	100	13,100	4,900	2.43	2.18	18.8
1989	47,575	7,800	20,300	720	900	100	12,900	4,900	2.48	2.26	19.3
1988	49,078	7,700	20,900	638	1,000	100	13,400	5,300	2.60	2.42	20.1
1987	48,290	7,500	20,700	554	1,000	100	13,200	5,200	2.63	2.51	19.9
1986	47,865	8,900	20,800	574	1,100	100	3,300	13,100	2.63	2.60	19.9
1985	45,901	8,500	19,900	538	1,100	100	3,200	12,600	2.59	2.59	19.2
1984	46,263	8,500	20,000	630	1,100	100	3,200	12,700	2.69	2.69	19.6
1983	44,452	8,200	19,200	520	1,100	100	3,100	12,200	2.62	2.68	19.0
1982	45,779	8,400	19,800	554	1,100	100	3,200	12,600	2.77	2.88	19.7
1981	51,385	9,400	22,200	668	1,200	100	3,600	14,200	3.13	3.30	22.4
1980	53,172	9,700	23,000	739	1,200	100	3,700	14,700	3.29	3.50	23.4
1979	53,524	9,800	23,100	826	1,200	100	3,700	14,800	3.35	3.50	23.8
1978	52,411	9,600	22,400	986	1,200	100	3,600	14,500	3.41	3.39	23.6
1977	49,510	9,100	21,200	902	1,100	100	3,400	13,700	3.33	3.35	22.5
1976	47,038	8,600	20,100	1,033	1,000	100	3,200	13,000	3.28	3.33	21.6
1975	45,853	8,400	19,550	979	1,000	100	3,130	12,700	3.33	3.45	21.3
1974	46,402	8,500	19,700	1,209	1,000	100	3,100	2,800	3.44	3.59	21.8
1973	55,511	10,200	23,600	1,194	1,000	100	3,800	15,600	4.28	4.24	26.3
1972	56,278	10,300	23,900	1,260	1,000	100	3,900	15,800	4.60	4.43	26.9
1971	54,381	9,900	23,100	1,378	800	100	3,800	15,300	4.68	4.57	26.3
1970	54,633	9,900	23,200	1,459	780	100	3,800	15,400	4.92	4.88	26.8
1969	55,791	10,100	23,700	1,495	800	100	3,900	15,700	5.19	5.21	27.7
1968	54,862	9,900	22,400	1,570	790	100	2,700	17,400	5.32	5.40	27.5
1967	52,924	9,400	22,000	1,620	750	100	2,350	16,700	5.35	5.50	26.8
1965	49,163	8,900	20,800	1,556	680	120	2,200	14,900	5.36	5.54	25.4
1960	38,137	7,850	14,800	1,368	460	80	1,700	11,900	5.12	5.31	21.2
1955	38,426	8,200	14,500	1,490	410	80	1,600	12,100	6.12	6.34	23.4
1950	34,763	9,000	11,650	1,541	440	70	1,300	10,600	7.07	7.59	23.0
1943-47 ave.	28,458	10,570	7,490	1,660	490	120	820	7,120	8.60	10.52	20.8
1938-42 ave.	33,549	12,430	9,500	1,624	748	140	1,048	7,848	10.41	11.49	25.4
1933-37 ave.	36,313	14,484	8,630	1,598	540	214	1,034	9,464	13.50	15.55	28.6
1928-32 ave.	31,050	12,300	5,700	1,850	—	274	700	9,100	12.10	15.60	25.3
1923-27 ave.	21,800	—	—	1,200	—	—	—	—	11.10	18.20	18.8
1918-22 ave.	12,700	—	—	—	—	—	—	—	13.90	11.90	—

SOURCE: National Safety Council.

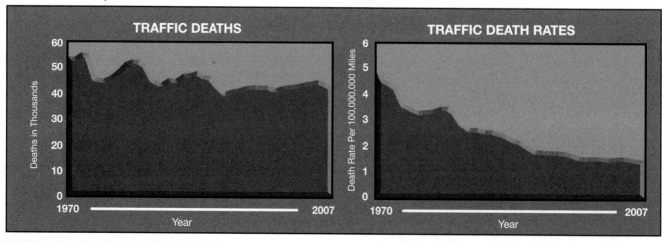

Vehicle Traffic Deaths and Traffic Death Rates by State

VEHICLE DEATHS AND DEATH RATES BY STATE

State	Traffic Deaths				Traffic Deaths Per 100,000,000 Vehicle Miles			
	2008	2007	2006	2005	2008	2007	2006	2005
Alabama	913	1,054	1,155	1,054	1.5	1.8	2.0	1.8
Alaska	62	85	74	72	1.2	1.7	1.5	1.4
Arizona	916	1,086	1,193	1,111	1.5	1.8	2.1	2.0
Arkansas	590	638	639	641	1.8	2.0	2.0	2.1
California	2,970	2,896	3,754	4,114	0.9	1.2	1.1	1.3
Colorado	543	554	533	586	1.1	1.2	1.2	1.3
Connecticut	292	302	325	293	0.9	1.0	1.0	0.9
Delaware	122	118	145	133	1.3	1.2	1.6	1.5
Dist. of Columbia	39	54	37	49	1.1	1.5	1.1	1.2
Florida	2,957	3,212	3,285	3,497	1.4	1.6	1.7	1.9
Georgia	1,446	1,594	1,637	1,652	1.3	1.4	1.5	1.5
Hawaii	97	124	147	139	0.9	1.3	1.6	1.5
Idaho	230	252	268	274	1.5	1.7	1.8	1.9
Illinois	1,039	1,246	1,260	1,355	1.0	1.2	1.2	1.3
Indiana	814	896	868	921	1.1	1.2	1.2	1.3
Iowa	405	443	439	433	1.3	1.4	1.4	1.4
Kansas	303	318	428	431	1.0	1.4	1.5	1.5
Kentucky	828	864	908	978	1.7	1.8	1.9	2.1
Louisiana	908	845	NA	729	2.0	1.9	NA	1.8
Maine	155	183	185	169	1.0	1.2	1.2	1.1
Maryland	557	593	632	572	1.0	1.1	1.1	1.0
Massachusetts	303	334	412	439	0.6	0.7	0.8	0.8
Michigan	970	1,084	1,057	1,072	0.9	1.0	1.0	1.1
Minnesota	453	508	476	551	0.8	0.8	0.8	1.0
Mississippi	NA	NA	NA	NA	NA	NA	NA	NA
Missouri	955	988	1,080	1,239	1.4	1.4	1.6	1.8
Montana	217	257	263	251	1.9	2.5	2.3	2.3
Nebraska	170	216	266	276	0.9	1.3	1.4	1.4
Nevada	322	371	432	423	1.5	1.8	2.2	2.2
New Hampshire	126	113	127	164	0.9	1.0	1.0	1.2
New Jersey	545	665	770	701	0.7	0.9	1.1	1.0
New Mexico	362	413	471	488	1.4	1.6	2.0	2.1
New York	NA	NA	1,317	1,353	NA	0.9	1.0	1.0
North Carolina	1,394	1,629	1,322	1,495	1.4	1.6	1.5	1.6
North Dakota	104	111	111	121	1.3	1.5	1.5	1.6
Ohio	1,207	1,257	1,243	1,331	1.1	1.1	1.1	1.2
Oklahoma	635	662	748	778	1.3	1.5	1.6	1.7
Oregon	421	452	477	479	1.2	1.3	1.3	1.3
Pennsylvania	1,349	NA	NA	NA	1.2	NA	NA	NA
Rhode Island	66	69	81	87	0.8	0.8	1.0	1.0
South Carolina	915	1,074	1,038	1,091	1.8	2.2	2.1	2.2
South Dakota	118	145	190	176	1.3	1.7	2.2	2.0
Tennessee	1,009	1,171	1,134	1,228	1.4	1.7	1.7	1.8
Texas	3,335	3,183	3,237	3,438	1.4	1.4	1.4	1.5
Utah	271	285	283	282	1.0	1.1	1.1	1.2
Vermont	NA	NA	NA	NA	NA	NA	NA	NA
Virginia	818	1,023	950	939	1.0	1.3	1.2	1.2
Washington	508	516	605	620	0.9	1.0	1.1	1.1
West Virginia	380	430	175	368	1.9	2.2	1.7	1.8
Wisconsin	589	741	715	800	1.0	1.2	1.2	1.3
Wyoming	159	147	195	170	1.7	1.6	2.1	1.8
Total*	39,800	43,100	44,700	45,800	1.3	1.5	1.5	1.6

NA - Not available.
* Total includes both traffic and nontraffic motor vehicle related deaths.
NOTE: Beginning with 2008, death rates may not be directly comparable to prior years due to differences in methodology.
SOURCE: National Safety Council.

Traffic Accidents and Fatalities

VEHICLE TRAFFIC DATA

Year	Crashes	Injuries	Fatalities
2007	6,024,000	2,491,000	41,059
2006	5,973,000	2,575,000	42,642
2005	6,159,000	2,699,000	43,443
2004	6,181,000	2,788,000	42,636
2003	6,328,000	2,889,000	42,643
2002	6,316,000	2,926,000	42,815
2001	6,323,000	3,033,000	41,877
2000	6,394,000	3,189,000	41,821
1999	6,279,000	3,236,000	41,717
1998	6,335,000	3,192,000	41,501
1997	6,624,000	3,348,000	42,013
1996	6,770,000	3,483,000	42,065
1995	6,699,000	3,465,000	41,817
1994	6,496,000	3,266,000	40,716
1993	6,106,000	3,149,000	40,150

SOURCE: U.S. Department of Transportation, National Highway Traffic Safety Administration.

TRAFFIC FATALITIES BY AGE AND GENDER OF VICTIM, 2007

Age of Victim	Gender of Victim Male	Female	Total
4 & under	268	240	508
5-9	259	211	470
10-15	612	432	1,044
16-20	3,651	1,686	5,338
21-24	3,532	997	4,530
25-34	5,178	1,617	6,796
35-44	4,486	1,596	6,082
45-54	4,474	1,656	6,130
55-64	2,899	1,202	4,101
65-74	1,673	929	2,602
75-98	1,912	1,418	3,330
Unknown	95	27	128
Total	29,039	12,011	41,059

Totals include 9 fatalities of unknown gender.
SOURCE: U.S. Department of Transportation, National Highway Traffic Safety Administration.

TRAFFIC FATALITIES BY AGE AND PERSON TYPE, 2007

Age of Victim	Person Type Drivers	Passengers	Pedestrians	Pedalcyclists	Total
4 & under	2	391	106	—	499
5-9	4	343	93	24	464
10-15	128	666	155	83	1,032
16-20	3,108	1,882	287	46	5,323
21-24	3,174	1,023	296	29	4,522
25-34	4,841	1,251	606	88	6,786
35-44	4,338	861	754	117	6,070
45-54	4,254	797	916	145	6,112
55-64	2,954	540	494	94	4,082
65-74	1,699	454	382	46	2,581
75-98	1,957	812	521	19	3,309
Unknown	21	55	44	7	279
Total	26,480	9,075	4,654	698	41,059

Total includes 152 unknown fatalities.
SOURCE: U.S. Department of Transportation, National Highway Traffic Safety Administration.

TRAFFIC FATALITIES BY HOUR OF DAY AND DAY OF WEEK, 2007

Hour of Day	Sun.	Mon.	Tues.	Wed.	Thurs.	Fri.	Sat.	Total
12 to 3 am	1,383	448	346	426	476	607	1,251	4,937
3 to 6 am	775	353	260	323	326	409	712	3,158
6 to 9 am	361	530	525	553	528	566	497	3,560
9 am to noon	456	503	462	500	487	529	551	3,488
noon to 3 pm	693	686	657	640	590	708	799	4,773
3 to 6 pm	869	869	814	775	807	908	905	5,947
6 to 9 pm	912	752	680	765	730	912	1,044	5,795
9 pm to 12 am	666	603	567	631	655	1,092	1,046	5,260
Unknown	54	38	28	40	38	49	83	330
Total	6,169	4,782	4,339	4,653	4,637	5,780	6,888	37,248

SOURCE: U.S. Department of Transportation, National Highway Traffic Safety Administration.

Traffic Deaths in Selected Countries and Countries with Safety Belt Use Laws

STATES WITH STANDARD/PRIMARY SEAT BELT ENFORCEMENT LAWS*

Alabama	Maryland
Alaska	Michigan
California	Mississippi
Connecticut	New Jersey
Delaware	New Mexico
District of Columbia	New York
Georgia	North Carolina
Hawaii	Oklahoma
Illinois	Oregon
Indiana	South Carolina
Iowa	Tennessee
Kentucky	Texas
Louisiana	Washington

*The safety belt use law may be enforced independent of another violation.
SOURCE: National Highway Traffic Safety Administration.

VEHICLE DEATHS IN SELECTED COUNTRIES

	2007	2006	Traffic Fatalities Per 100,000 Registered Vehicles 2007	2006
Australia	1,616	1,598	11.4	11.9
Austria	691	730	14.9	15.9
Belgium	1,067	1,067	18.5	18.8
Canada	2,729	2,889	13.6	14.8
China	80,850	98,738	NA	282.1
Denmark	406	315	15.5	12.4
Finland	380	330	12.7	11.5
France	4,620	4,722	12.5	12.9
Germany	4,949	5,107	11.2	10.3
Hungary	1,232	1,304	35.8	38.6
Italy	NA	5,235	NA	13.1
Japan	5,744	8,224	7.7	11.1
Netherlands	791	809	9.1	9.5
Norway	233	244	8.7	9.4
Poland	5,583	5,243	32.5	33.4
Portugal	854	1,103	14.9	19.6
Spain	3,823	4,118	14.1	15.8
Sweden	471	431	9.9	9.2
Switzerland	384	372	8.9	8.7
Turkey	5,004	4,516	51.8	49.7
United Kingdom	3,059	3,307	8.6	9.5
United States	41,059	42,642	16.5	19.1

NA - Not available.
NOTE: Data varies significantly between countries both definitionally and quantitatively
SOURCE: Compiled by *Ward's* from various sources.

COUNTRIES WITH SAFETY BELT USE LAWS

Country	Effective Date	Country	Effective Date
Argentina	7/1/92	United States and Territories	
Australia	1/72	Alabama	7/18/91
Austria	7/76	Alaska	9/12/90
Belgium	6/75	Arizona	1/1/91
Brazil	6/72	Arkansas	7/15/91
Bulgaria	1976	California	1/1/86
Canadian Provinces		Colorado	7/1/87
Alberta	7/87	Connecticut	1/1/86
British Columbia	10/77	Delaware	1/1/92
Manitoba	4/84	District of Columbia	12/12/85
Newfoundland	7/82	Florida	7/1/86
New Brunswick	11/83	Georgia	9/1/88
Nova Scotia	1/85	Hawaii	2/16/85
Ontario	1/76	Idaho	7/1/86
Prince Edward Island	1/88	Illinois	7/1/85
Quebec	7/76	Indiana	7/1/87
Saskatchewan	7/77	Iowa	7/1/86
Croatia	—	Kansas	7/1/86
Cyprus	—	Kentucky	7/13/94
Czech Republic	1/69	Louisiana	7/1/86
Denmark	1/76	Maine	12/26/95
Finland	7/75	Maryland	7/1/86
France	10/79	Massachusetts	2/1/94
Germany	1/76	Michigan	7/1/85
Greece	12/79	Minnesota	8/1/86
Hong Kong	10/83	Mississippi	3/20/90
Hungary	7/77	Missouri	9/28/85
Iceland	10/81	Montana	10/1/87
India	—	Nebraska	1/1/93
Ireland	2/79	Nevada	7/1/87
Israel	7/75	New Hampshire	—
Italy	7/03	New Jersey	3/1/85
Ivory Coast	1970	New Mexico	1/1/86
Japan	12/71	New York	12/1/84
Jordan	12/83	North Carolina	10/1/85
Luxembourg	6/75	North Dakota	7/14/94
Malaysia	4/79	Ohio	5/6/86
Netherlands	6/75	Oklahoma	2/1/87
New Zealand	6/72	Oregon	12/7/90
Norway	9/75	Pennsylvania	11/23/87
Peru	—	Puerto Rico	1/19/75
Poland	1/84	Rhode Island	6/18/91
Portugal	1/78	South Carolina	7/1/89
Singapore	7/81	South Dakota	1/1/95
Slovenia	—	Tennessee	4/21/86
South Africa	12/77	Texas	9/1/85
Spain	10/74	Utah	4/28/86
Sweden	1/75	Vermont	1/1/94
Switzerland	1/76	Virginia	1/1/88
Turkey	10/84	Washington	6/11/86
United Kingdom	1/83	West Virginia	9/1/93
USSR	1/76	Wisconsin	12/1/87
Zimbabwe	7/80	Wyoming	6/8/89

SOURCE: Compiled by Ward's from various sources.

INDEX

INDEX

Contact Ward's Information Products for
more details or pricing on the products below:
Amber McLincha • 248.799.2622 • amclincha@wardsauto.com

Contact Customer Service for more
details or pricing on the products below.
Barbara Liske • 248.799-2645 • bliske@wardsauto.com

Online Subscription Services

Call for pricing
(based on number
of users)

WardsAuto.com
All of Ward's in one online subscription --
news, data, analysis and more.
_____

Ward's AutoInfoBank™ on the web
Powerful web-based data reporting tool
_____

Forecast Report Products

Ward's AutoForecasts
Knowledgable forecasts on where the
automotive manufacturing industry is headed
_____

Call for pricing
(multiple forecast
products available)

Ward's Monthly Auto Data Reports

Call for details and pricing on these reports:
• Retail sales   • Production/factory sales

Magazines

Call 866-505-7173 to order or for more details:

	US & Mexico	Canada	Airmail Overseas
Ward's AutoWorld®* 1 yr. (12 issues)	$63	$79	$95
Ward's Dealer Business®* 1 yr. (12 issues)	$48	$66	$95

Newsletters

Ward's Automotive Reports®*
❏ One year (52 issues) with Yearbook $1,450 (airmail overseas, add $50)
❏ 13-week trial ....$275 (airmail overseas, add $12)

**Ward's Engine and
Vehicle Technology Update**®*
❏ One year (24 issues).............................$1,050 (airmail overseas, add $25)
❏ Half-year (12 issues) ....$495 (airmail overseas, add $12)

Reference Annuals

Ward's Automotive Yearbook®**
❏ 2009 Yearbook ....$560 (airmail overseas, add $30)
❏ 2009 Yearbook and CD-ROM set........$895 (airmail overseas, add $30)
❏ 2008 Yearbook ....$550 (airmail overseas, add $30)
❏ 2008 Yearbook and CD-ROM set........$895 (airmail overseas, add $30)

Ward's World Motor Vehicle Data™
❏ 2009 Data Book...................................$300 (airmail overseas, add $25)
❏ 2009 Data Book and CD-ROM set........$385 (airmail overseas, add $25)
❏ 2008 Data Book ....$285 (airmail overseas, add $25)
❏ 2008 Data Book and CD-ROM set........$515 (airmail overseas, add $25)

ALL ORDERS MUST INCLUDE APPLICABLE TAXES. If tax-exempt and not a govt.
agency, please provide copy of tax exempt certificate.
* Subject to sales tax in AL, CO, FL, GA, IN, KS, KY, MO, SC, TN, WA and Canada.
** Subject to sales tax in AL, AK, CA, CO, CT, FL, GA, IL, IN, KS, KY, MA, MI, MN,
MO, MS, NE, NJ, NY, OH, PA, SC, TN, TX, VA, WA, WI and Canada.

Please make checks payable to: Penton Media, Inc. in U.S. funds, drawn on a U.S. bank.

Payment enclosed $ _____ Signature _____
(Please do not use this form to order Ward's AutoWorld or Ward's Dealer Business.
Please call 866-505-7173 to order either monthly magazine.)

Bill to my: ☐ VISA   ☐ Mastercard   ☐ American Express   ☐ Discover

Card number_____ Exp. Date _____

Name/Title (Please print) _____

Company/Division_____

Street Address _____

City_____ State/Province _____

Zip/Postal Code_____ Country_____

Phone _____ Fax _____

E-mail Address _____

Mail Orders to: Penton Media, Inc. - Ward's Automotive Group • 24653 Network Place • Chicago, IL 60673-1246
Customer Service Inquiries: Contact Barbara Liske by phone: (248) 799-2645, by fax: (248) 357-9747, or email: bliske@wardsauto.com